✓ S0-BIP-930

DAMAGE NOTED

DATE: 7/29/2014 INITIALS: CE
highlighting on several pages

Methamphetamine

Elgin Community College Library
Elgin, IL 60123

DAMAGE NOTED

DATE:

INITIALS:

Methamphetamine

ITS HISTORY, PHARMACOLOGY, AND TREATMENT

RALPH WEISHEIT, PH.D.
and
WILLIAM L. WHITE, M.A.

HAZELDEN®

ECC Library

362.299
W427m

Hazelden
Center City, Minnesota 55012
hazelden.org

© 2009 by Ralph Weisheit and William L. White
All rights reserved. Published 2009
Printed in the United States of America

No part of this publication may be reproduced, stored in a retrieval system, or transmitted in any form or by any means—electronic, mechanical, photocopying, recording, scanning, or otherwise—without the express written permission of the publisher. Failure to comply with these terms may expose you to legal action and damages for copyright infringement.

Library of Congress Cataloging-in-Publication Data
Weisheit, Ralph A.
  Methamphetamine : its history, pharmacology, and treatment / Ralph Weisheit and William L. White.
     p. cm.
  Includes bibliographical references and index.
  ISBN 978-1-59285-717-3
  1. Substance abuse. 2. Methamphetamine. I. White, William L., 1947- II. Title.
  HV5801.W384 2009
  362.29'9—dc22
                                                                      2008055458

13 12 11 10 09 1 2 3 4 5 6

Cover design by Theresa Jaeger Gedig
Interior design and typesetting by Madeline Berglund

To my parents, Lenus and Sarah Weisheit,
who have stood by me these many years.
They have not only given their unwavering support,
but have been models
of good parents and good people.
—RAW

This book is also dedicated to the individuals
and families who offer living testimony
that long-term recovery from methamphetamine dependence
is a reality and to the professionals and recovering peers
that help make this possible.
—WW

The authors would like to thank the Coalition Against Methamphetamine Abuse (CAMA) in Edgar and Clark counties in Illinois for generously facilitating the research in which we were able to see and hear firsthand the many ways that the effects of methamphetamine ripple through a community. We also had the opportunity to see CAMA in action and found their dedication and focus inspiring. CAMA provides a model for how citizens can come together to effectively respond to the problem of drug use in their community.

CONTENTS

PREFACE

In the 1990s, methamphetamine gained national attention, although it was hardly a new drug. It had been associated with a host of social problems in Hawaii and the Far West for many years. One sign of methamphetamine's popularity is the hundreds of slang terms for it, including *Barney dope, blizzard, candy, chalk, crank, crystal, glass, go, go fast, hillbilly crack, ice, juice, Nazi dope, powder, rock, shit, sparkle, spin, Teena, Tina, tweak, white, yaaba, zoom.* There are nearly four hundred nicknames for methamphetamine and more than thirty nicknames for methamphetamine users.[1]

Methamphetamine is a global problem and in some parts of the world it is the leading drug problem. Throughout this book we include references to its use and manufacture in other countries, but the primary focus is on its use, production, and social consequences in the United States. This is done for several reasons. First, the problem is large, and by concentrating on one country, we were able to study the problem in depth. Second, while research continues to expand worldwide, much of the published work thus far has been conducted in the United States. Other countries, most notably Thailand, have generated a substantial body of research on methamphetamine (much of it is referenced in this book), but the volume of work done there still pales when compared with the amount done in the United States.

This book provides a comprehensive overview of what is known about methamphetamine, from its origins to contemporary ideas about treatment. Chapter 1 introduces the reader to methamphetamine. It describes how the drug has been portrayed in the media and gives a brief overview of the methamphetamine problem in the United States. Overall patterns of use—as well as variations by region, race, and gender—are described, setting the stage for the chapters that follow.

Chapter 2 provides a context for understanding the current methamphetamine problem by tracing its history and patterns of use over time. Since it was first synthesized in 1887, methamphetamine has been used both as a medicine and as a recreational drug, and there has been a range of consequences.

Chapter 3 uncovers the myths and realities of methamphetamine's impact on the mind and body. Where there are gaps in knowledge—and there are many—inferences about methamphetamine can be drawn from studies of other stimulant drugs. Methamphetamine can be benign and beneficial for some people while a curse and destructive force for others.

The social effects of meth are addressed in chapter 4. Methamphetamine affects not only the mind and body, but society as well. This chapter shows the impact of methamphetamine on families, work, and the social lives of users, including its connection to violence. The chapter notes how the drug has played a role in the gay community, particularly in clubs and bars.

Chapter 5 takes the reader on a journey through the meth-cooking world. Methamphetamine is smuggled into the country, but it is also a domestic industry, with producers ranging from mom-and-pop operations to super labs that generate hundreds of pounds of the drug. This chapter considers issues surrounding the production of methamphetamine, including environmental contamination, fires, and the exposure of public safety officers to toxic materials.

Chapter 6 examines meth in rural communities. It presents a case study of two rural counties in which methamphetamine has been a particularly troublesome problem. The impact of methamphetamine on a variety of community groups is considered, as is the effort of community members to respond to the problem.

Finally, Chapter 7 covers what is known about treatment and recovery support resources for methamphetamine dependence. Treating methamphetamine dependence has proven possible but challenging. This chapter also considers how the problem and responses to it might evolve over time.

Throughout the book we have tried to look beyond raw emotions to uncover the "facts"—to the extent that ultimate truth about such issues can ever be known. Our purpose is not only to educate the reader but also to encourage rational discourse about a subject that causes such angst at the individual, community, and societal levels.

CHAPTER 1

Does Methamphetamine Matter?

The headlines and anecdotal stories about methamphetamine are sometimes horrific. Such terms as *scourge* and *epidemic* are often used when describing the methamphetamine problem in the United States. The media, including sources that offer a moderating voice on other issues, have done their share to fuel the perception that methamphetamine is not simply a problem, but a problem of crisis proportions. For example:

- *Frontline,* a PBS documentary series not ordinarily given to exaggeration, addressed the issue with a documentary titled "The Meth Epidemic."

Woman loved meth more than her son, prosecution says at trial

—During a drug-induced sleep the woman rolled over on her three-month-old son suffocating him.[1]

Schoolgirls questioned in sex-for-drugs case

—Schoolgirls as young as twelve trade sex for methamphetamine.[2]

A drug scourge creates its own form of orphan

—The foster care system in Oklahoma is overwhelmed by the number of children removed from homes where their parents were using or making methamphetamine.[3]

Breast milk cited in meth fatality

—A California woman is convicted in the death of her three-month-old son after he ingests methamphetamine-tainted breast milk.[4]

Man who killed 5 is sentenced to death

—The first person sentenced to death in Iowa in forty years was convicted of killing five people to protect his methamphetamine operation.[5]

Meth fallout: "I felt my face just melting"

—Burn units in Tennessee struggle to handle cases arising from explosions and fires from methamphetamine labs.[6]

- The National Association of Counties issued a series of reports under the general heading "The Meth Epidemic in America." Citing one of those reports, National Public Radio ran a story titled "Meth Epidemic Fueling Family Breakups."

- A *Newsweek* cover headline read "The Meth Epidemic: Inside America's New Drug Crisis," and the story inside was titled "Meth: America's Most Dangerous Drug."

- Even the U.S. Congress has been drawn to the use of the word *epidemic*. Legislation to restrict access to ephedrine, a chemical precursor, or ingredient, used in the production of methamphetamine, was titled "Combat Methamphetamine Epidemic Act of 2005."

- A Google search for the phrase "methamphetamine epidemic" finds about thirty thousand results, and a search for both words appearing separately on a Web page brings nearly188,000 results (as of Oct. 7, 2008).

- The National Geographic Channel, which usually focuses on the more mundane, ran a documentary about methamphetamine titled "The World's Most Dangerous Drug." With this label, methamphetamine joins the ranks of such previous designees as heroin, cocaine, LSD, and Ecstasy.[7]

Methamphetamine has not just been fodder for journalists or documentary filmmakers. It has also made its way into popular culture, appearing in books *(Tweak: Growing Up on Methamphetamine; Beautiful Boy: A Father's Journey Through His Son's Addiction; Almost Midnight; Crank; Glass; Leaving Dirty Jersey; Tweaked; The King of Methlehem)*, movies *(Spun, The Salton Sea)*, and music ("Methamphetamine" by Son Volt, "You and Your Crystal Meth" by the Drive-By Truckers, "Semi-Charmed Life" by Third Eye Blind). The AMC television network has developed a television series entitled *Breaking Bad*, which is a fictional account of a financially strapped high school chemistry teacher who teams up with a former student to make and sell methamphetamine. Methamphetamine, it seems, is everywhere.

Not everyone agrees, however, that the problem of methamphetamine rises to epidemic proportions. A lengthy report by the Sentencing Project concludes that applying a term such as *epidemic* to methamphetamine is misleading, inflammatory, and ultimately counterproductive in responding to the problem.[8] While acknowledging that methamphetamine use is substantial in some communities, the report says there is no evidence for a national epidemic because (1) studies of arrestees in large cities find that meth is reported in high percentages only in Western cities; (2) where meth is reported, it appears to replace cocaine rather than add to the overall number of drug users; (3) studies may show meth to be a problem in rural areas, but such areas are not representative of the entire country; and (4) overall rates of use did not increase substantially from 1999 to 2004. The implication is that the term *epidemic* should only be applied to problems that affect all parts of the country, that are on the increase, and for which there is no obvious ameliorative treatment—a high standard indeed.

In his book *No Speed Limit: The Highs and Lows of Meth*, Frank Owen painstakingly details how methamphetamine has swept across the country and the many ways in which the drug has wreaked havoc on users, their families, and their communities.[9] In the end, however, he concludes that reactions to the problem largely have been overblown, noting that although the devastation from methamphetamine is real, it pales compared with the devastation caused by alcohol or cocaine.

Taken from the field of medicine, the term *epidemic* refers to a large number of people who have been infected with a disease, either in a community or more broadly. Certainly there are communities in which *epidemic* would aptly describe the methamphetamine problem, and there are communities in which that epidemic would appear to have been brought under control (see chapter 6). The problem with using the term is not whether it technically applies to the methamphetamine situation. The problem is that the term is emotionally loaded and lacks precision. Ultimately, *epidemic* and *scourge* are judgment calls, having no empirical markers. There is, for example, no magic number of users above which we say there is an epidemic and below which we say there is none.

Methamphetamine is not the first drug for which problems have been exaggerated or overblown. Marijuana, cocaine, heroin, and alcohol all have been demonized as instantly addictive substances; using them would inevitably lead to the social, moral, and physical destruction of the user.[10] But to argue that the addictive nature and destructive consequences of methamphetamine have been overblown is not to argue that the drug is harmless.

Is methamphetamine a new problem and do such headlines and terminology accurately reflect the nature and extent of the methamphetamine problem in the United States? Is it even accurate to describe the situation as a national problem? Is the drug truly deadly to the user and is treatment possible? Such questions provided the impetus for this book. The chapters that follow will discuss many aspects of the issue—history, physiology, social effects, manufacturing, community consequences, and treatment for those who have become dependent on the drug. The intent is to separate "fact from fiction" about methamphetamine—to the extent that is possible when describing such an emotionally charged subject. This chapter lays the foundation for those that follow by describing the extent of the problem in the United States.

Is There a Methamphetamine Epidemic?

Most methamphetamine use is illegal; consequently, users, manufacturers, and distributors have strong incentives to hide their behavior. This means the nature and extent of the problem are difficult to measure. The absence of any concrete data about the problem makes it easy to either exaggerate or diminish the impact of the drug on society. Although current knowledge is incomplete, it is possible to draw on a number of sources to get a general sense of the problem.

Those who believe the methamphetamine *epidemic* has been overblown, or who dismiss the problem outright, often turn to national indicators of use to make their point, while ignoring or minimizing regional or local variations. And, utilizing national data does lead one to view the problem as minor when compared with that of other drugs. Perhaps the most commonly used source of national data about drug use prevalence is the National Survey on Drug Use and Health (NSDUH). Conducted annually by the Substance Abuse and Mental Health Services Administration (SAMHSA) since 1996, the survey has undergone changes over the years. Methamphetamine was not specifically included in the survey until 1999, and questions about the recreational use of legally manufactured methamphetamine and about methamphetamine use via injection were not included until 2006. In 2006, the NSDUH was administered to 67,802 individuals age twelve or older representing all fifty states. The survey did not include homeless people or prison inmates, two groups that might be expected to have higher-than-average drug abuse rates. Although respondents were promised confidentiality and no identifying information was stored with the responses, the survey did ask people to self-report drug use to a federal agency—a circumstance almost certain to encourage underreporting.

Despite these limitations, the NSDUH is one of the few data sources of its kind and is routinely used as a gauge of drug use prevalence. For 2006, the NSDUH reported that an estimated 731,000 people age twelve or older in the United States were current methamphetamine users and 259,000 people were new users.[11] These numbers had not significantly changed since 2002. Putting these numbers in perspective, figure 1.1, created using numbers from the 2006 NSDUH, shows how the estimated number of people who used methamphetamine in the previous month compares with the number of people who used other illicit drugs in that same period.

Figure 1.1

Number of People Who Reported Using Drugs
in the Past Month, 2006

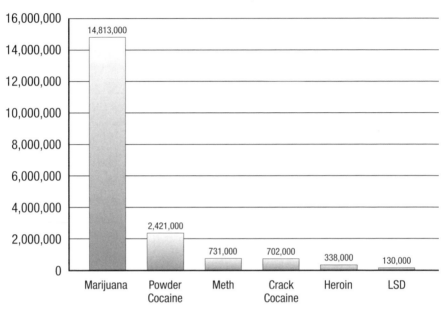

As seen in figure 1.1, the number of current methamphetamine users was slightly greater than the number of crack cocaine users, but was more than double the number of heroin users. The numbers pale, however, compared with those for alcohol and marijuana. The 2006 NSDUH estimated that half of the U.S. population age twelve and older (125,309,000 people) had used alcohol in the previous month. If one wishes to use the term *epidemic* based purely on large national numbers, then alcohol and to a lesser extent marijuana are the drugs that best fit that characterization.

Another source of national data about the extent of methamphetamine use can be found in treatment admissions data, collected and reported by SAMSHA and known as the Treatment Episode Data Set, or TEDS.[12] TEDS represents data gathered from the 1.8 million people admitted to state-recognized treatment facilities throughout the United States. Admissions data have been reported annually since 1992. In 2000, TEDS included a second series of annual data focused on reports from individuals discharged from treatment.

The TEDS data have their limitations. The data are drawn from treatment programs reporting to the states; however, criteria for including facilities in the count vary considerably among the states, as do the speed and thoroughness with which they report. For example, some states include only facilities receiving public funding while others include private facilities. People who receive treatment from the Department of Defense or Veterans Affairs are not included, nor are federal prison inmates, even though over half are in prison on drug-related charges. Those who enter treatment more than once in a year or who switch treatment providers will have each admission counted separately. Many drug users do not enter treatment, many are not dependent and thus do not need treatment, and many who are dependent are able to quit without entering a formal treatment program—either quitting on their own or through peer support groups. The number of drug users in any of these categories is unknown. However, if other drugs provide any indication, the number of methamphetamine users whose use is short-term, periodic, or limited far outnumbers those whose use has spun out of control. Further, treatment sites are not geographically distributed in such a way as to be equally accessible to all. As many as one in ten drug users who believe they need treatment do not access it because of transportation problems or because treatment is not convenient.[13] Still, despite these limitations, treatment admissions data provide another piece of the puzzle and may provide some insight into the extent to which drugs cause problems for their users or for society in general.

Figure 1.2[14] shows that marijuana and heroin accounted for most drug treatment admissions in 2005 (the most recent year that numbers are available). Methamphetamine, which was reported only one-third as often as powder cocaine in recent use (see figure 1.1), accounted for twice as many drug treatment admissions as powder cocaine. This suggests that methamphetamine use is substantially more likely to cause users the kinds of problems that lead to treatment. Heroin, which hardly registered among those reporting drug use in the past month, accounted for over one-fifth of admissions for illicit drugs. Alcohol, not shown in figure 1.2, accounted for 39.1 percent of treatment admissions, more than double the number for marijuana, almost triple the number for heroin, and almost five times the number for methamphetamine. On the basis of treatment data it appears that methamphetamine may not be appropriately described as an epidemic, but is likely more problematic than powder cocaine.

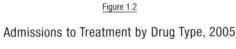

Figure 1.2

Admissions to Treatment by Drug Type, 2005

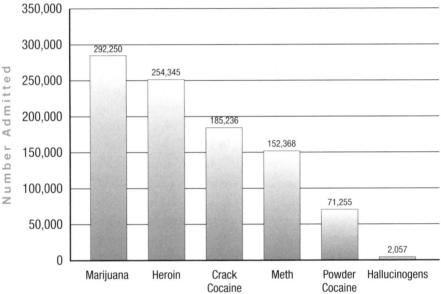

A third source of national data targets children in secondary schools. Monitoring the Future is a project that conducts annual surveys of students in grades 8, 10, and 12.[15] The sample is large, including more than fifteen thousand students from each grade, and designed to be nationally representative. In grades 8 and 10 the surveys are anonymous, but in grade 12 identifying information is recorded to facilitate postgraduation follow-up. This restriction seems likely to discourage honest reporting. The data are further limited because they miss dropouts and students absent on the day of the survey, two groups that are likely to be at greater risk for drug use.

Although the annual surveys began in 1975, questions about methamphetamine were not included until 1999. Self-reported methamphetamine use showed a relatively consistent decline between 1999 and 2007. In 1999, for example, 8.2 percent of high school seniors reported having used methamphetamine in their lifetime, but by 2007 that rate had dropped to 3.0 percent.

Table 1.1[16] shows that among major drugs, only heroin was used less frequently than methamphetamine, and methamphetamine was used almost as frequently as crack cocaine. That 3 percent of high school seniors reported having used methamphetamine is by no means trivial, but it is also far removed from a national epidemic.

Table 1.1

Percent of High School Seniors Reporting Drug Use, 2006

Drug	Past Month	Past Year	Lifetime
Alcohol	44.4	66.4	72.2
Marijuana	18.8	31.7	41.8
Hallucinogens	1.7	5.4	8.4
Powder Cocaine	2.0	5.2	7.8
Crack Cocaine	0.9	1.9	3.2
Methamphetamine	0.6	1.7	3.0
Heroin	0.4	0.9	1.5

Although the survey did not ask about methamphetamine in general until 1999, in 1991 it began asking about a crystalline form of methamphetamine known as *ice.* Also included were questions about the perceived availability of ice and the perceived risk of using ice. While methamphetamine use in general declined rather steadily over time, the use of ice changed little between 1991 and 2007. By 2007 the percentage of high school seniors reporting the use of ice slightly exceeded the number reporting methamphetamine use in general (3.4 percent versus 3.0 percent lifetime use). Most seniors (about 60 percent) thought there was a great risk in using ice even one or two times. Further, the percentage of seniors reporting that ice was very easy or somewhat easy to get held steady over time at around 27 percent.

Overall, these three sources of national data about methamphetamine—the NSDUH, treatment admission data, and the survey of high school seniors—suggest that methamphetamine is a significant problem, but one that is far short of a national epidemic. However, national data may mask important regional and local variations. There may well be local epidemics that are lost when made part of a national average. The problem with averages is they obscure important extremes. One is reminded of the tongue-in-cheek saying "My head is in an oven and my feet are in a bucket of ice, and so on average I'm comfortable."

Where Is Methamphetamine a Problem?

The problem of methamphetamine is not evenly distributed across the country. There are two respects in which this variation manifests itself: regional differences and rural–urban differences. Some of the same data sources used to describe the methamphetamine problem on a national scale can be used to consider geographic patterns. In addition, there are some data sources that tend to draw on urban populations and by doing so reveal regional variations.

Regional Differences in Methamphetamine Use

One of the most striking observations about methamphetamine use is that it began in the western region of the United States (see chapter 2), and it is in the West where methamphetamine remains the biggest problem. A 2007 report from the NSDUH rather dramatically illustrates this regional variation. Figure 1.3 shows the percentages of people who reported using methamphetamine in the previous year (2006) by region: 1.2 percent in the West, 0.5 percent in the Midwest, 0.5 percent in the South, and 0.1 percent in the Northeast.[17]

Drug treatment admissions data also reflect the high concentrations of methamphetamine users in the West.[18] The states with the highest treatment admission rates in 2005 were Oregon, Hawaii, Iowa, Washington,

Figure 1.3

Percent of People Reporting Methamphetamine Use
in the Past Year by Region, 2006

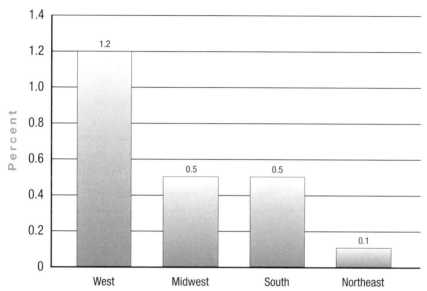

California, South Dakota, and Utah. All are west of the Mississippi River. These states each had more than two hundred methamphetamine treatment admissions for every one hundred thousand people in the state. Conversely, the states with the lowest treatment admission rates were in the East—New Jersey, Rhode Island, New York, Massachusetts, Maryland, Connecticut, and Pennsylvania. Each of these states reported four or fewer methamphetamine treatment admissions per one hundred thousand people in the state. Drug treatment admissions data also indicate that when viewed over time methamphetamine appears to have first taken hold on the West Coast and then moved eastward (see chapter 2). Whether this trend will continue is unknown.

Another source of information about the geographic distribution of methamphetamine is the Arrestee Drug Abuse Monitoring program, also known as ADAM.[19] Under the ADAM program, offenders brought to city or county detention facilities were interviewed about their drug use and asked to confirm their self-reports with a urinalysis. Interviews and drug screens were usually conducted on the day they were arrested and always within forty-eight hours of their detention. In 2003, the last year of the program, ADAM collected data from thirty-nine cities from across the United States. The information was not used against arrestees in their legal proceedings and cooperation was high, with over 90 percent agreeing to be interviewed and, of those, over 80 percent agreeing to provide a urine screen. Because the data were gathered primarily from large cities, they are not representative of the country as a whole, but they do provide insight into regional variations in methamphetamine use.

The ADAM data show that regional variations in methamphetamine use are strong. Each of the twenty cities that fell at or above the median percentage of arrestees testing positive for methamphetamine are located west of the Mississippi River. Table 1.2 shows the five cities reporting the highest percentage of arrestees testing positive for methamphetamine.[20] All five cities are in the Western United States. Table 1.3 shows the states with the highest percentage of arrestees testing positive for cocaine.[21] Except for Tucson, Arizona, the remaining four cities are all east of the Mississippi River. Of the nineteen cities above the median in the percent of arrestees testing positive for cocaine, thirteen are east of the Mississippi.

Tables 1.2 and 1.3 illustrate another interesting pattern regarding the geographic dispersion of methamphetamine. Methamphetamine and

Table 1.2

Top Five Cities with Arrestees Positive for Meth, 2003

City	% Positive for Methamphetamine	% Positive for Cocaine
Honolulu, HI	40.3	11.6
Phoenix, AZ	38.3	23.4
Sacramento, CA	37.6	21.6
San Jose, CA	36.9	12.9
San Diego, CA	36.2	10.3

Table 1.3

Top Five Cities with Arrestees Positive for Cocaine, 2003

City	% Positive for Cocaine	% Positive for Methamphetamine
Chicago, IL	50.6	1.4
Atlanta, GA	49.8	2.0
New Orleans, LA	47.6	2.6
Miami, FL	47.1	0.4
Tucson, AZ	42.5	16.0

cocaine are both powerful stimulants, and, in those places where methamphetamine becomes popular, it is at the expense of cocaine. This pattern is also seen in the treatment admissions data[22] in which methamphetamine treatment admissions are heavily concentrated in the West while cocaine treatment admissions are heavily concentrated in the East. Whether the tendency of methamphetamine to displace cocaine is the result of distribution networks, user preference, or some combination of the two is difficult to determine.

Regional Differences in the Method of Administration

Like many other drugs, methamphetamine can be taken in a variety of ways. It can be smoked, eaten, snorted, injected (into the blood, muscle, or skin), or even taken in suppository form. The method of administration influences "the timing and intensity of the 'rush' that accompanies the use of MA [methamphetamine]. . . . The effects are almost instantaneous when MA is smoked or injected; they occur approximately five minutes after snorting or 20 minutes after oral ingestion."[23] Injecting the drug produces the shortest time from first use to abuse and from abuse to treatment. Injection also places the user at risk for HIV and for hepatitis C.

Not only are there regional variations in the extent of methamphetamine use, there are also regional and local variations in the manner in which the drug is used. For example, in San Diego methamphetamine is most commonly smoked. In Texas injection is the preferred method of administration, while in Minnesota methamphetamine is most commonly taken by snorting.[24] While in many parts of the country methamphetamine is purchased in powdered form, in Hawaii it is purchased in crystal form (aka *ice*) and smoked. Why one form of use is preferred over others in any particular location is probably related to custom,[25] and perhaps to the way the drug was introduced into the area. For example, it has been speculated that smoking is the preferred method of administration in Hawaii because Hawaiians have a history of smoking marijuana.[26] In fact, ice is such a dominant form of methamphetamine in Hawaii that many users think that ice and methamphetamine are different drugs, or that methamphetamine is a form of ice, rather than ice being a form of methamphetamine.[27]

Rural–Urban Differences

Public perceptions, fueled by the media, are that methamphetamine is primarily a rural problem. This perception is bolstered by the reality that methamphetamine labs in the United States are found primarily in rural areas—partly because the odors from the labs are less likely to be noticed in sparsely populated areas and partly because small methamphetamine labs use ingredients that are more readily accessible in rural areas (see chapter 5).

Although the popular press frequently emphasizes the rural nature of domestic methamphetamine *production,* the data on methamphetamine *use* are more mixed. A few studies suggest that rural–urban differences in the percentage of users are minor. For example, the National Survey on Drug Use and Health found that among respondents age twelve and over in nonmetropolitan counties in 1999, 0.8 percent reported using methamphetamine in the past year, compared with 0.5 percent of respondents from large metropolitan areas.[28] A study of recent arrestees in Omaha, Nebraska, and four rural Nebraska counties found few rural–urban differences, observing greater variation among the rural counties than between the urban and rural counties.

Arrestee data and national survey data obscure an important rural–urban difference in methamphetamine use. As noted in chapter 4, a substantial body of literature suggests that methamphetamine is of concern in a particular subset of the population in major urban areas, including large cities east of the Mississippi River. These urban users are males who are active in the gay club scene or who seek anonymous gay sex partners through the Internet. These individuals are unlikely to appear in studies of arrestees or to have much impact on the outcome of general population surveys. While such groups of methamphetamine users in rural communities may exist, they do not appear in any reports.

Some research presents a mixed picture of rural–urban differences in methamphetamine use. A study by the National Center on Addiction and Substance Abuse at Columbia University considered a variety of data sources and concluded that young people in rural areas were substantially more likely than young people in urban areas to have used methamphetamine in the previous year, but that rates of lifetime use were similar across community sizes.[29]

More common, however, is a finding of considerably more methamphetamine use in rural areas, particularly in the Midwest. Bauer reported that in Illinois 71 percent of all methamphetamine arrests were carried out by rural police units and that 71 percent of drug treatment admissions for methamphetamine were in rural counties.[30] Thus, the admission rate for methamphetamine treatment in rural counties was five times that for the state as a whole. As illustrated in figure 1.4, data on drug-related admissions to the Illinois Department of Corrections also reflect the extent to which methamphetamine is a rural phenomenon in the Midwest.

In their study of incarcerated offenders, Warner and Leukefeld found large differences between urban and rural prison inmates in their reported use of amphetamines prior to incarceration.[31] Among urban inmates 10.6 percent reported having used amphetamines in the thirty days prior to their arrest, compared with 23.1 percent of rural inmates and 30.0 percent of inmates from the most rural areas. Unfortunately, inmates from the most rural areas were also less than half as likely to have sought drug treatment prior to incarceration (23 percent versus 49 percent).

A study of urban and rural admissions for methamphetamine at five midwestern treatment sites found several respects in which rural users exhibited more problematic patterns of abuse. Rural methamphetamine

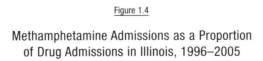

Figure 1.4

Methamphetamine Admissions as a Proportion
of Drug Admissions in Illinois, 1996–2005

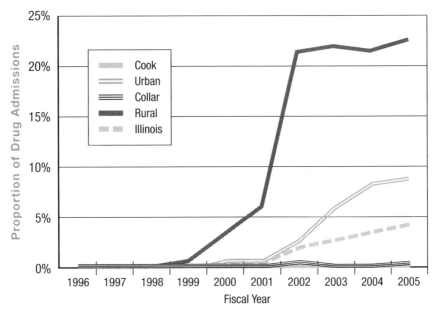

Source: Illinois Department of Corrections

users began using at a younger age, and subsequently entered treatment at a younger age. Rural methamphetamine users also reported more alcohol dependence, more frequently experienced methamphetamine-related psychosis, and an earlier onset of methamphetamine-related psychosis.[32] Rural methamphetamine users in this midwestern study were more likely than urban users to take the drug intravenously. This finding is consistent with national data indicating that rural methamphetamine users are almost three times more likely than those in the largest cities to use methamphetamine intravenously.[33]

One population, most of whose citizens live in rural areas, has been particularly hard hit by methamphetamine. Nearly three quarters (74 percent) of surveyed Indian law enforcement agencies in the United States reported methamphetamine as the drug posing the greatest threat to residents of tribal lands.[34] Only 3 percent of the agencies reported that methamphetamine was not available in their communities and most (69 percent) said there was no tribal-sponsored center or program to treat methamphetamine addicts.

Although not unique to rural areas, methamphetamine appears to present particular challenges for rural communities. Even if the percentage of the population using methamphetamine were the same in rural and urban areas, the problems arising from methamphetamine use may be more substantial in rural areas where the tax base is smaller, thus limiting resources for prevention, treatment, and enforcement.[35] In rural communities, with tightly knit social networks, concerns about the stigma of drug use may discourage users from seeking treatment and thus risking public disclosure of their problem.[36] Closely knit social networks also make undercover police work more difficult and complicate the conduct of research on rural methamphetamine users.[37] Finally, the distances that must be traveled complicate access to treatment. All of these factors combined may mean that reported rural–urban differences in methamphetamine use may substantially understate rural–urban differences in the drug's impact.

Who Is the Methamphetamine User?

Methamphetamine has been stereotyped as a "white trash" drug that has particular appeal to women. As with any illicit drug, methamphetamine users come in all ages, races, genders, and incomes. The question is whether there is a grain of truth to the stereotype—are methamphetamine users more likely than other drug users to be white, female, and blue collar?

Race and Methamphetamine Use

The public perception is that methamphetamine is a drug primarily used by white people, and this appears to be only partly true. As illustrated in figure 1.5, the 2005 National Survey on Drug Use and Health shows that by far the most use is reported by the category "American Indian or Alaska Native" (1.5 percent), a rate about double that for Hispanics (0.9 percent), white people (0.8 percent), or Asians (0.7 percent).[38] Black people were among the least likely users of methamphetamine, with a rate (0.2 percent) that was only a fraction of the rates reported by other groups.

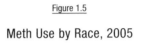

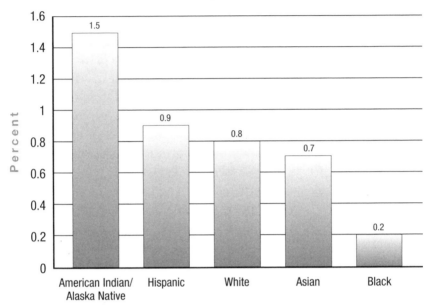

Monitoring the Future, the annual survey of high school seniors, reports drug use by only three racial/ethnic categories: white, black, and Hispanic. Among high school seniors in 2006, the group reporting the highest percentage of methamphetamine users was Hispanic (3.7 percent of respondents), followed by white students (2.6 percent).[39] By comparison, the percentage of methamphetamine users among black high school seniors was relatively small (0.4 percent).

Treatment admissions data also report methamphetamine-related admission by race. For 2006, these data show that among the three largest racial groups 11.8 percent of Hispanics admitted for treatment were admitted for methamphetamine as their primary substance of abuse, compared with 11.1 percent of white people and 1.1 percent of black people.[40] There are, however, other groups that are smaller in number but for whom methamphetamine is a particular problem. For example, among Asian/Pacific Islanders admitted for drug treatment, 28.6 percent were admitted for methamphetamine as their primary drug of abuse and among American Indians, 10.4 percent were admitted for methamphetamine.

There also appear to be significant differences among Hispanic subgroups. As table 1.4 shows, Mexicans were not only the subgroup with the largest number of drug treatment admissions overall, but also among those admissions they were most likely to have methamphetamine as their primary drug of abuse.[41]

Table 1.4

Differences Among Subgroups of Hispanics Admitted for Drug Treatment, 2006

Subgroup	Number Admitted for Any Drug	Percent Admitted for Methamphetamine
Mexican	99,017	21.4
Puerto Rican	73,389	0.8
Cuban	9,291	4.0
Other	69,021	10.6

Overall, the data from several national sources suggest that while methamphetamine is relatively popular among white people, it is also a popular drug among Hispanics, American Indians, and Asian/Pacific Islanders. Perhaps the most consistent finding across various sources is the very small representation of black people among methamphetamine users and among those seeking treatment for methamphetamine abuse. Of course, these national patterns obscure regional and local variations. In Hawaii, for example, Pacific Islanders are heavily represented among methamphetamine users. In the Midwest, where minority populations are small or nonexistent in many communities, it is not surprising that white people are heavily represented among the user and treatment populations. Still, the notion that methamphetamine is "white man's crack"[42] is an exaggeration.

Gender and Methamphetamine Use

According to the 2005 NSDUH, men were twice as likely as women to report having used methamphetamine in the previous month. This is similar to the pattern for marijuana, cocaine, and inhalants.[43] The difference between men and women was smaller for other stimulants, pain relievers, hallucinogens, and psychotherapeutics.

Among high school seniors, the percentage of males using drugs exceeded that for females for most drugs.[44] Methamphetamine, however, displayed an interesting gender-related pattern. When seniors were first asked about methamphetamine use in 1999, boys were more likely than girls to report use, though by a narrow margin (5.0 percent versus 4.5 percent). The difference favoring males remained, and remained slim until 2006, when the percentage of females using methamphetamine exceeded that for males, though the difference was small (2.0 percent for males and 3.0 percent for females). In any of the years reported, the male-female differences were likely too small to be of practical importance for prevention or treatment programs.

National treatment admissions for methamphetamine also find that males outnumber females in treatment admissions, but the gap is much smaller (53.8 percent versus 46.2 percent) than that for self-reported methamphetamine use in the adult population.[45] The gap between men and women regarding treatment for methamphetamine is smaller than the gap for heroin, powder cocaine, marijuana, hallucinogens, or inhalants.

Taken together, these national data on methamphetamine use and on treatment suggest it is not a drug that is uniquely appealing to women. It may be true, however, that women use the drug for different reasons. Women may be more likely to use the drug for weight loss and less likely to use the drug as a sexual stimulant (see chapter 4). Further, women who use methamphetamine may be more willing to seek treatment than are men.

Other Characteristics

Treatment admissions data provide insight into other characteristics of methamphetamine users. As table 1.5 shows, methamphetamine users entered treatment at a younger age than did the users of most other drugs, except for marijuana.[46] Methamphetamine users were also less likely than heroin or crack cocaine users to enter treatment by self-referral and were more likely than the users of other drugs (except marijuana) to have entered treatment as a result of a criminal justice referral. Methamphetamine users were more likely than the users of other drugs (except marijuana) to report this was their first admission to treatment.

Table 1.5

Characteristics of Methamphetamine and Other Drug Users in Treatment

Characteristic	Meth	Heroin	Crack	Powder Cocaine	Marijuana
Average Age at Admission	31	36	38	34	24
Daily Use (%)	27.9	75.2	40.2	27.0	26.1
First Use under Age 15 (%)	16.3	9.8	8.1	11.2	55.7
Self-Referral to Treatment (%)	23.8	59.3	37.6	31.7	15.9
Criminal Justice Referral (%)	49.2	14.2	26.4	33.7	56.7
No Prior Treatment (%)	52.5	25.5	37.3	45.8	59.6
Employed Full-Time (%)*	17.2	11.9	11.5	22.6	20.5
Public Aid (%)	6.2	13.8	11.8	9.4	7.8
High School or More (%)**	61.5	62.5	64.7	66.3	56.8
Yes Pregnant (%)***	6.8	4.0	4.5	4.3	5.5
Psychiatric Problems (%)	14.2	20.5	26.7	26.2	20.0
No Health Insurance (%)	73.0	57.8	67.4	63.5	57.4

*Among those 16 and over; **Among those 18 and over; ***Females only

While meth users were more likely than heroin or crack cocaine users to be employed full-time, only 17 percent were full-time employees, though they were less likely than the users of any other drug to have public aid as their primary source of income. Methamphetamine users were less likely than any other type of user to have health insurance. Methamphetamine users were somewhat less likely than the users of heroin, crack, or powder cocaine to have a high school diploma or more. Finally, despite the ability of extended methamphetamine use to induce psychosis (see chapter 3), methamphetamine users admitted to treatment were less likely than the users of any other major category of drug to have other psychiatric problems.

Overall, the characteristics of substance abusers admitted to treatment suggest that methamphetamine users are unique, but probably have more in common with powder cocaine and marijuana users than with those who use heroin or crack cocaine.

CONCLUSION

Describing the methamphetamine problem with such terms as *epidemic* and *scourge* does more to inflame than to inform. However, arguing about whether these terms accurately describe the nature and extent of the problem is, to use a biblical phrase, straining at gnats. It's simply not very helpful. The drug clearly poses significant problems for some communities and not for others and is incredibly destructive for some users but not for others. What these terms do reflect is a visceral reaction to the drug and its attendant problems. Such a reaction can make it difficult to separate truth from fiction. This chapter has begun the process of separating fact from fiction by looking at the issue in its broadest sense, including national-level indicators of methamphetamine use and treatment, regional variations in use, and characteristics of those who use the drug. By almost any measure the problems created by methamphetamine are small compared with those that arise from alcohol abuse. Beyond alcohol, methamphetamine is used by about as many people as use crack cocaine, but is more commonly found in the West and in rural areas than are either crack or powder cocaine. Both cocaine and methamphetamine are powerful stimulants and so it is not surprising that where one is popular the other is considerably less so. One of the most striking differences between methamphetamine and other illicit drugs is the relatively small percentage of meth users who are black.

This chapter has outlined the broad patterns of methamphetamine use in modern times. The chapters that follow examine more specific dimensions of the drug and its impact on society. Chapter 2 takes us back to the beginning, detailing the origins and evolution of methamphetamine's use as a recreational drug.

Listening to Methamphetamine:

The Lessons of History

As noted in chapter 1, sudden increases in drug use that result in significant personal and social problems are often, questionably, referred to as *epidemics*. Chapter 2 and coming chapters will refer to such sudden increases in methamphetamine use as a *surge* and the accompanying public alarm as a *drug panic*. Each real or perceived surge has something to teach us. Harvesting these lessons is only possible if we listen carefully to each drug and how its pattern of use is spawned and then either sustained or aborted. If we listen with sufficient skill and understanding, a drug may not have to, historically speaking, repeat itself.

In this chapter,[1] we will listen to the story of methamphetamine from its birth in 1887 until the present. We will focus on a series of surges in amphetamine and methamphetamine use in Japan, Hawaii, and the mainland United States as well as localized surges in the use of "ice" (a smokable form of methamphetamine) in these two countries. There have also been methamphetamine surges in the Philippines, Thailand, Korea, England, Ireland, and Sweden,[2] but the Japanese and American methamphetamine surges are the most fully documented.

There have been two major methamphetamine surges in Japan, one spanning the years 1945 to 1955 and the second beginning in 1970 and extending to the present. Each of these two surges was seeded through

25

isolated methamphetamine exposure in medicine and the military, moved to Japanese criminal societies, and then expanded to the larger Japanese culture. The first of these surges eventually involved more than two million Japanese citizens.[3]

Similarly, three methamphetamine surges in the United States grew out of widespread medically prescribed amphetamine use from 1944 into the 1960s. Such use peaked in 1967 at thirty-one million amphetamine prescriptions per year.[4] This set the stage for two brief methamphetamine surges, one from 1959 to 1962 and a second from 1968 to 1972. The first grew out of medically treating heroin addicts with injectable methamphetamine in the late 1950s and early 1960s.[5] A subsequent surge of intravenous (IV) methamphetamine use emerged in the late 1960s within California's polydrug subculture and rapidly moved eastward through American urban centers. In this latter surge, prolonged "speed runs" of injected methamphetamine became associated with crime, violence, and acute psychotic episodes. "Speed freaks" of that era lived in what rapidly became a paranoid and predatory underworld. Survivors of this methamphetamine subculture helped spread the mantra "Speed Kills!"[6]

Following the waning of these methamphetamine subcultures in the 1970s, there were local surges in the use of ice (a pure, highly potent, and smokable form of d-methamphetamine hydrochloride) in Hawaii (1980s), San Diego (1989), and the Upper Peninsula of Michigan (early 1990s).[7] These surges stirred local drug panics and the prediction that ice would become the cocaine of the 1990s, but the use of ice remained an isolated phenomenon.[8]

The latest surge in methamphetamine use began in the early 1990s and extends into the present. This recent spread of methamphetamine use emerged on the heels of the 1980s cocaine surge but, in contrast to earlier drug surges, was mostly concentrated in rural areas of the United States.[9] We will "listen" to the detailed stories of these surges to see what they tell us about the rise, fall, and cyclical return of particular patterns of drug use.

Meth's Birth and Prolonged Dormancy

Ephedrine, the active ingredient in amphetamine, was first synthesized in

1887 by the German chemist Lazar Edeleano, and methamphetamine was later synthesized by Nagayoshi Nagai, a pharmacologist, in Japan in 1893 and by Akira Ogata in 1919.[10] Amphetamine and methamphetamine each arrived on the world stage with little fanfare. However, amphetamine took the spotlight in 1929 after Gordon Alles studied its psychoactive effects. The discovery of such properties led the Philadelphia pharmaceutical firm Smith, Kline & French to introduce the Benzedrine inhaler in 1931, which was promoted to relieve the nasal congestion associated with asthma.[11] The inhaler was shortly followed by Benzedrine tablets, both of which were available without a prescription until regulatory controls began in the 1950s.

Amphetamine rapidly acquired a "wonder drug" status in the United States. Within a few years, the drug was recommended in the treatment of more than thirty conditions, including narcolepsy, epilepsy, fatigue, depression, schizophrenia, alcoholism, morphine and codeine addiction, nicotine addiction, barbiturate intoxication, enuresis (bed wetting), radiation sickness, sea sickness, dysmenorrhea (painful menstruation), colic, obesity, persistent hiccups, stimulation of sexual libido, and the treatment of hyperactive children.[12] In 1936, Dr. Charles Bradley, a psychiatrist, began the first experiments using amphetamine to treat children with learning disabilities—a trend that would increase dramatically in the seventy years following his pioneering work.[13]

Early on, the drug was universally viewed as safe and nonaddicting. In 1938, two prominent physicians proclaimed, "There is no evidence in the entire literature of medicine that stimulants become habit-forming."[14] Six years later, reports of the safety of amphetamine had only been slightly tempered: ". . . addiction is very rare and only occurs in the severe psychopath who would have probably become addicted to some drug or other anyway."[15]

This early perception of amphetamine's safety set the stage for the broad exposure of American citizens to the drug. More than two hundred million amphetamine tablets were freely distributed to suppress fatigue among American soldiers in World War II. Sales of Benzedrine exploded in the years following the return of American soldiers to the United States at the end of the war.[16] Medical warnings about the addiction potential of amphetamine that were first published in the late 1930s increased dramatically in the following decades and triggered calls for control over the drug's manufacture and distribution.

In Japan, the use of amphetamines and methamphetamine followed a similar pattern. There was widespread use of the drugs by soldiers and civilian workers in World War II. Methamphetamine was introduced in 1941 as an over-the-counter medication sold as Philoppon and Sedrin. In a short time span, the stage was set for the first methamphetamine surge.[17]

The localized IV methamphetamine surge in the United States in the early 1960s was distinctive in several ways. First, there was almost no dormancy period in the rise of this surge. This was attributable to a new, liquid form of the drug and a new and more efficient method of ingestion (injection versus oral administration) that developed in a fringe culture of heroin addicts. Second, while this initial surge was quickly contained, it retained enough hard-core underground users to serve as a fuse that ignited a broader IV methamphetamine subculture later in the decade. Such hard-core users may be considered carriers who lie dormant in the culture until conditions return for the wider dissemination of their drug of choice.

There are several striking lessons we can take from this earliest history of amphetamine use in the United States and Japan. The first is that psychoactive drugs can be used in medicine for some time before their addictive properties are recognized. The second is that psychoactive drugs can lie dormant in a culture for many years if not decades before they break into widespread use and generate significant personal and social problems. Both amphetamine and methamphetamine exhibited a long incubation period between their discovery and their emergence and association with addiction. So, if we were going to predict what new drugs would emerge as problems in the coming decades of the twenty-first century, we might begin by looking at drugs that are already here, but that have not yet achieved cultural visibility. Listening to the earliest history of methamphetamine would also offer two other clues to the sources of such substances: drugs currently used in medicine and drugs recommended in the treatment of addiction. Another lesson from this early history is that war can play a role in setting the stage for drug surges (e.g., the widespread use of amphetamine by soldiers in Germany, Japan, the United States, and

Britain during World War II). There is also evidence that disruption of established availability of one drug can trigger onset of a new (and potentially more dangerous) pattern of use as was the case in Hawaii when crop eradication of pakalolo (marijuana) created an opening for Asian distributors to aggressively market and distribute ice in Hawaii.[18]

Third, each psychoactive drug whose use reaches surge proportions brings unique features that distinguish it from its predecessors. Methamphetamine was distinctive in the lack of need for any plant-based precursor like the opium poppy or the coca bush, the widespread availability of the ingredients required for its manufacture, the minimal skill required for such manufacture, the toxic by-products resulting from its illicit manufacture, its initial concentration in predominately white and Native American rural communities, and the long duration of its effects.

Before the Surge

Both the United States and Japan experienced their first amphetamine surges in the late 1940s and 1950s, but under different circumstances. The U.S. surge unfolded among explosive postwar prosperity, while Japan's surge rose amid poverty, unemployment, food scarcity, and cultural demoralization. The first Japanese methamphetamine surge underscores the role cultural demoralization can play in the rise of such surges.[19] Interestingly, during the 1980s and 1990s rural American communities that were socially and economically disrupted and demoralized were similarly vulnerable to the ravages of methamphetamine.

Both the early amphetamine and methamphetamine surges in the United States and Japan started with a core of people exposed to amphetamine through medicine and the military and then spread outward into the mainstream population through new forms of the drug, excessive drug supply (from overproduction), and overprescribing. In the United States, use of amphetamines spread from military personnel and those being prescribed the drug for medical purposes to Bohemian groups (jazz, bebop, and beat subcultures), to students, truck drivers, and others seeking to suppress fatigue, and then to a broad segment of the population who considered "pep pills" something of a fad.[20] In Japan, amphetamine use spread from military personnel and those working in military support industries to others using the drug to enhance work efficiency (students, artists, writers, factory workers) before it moved to fringe elements of society (school dropouts, delinquent gangs, criminal syndicates) who began using the drug as a source of pleasure and escape.[21]

When we look at these early methamphetamine surges, several things stand out. First, it can take a period of sustained population exposure before the drug's casualties become visible. In the case of amphetamine, the first report of amphetamine psychosis and the first report of amphetamine dependence did not appear in the medical literature until 1938—six years after the introduction of Benzedrine.[22] There is a slow rippling effect with new drugs, starting with those individuals who have been most directly involved with the drug's introduction who begin using the drug outside medical boundaries. In the case of amphetamine, one of the earliest reports of misuse of the drug was by students at the University of Minnesota who had participated in clinical trials of the drug and, liking its effects, continued their own uncontrolled experiments. Within two years, there were reports of student amphetamine use on many campuses.[23]

This period of initial exposure is followed by a period of wide cultural infatuation with the drug—an infatuation often spurred by the cultural media and celebrities. The American media of the 1940s and 1950s played a significant role in the promotion of amphetamine, labeling it the "Confidence Drug" and printing stories with headlines such as "Reach for a Pill instead of a Cocktail."[24] Amphetamine became associated with the sophisticated, whom columnist Earl Wilson christened as "New York's Benzedrine Set."[25] These stories portrayed amphetamine as a source of pleasure rather than of medicinal benefit. They also noted the practice of "bolt and jolt"—using a combination of amphetamines and barbiturates for increased pleasure. The broad cultural acceptance of amphetamine in this period is evident in the popularity of songs such as Harry Gibson's "Who Put the Benzedrine in Mrs. Murphy's Ovaltine?" The mainstream infatuation with amphetamine was fed by a pharmaceutical industry that increased its production of amphetamine from 16,000 pounds in 1949 to more than 75,000 pounds in 1958. Within another ten years, that production had grown to more than 160,000 pounds.[26]

Some drug surges have a clearly identifiable inciting source. This is clearly the case in the 1960–1962 methamphetamine surge in California. The seed of this sudden shift was a small number of physicians who began prescribing injectable ampoules of methamphetamine as a treatment for heroin addiction. The drug was legally manufactured by two pharmaceutical firms, Abbott and Burroughs Wellcome, under the trade names Desoxyn and Methedrine.[27] As these heroin addicts developed a primary addiction to methamphetamine, unscrupulous physicians and pharmacists began prescribing and distributing liquid forms of the drug. This practice illustrates a theme in the history of addiction—harmful effects that grow out of efforts to treat addiction. Such harm within the practice of medicine is referred to as an iatrogenic (physician-caused or treatment-caused) illness.

Surges can reflect deep cultural changes that alter personal appetites for certain kinds of experiences and imbue certain drugs with symbolic value. The challenging of traditional values and the protest movements of the 1960s whetted the cultural appetite for introspection while elevating the values of nonconformity and activism. Marijuana and LSD facilitated nonconformity and became symbols of youthful protest. Similarly, the roaring financial markets of the 1980s elevated the value of high-priced, high-status drugs and fueled the rise in cocaine use. But the lower-priced stimulants are harder to interpret in terms of their cultural popularity because they, like alcohol, can serve so many needs, from the search for stimulating euphoria to suppression of fatigue and appetite within an overweight, overworked populace. Perhaps it is enough to note that the latest methamphetamine surge rose within a larger cultural context that found drug stimulation very attractive, via the explosion of coffee shops, caffeine-spiked drinks, and over-the-counter "pick-me-ups." It is similarly worth noting that some drug surges end not because of drug supply reduction efforts or public education related to the drug's effects, but because appetite for that particular type of drug experience rapidly wanes as a by-product of larger cultural changes that occur.

Transmission of Drug Surges

We have already seen that an emerging drug can move either from a deviant subgroup to the mainstream culture or from the mainstream culture to deviant subgroups. Several rules seem to govern the transmission of drug surges.

First, drug surges can ignite quickly in conditions characterized by high availability, the absence of drug controls, a vulnerable population of potential users, and social and economic distress resulting from conditions such as cultural demoralization, mass unemployment, poverty, or mass migration.[28] They also may arise in conditions of sudden economic prosperity, excess income, and the search for new symbols of status and pleasure—conditions that spawned American amphetamine use after World War II and the cocaine surges of the 1980s.

Second, drug diffusion is an interpersonal process. Reports of the situations in which nonprescribed amphetamine and methamphetamine are first used nearly always refer to friends and acquaintances as the instigators and not the mythical drug peddler seeking new victims.[29] Early stage stimulant use generates euphoria, confidence, and overall feelings of well-being that turn many neophyte users into effective marketers for the drug. Drug supply is a critical factor in drug surges, but the process of initiating use is a highly social one.

Third, diffusion often follows predictable geographical pathways, with some exceptions to this rule. Both the general rule and the exceptions are illustrated in the following maps,[30] which plot the geographical progression of the 1990s methamphetamine surge in the United States.

Tracking the west to east movement of methamphetamine use and dependence across the United States allows public health officials to prepare for drug surges by increasing community resiliency and resistance. If, for example, you were located (as the authors were) in Illinois in 1996, it would not have been difficult to predict the movement of methamphetamine into Illinois from Iowa and Missouri and to track its eastward movement across Illinois treatment centers, courts, and child welfare agencies. Seen as a whole, methamphetamine surges have tended to move from large cities to small towns, but the reverse of this has occurred in the latest U.S. methamphetamine surge.[31]

The maps also illustrate how certain areas, such as the state of Iowa in the early 1990s, experience combinations of vulnerability factors, which can accelerate the arrival of an otherwise predictable drug trend. Those vulnerability factors in Iowa included ethnic migrations, ready availability of ingredients to manufacture methamphetamine, and a depressed economy.[32]

The maps do not show another phenomenon, which was methamphetamine moving across Illinois but leaving some communities untouched. This was most dramatically illustrated in Chicago. At a time when nearly all other urban areas of Illinois and northwest Indiana were seeing meth lab seizures, increased meth possession and sales arrests, and increased meth-related treatment admissions, there was not a whisper of methamphetamine in Chicago. The answer to this anomaly is an interesting one. It appears that methamphetamine does not easily penetrate communities that already have an established stimulant drug market.[33] The forces that controlled Chicago's lucrative cocaine market collectively decided not to distribute methamphetamine on the grounds that it would reduce income from the more profitable cocaine trade.

The Spread of Methamphetamine Abuse Treatment Admissions, 1992

Methamphetamine Admission Rates (per 100,000)

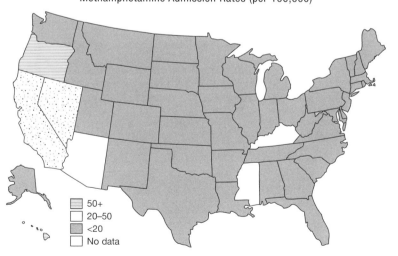

50+
20–50
<20
No data

The Spread of Methamphetamine Abuse Treatment Admissions, 1993

Methamphetamine Admission Rates (per 100,000)

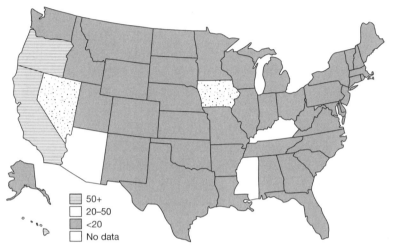

50+
20–50
<20
No data

The Spread of Methamphetamine Abuse Treatment Admissions, 1994

Methamphetamine Admission Rates (per 100,000)

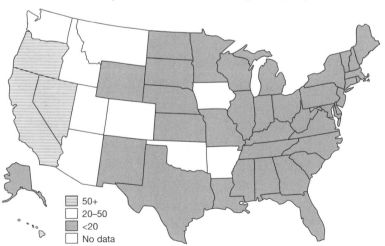

50+
20–50
<20
No data

The Spread of Methamphetamine Abuse Treatment Admissions, 1995
Methamphetamine Admission Rates (per 100,000)

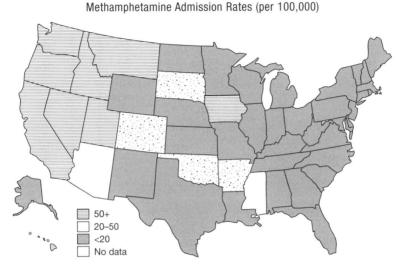

50+
20–50
<20
No data

The Spread of Methamphetamine Abuse Treatment Admissions, 1996
Methamphetamine Admission Rates (per 100,000)

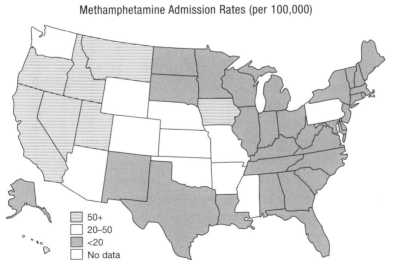

50+
20–50
<20
No data

Viewing the country as a whole, observers can detect shifts within the larger west to east migration of methamphetamine use. That trend within a trend involves the movement of methamphetamine use from rural white and Native American populations to use among urban ethnic and sexual minorities. Age (a move toward younger use) and gender (increased use by women) also are reflected in the maturing of local methamphetamine surges.[34]

Fourth, the surge and alarm stage can be triggered by changes in the characteristics of the drug, by ingestion rituals, and/or by changes in the characteristics of drug consumers.[35] An early warning signal of a methamphetamine surge was the practice of "speedballing" (injecting mixtures of methamphetamine and heroin) by American soldiers stationed in Japan and Korea in the 1950s. Future drug surges may involve such planned synergism—purposefully combining two or more drugs to achieve an intensified effect. The localized ice surges, particularly the Hawaiian ice surge of the late 1980s and early 1990s, similarly illustrate how a shift in a drug's potency, purity, and method of administration (creating rapid onset of effects) can quickly trigger social alarm.[36]

Surge and Alarm: Drug Panics

There is a point at which growing methamphetamine use and its related problems break into cultural visibility. This visibility can result from a slow accumulation of problems or, more often, from a deviant group pushing the boundaries of the drug (dosage, frequency, method of administration, context in which use occurs) in ways that rapidly escalate problems related to its use. The mainstream use of amphetamine in Japan in the 1940s achieved little visibility until amphetamine was adopted by young criminal elements.[37] Amphetamines in the United States in the 1950s and 1960s also had little visibility as a problem until amphetamine use spread to adolescents and young adults in the 1960s.

Cultural alarm is often triggered by fringe use. Jackson has described an early amphetamine injection subculture in the 1950s made up of youth extracting the medicated strips within amphetamine inhalers, soaking them in water, and then injecting the resulting amphetamine solution.[38]

Experimenting youth also placed the strips, in whole or in pieces, in beverages and gum or simply swallowed them.[39] Cultural alarm about drug use often comes fol-lowing exposure of a new drug to

Benzedrine inhaler used in the treatment of asthma.

a particularly vulnerable population (e.g., teenagers, pregnant women, and people working in safety-sensitive occupations or positions of cultural leadership).

This breaking into visibility of a new drug trend triggers what is some-times called a "drug panic."[40] The drug panic often follows on the heels of a highly publicized drug incident. Examples of such incidents can be drawn from the Japanese methamphetamine surges. In 1954, the killing of a ten-year-old girl by a youth under the influence of methamphetamine in Kyoko-chan led to a public outcry and passage of a stimulant control law. During the second Japanese methamphetamine surge, the killing of two housewives and two children by a methamphetamine addict in Tokyo sparked a similar intensification of drug control policies.[41]

All of the methamphetamine surges we are exploring created drug pan-ics of varying degrees of intensity. Several lessons emerge in studying the history of drug panics related to amphetamine, methamphetamine, and ice that parallel panics related to other psychoactive drugs.

1. Early reports emerging from drug panics on the pharmacology of the drug, the extent of its use, and the problems resulting from such use are notoriously unreliable.

2. Early reports emanating from drug panics employ rhetorical devices (e.g., "Speed Kills!") that are purposely designed to inflame citizen demands for action.

3. The targeted drug is associated with a hated or marginal sub-group of the society, or a perceived foreign enemy.

4. The drug is linked to crime, violence, insanity, and the sexual corruption of women and youth.

5. The drug is linked to an already stigmatized drug (usually

heroin or cocaine) and its effects are portrayed as far beyond
the already demonized substance.

6️⃣ The drug is described in language that conveys uncontrollable
contagion, for example, *epidemic, plague, scourge, menace.*[42]

To describe these themes is not to discount the very real personal and
social problems that can result from drug use. This observation does suggest two things. First, early reports on an emerging drug are often scientifically inaccurate and result in later retractions. Second, and most
importantly, great harm can be done in the name of good through the
precipitous actions that emerge in the heat of drug panics. Bad policy and
law can be passed in hours or days in the heat of a drug panic, but often
require years or decades to change. One could build a case that the United
States has the largest prison population in the world today due in great
measure to the laws and policies that emerged as part of the cocaine panic
of the 1980s. Drug panics are a natural response to any threatening problem, but such panics are often exploited to advance the power, prestige, or
financials interests of individuals and institutions claiming ownership of
the problem.[43]

The greatest panics are linked not so much to what drug is being used
but to who is using the drug and for what reasons. Alarm is greatest in
Western cultures when the "who" shifts from the mainstream "we" to the
disfranchised "they" and the reasons for using shift from medicinal or
instrumental (for enhanced performance) use to using for purposes of
pleasure or escape.[44]

Problem Definition and Response

The stage of panic is often followed by more reasoned actions that can
serve to slow, constrict, or end the drug surge. The good news in the historical episodes we are reviewing is that peak periods of amphetamine and
methamphetamine use have been constricted and sometimes contained,
at least in the short run, by decisive action. Such actions often involve a
combination of strategies. Responses that have exerted positive effects in
containing these amphetamine surges include the following:

 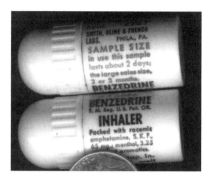

Benzedrine inhalers introduced in medicine in 1931.

- Voluntary actions by the pharmaceutical industry to remove a drug from the market, for example, Smith, Kline & French's 1949 decision to remove the Benzedrine inhaler from the market
- The Food and Drug Administration's 1954 crackdown on amphetamines
- Law or regulatory actions requiring physician prescription for access to amphetamine/methamphetamine, for example, the Food and Drug Administration's 1959 use of the Drug Control Amendments of 1951 to require prescriptions for amphetamine inhalers
- Laws specifically aimed at reducing amphetamine availability, for example, Japan's Stimulant Control Laws of 1951, 1954, 1955; the U.S. Drug Abuse Control Amendments of 1965; the U.S. Controlled Substances Act of 1970
- Laws targeting clandestine meth labs and controlling precursor chemicals and lab equipment, for example, the U.S. Chemical Diversion and Trafficking Act of 1988
- Responses of indigenous helping organizations, for example, the Haight-Ashbury Clinic in San Francisco, which actively responded to use of IV methamphetamine injectors in the late 1960s
- Provision of treatment resources for those impacted by amphetamine and methamphetamine

Problem Morphing

Drug surges are living entities that evolve dynamically even as efforts are made to end them. Two particularly important lessons illustrate this dynamic quality.

Successful efforts to control legal supplies of a drug are often followed by new sources of drug supply. When Smith, Kline & French withdrew its Benzedrine inhaler from the market in 1949 and its patent for the inhaler expired in 1952, other amphetamine inhalers appeared, such as Valo inhaler, Wyamine inhaler, and Nasal-Ato inhaler.[45] When the Drug Abuse Control Amendments of 1965 successfully shrank supplies of amphetamine produced by the pharmaceutical industry, new supplies emerged from criminally run clandestine labs. This resulted in a precipitous drop in purity of street amphetamine and methamphetamine, led to adulterated or misrepresented products (ephedrine-caffeine mixtures sold as amphetamine), and sparked the phenomenon of "look-alike drugs" (drugs illicitly manufactured to mimic the appearance of pharmaceutical amphetamine and methamphetamine). Morgan characterized this change in the amphetamine street market as "near complete counterfeiting and deception."[46]

As domestically manufactured supplies of amphetamine shrank, imported supplies from other countries increased. The rapid spread of methamphetamine use across the United States has been similarly matched by an increase in seized laboratories—a number that rose nationally from eighty-eight in 1981 to over eight thousand in 2001.[47] Supply reduction efforts must be sustained and evolve dynamically in tandem with evolving drug markets.

Drug surges may morph into something else as drug casualties increase and as successful containment efforts emerge. There is considerable historical evidence that a period of widespread use of one drug can pave the way for the use of other drugs. This lesson has been repeated in nearly every stimulant surge (including cocaine surges not reviewed in this chapter). The first Japanese surge of amphetamine and methamphetamine use, which abated in 1955 and 1956, was immediately followed by a period (1957–1963) of increased consumption of, first, sedatives and then heroin.[48] Similarly, many of the IV methamphetamine users of the late 1960s migrated into increased use of alcohol, sedatives, and narcotics. Many entered addiction treatment programs in the 1970s with drug choices other than stimulants. The current methamphetamine surge in the United States has spawned increased use of heroin and prescribed narcotics (e.g., Vicodin, OxyContin). Communities and community institutions must both prepare for and respond to the current methamphetamine surge and anticipate the rise in alcoholism, sedativism, and narcotic addiction that this surge often leaves in its wake. Seen historically, methamphetamine may be the Trojan horse that brings heroin and other narcotics into communities—particularly rural communities—that have been immune to opiate addiction.[49] Anecdotal incidents tell of heroin working its way into rural areas that had experienced high levels of methamphetamine use. Only time will tell if these incidents reflect an emerging pattern.

Hibernation, Amnesia, and Incubation

When successful suppression occurs, it seems as if a drug surge can wane or disappear overnight, as did the first methamphetamine surge in Japan.[50] Such drug surges return to a stage of dormancy or, more accurately, hibernation. But another important lesson from the early methamphetamine surges is that drug surges can be constricted to a point of cultural invisibility, but are rarely fully contained. They often leave behind an underground colony of chronic, hard-core users whose problems are quite severe and who pose a sustained drain on the criminal justice, health care, and social service systems. These users may sustain their drug choice and lifestyle for a number of years, even as the group is depleted by periodic institutionalization and premature death. Such colonies serve as a wick for the potential ignition of a new drug surge. Suwaki has described how "veterans" of the first Japanese methamphetamine surge survived to eventually spark a second surge in the 1960s.[51]

Of all the patterns in drug use, one that is most baffling is the propensity for particular drug choices to recycle into renewed popularity long after they were thought to be fully suppressed. While there is evidence of intragenerational learning and maturing out of drug choices that create visible negative effects, there is little historical evidence for intergenerational learning. The "war babies" who came of age in the midst of amphetamine experimentation in the 1960s and early 1970s were able to shed this drug choice as they reached maturity, but they were unable to pass that experiential wisdom on to their children as a protective factor. Drug surges are often followed by cultural amnesia related to the drug's untoward consequences.[52] When these consequences have not been culturally implanted, a new generation of users is vulnerable to experience and extol the drug's early euphoric effects and to rediscover in potentially disastrous ways the drug's hidden long-term effects.

History does tell us that when a particular drug returns, it usually does so in a different and often more virulent form. This is not just a repetition of the old cycle. The new episode often involves changes in the drug, its source, and the characteristics of users and changes in the problems created by use. For example, between Japan's first and second methamphetamine surges, sources of methamphetamine supply shifted almost completely from legal to illegal sources.[53] The evolution of surges can often be tracked by the transition from licit to gray market (legally manufactured products diverted from authorized channels without the manufacturer's knowledge) to black market (illicit manufacture and distribution) supply routes.

Finally, there is danger in overapplying the lessons of past drug surges to a newly emerging surge. Each has its own character, suggesting the need to listen to the present as well as the past.

CONCLUSION

Several factors seem important in the successful constriction of the earliest amphetamine and methamphetamine surges in the United States and Japan.

1 Limits on legal production and promotion play an important role in containing widespread drug use and in preventing the further expansion of an emerging drug surge.

2. Placing physicians and pharmacists in the role of gatekeepers for psychoactive drugs restricts access, but prescribing patterns continue to be shaped by the marketing practices of the pharmaceutical industry.

3. Education and monitoring of physicians and pharmacists (including warnings and indictments for inappropriate and excessive prescribing) can temper efforts by the pharmaceutical industry to promote use of the targeted drug.

4. Laws and enforcement strategies aimed at containing the illicit manufacture and distribution of a drug can help stem illicit drug supplies that increase in tandem with the reduction in licit drug supplies.

5. Prevention efforts can serve to stigmatize a drug and its use by the general public, but may have little effect on deeply disenfranchised elements of society.

6. Early identification of drug users and those experiencing drug-related problems via outreach, drug testing in schools and the workplace, and criminal justice diversion for assessment and treatment can potentially shorten addiction careers (reduce the time span from first to last use).

7. Increasing access to treatment and recovery support resources and the development of specialty resources (e.g., Crystal Meth Anonymous) can open pathways of escape from methamphetamine addiction.

8. Enhancing the visibility of recovery role models to instill hope for recovery and spark help-seeking has worked well with other drug choices, but we have yet to see a celebrity methamphetamine addiction/recovery story published.

9. Communicating the accumulation of drug-related casualties through the mainstream press and within active drug cultures (via outreach workers) can speed the deceleration of a drug surge.

⑩ A stigmatizing event that alters the image and attractiveness of a drug can speed the deceleration of a drug surge.[54]

⑪ The quarantine of hard-core users via treatment or incarceration at a presurge stage may diminish the social contagion that sparks wider use and its personal and social consequences.

⑫ Cultural/religious revitalization and economic development have played important roles in containing and reversing the effects of communitywide drug surges.[55] For example, the rapid decline of the first Japanese methamphetamine surge was closely tied to cultural and religious revitalization and the eventual revitalization of the nation's economy following World War II.[56]

⑬ Active management of the surge and its aftermath seems to be a key in shortening methamphetamine surges and reducing the personal and social toll of such surges. National, state, and local task forces seem to be an effective way to mobilize and coordinate the resources of multiple social institutions to respond to a drug surge.[57]

Chapter 3 continues our exploration of methamphetamine by looking at the drug's effects on the body and mind.

The Physiological Effects of Methamphetamine

Amphetamine and methamphetamine are members of a family of drugs known as central nervous system (CNS) stimulants. Drugs in this class also include cocaine, ephedrine, and methylphenidate. The drugs in this family are similar in many respects, including their effects. Further, drug abusers with a preference for a particular stimulant drug may turn to other drugs in this family when their first choice is in short supply. Thus, research involving other stimulant drugs can provide a fuller understanding about methamphetamine.

General Effects of Central Nervous System (CNS) Stimulants

CNS stimulants tend to elevate mood, suppress the appetite, raise the body's temperature, increase alertness, and relax bronchial muscles. As a central nervous system stimulant, methamphetamine is two to three times more potent than amphetamine[1] and its effects last longer. Curiously, however, neither users nor clinicians who observe their effects are able to distinguish among amphetamine, methamphetamine, and methylphenidate in blind tests.[2] The effects of amphetamine and methamphetamine are dose-dependent; that is, the effects at small doses may be very different from those at high doses. In general, low doses are relatively benign, particularly when taken on a short-term basis and under the supervision of a physician. In contrast, high doses can be highly destructive to the brain and to the body, particularly when taken over time in uncontrolled doses. Thus, because methamphetamine is so much more potent than amphetamine, the methamphetamine user's body may be hit with a substantially stronger stimulant, and in that respect its effects may also be different from those of other stimulant drugs.

There is relatively little information comparing the psychological or physiological effects of amphetamine versus methamphetamine, or comparing their addictive nature. There are, however, discussions comparing methamphetamine with cocaine and other drugs. Both methamphetamine and cocaine are CNS stimulants that generally lead to an increased heart rate and to a reduction in fatigue. There is some evidence that methamphetamine can facilitate the development of heart disease.[3] In limited doses both drugs lead to an increased ability to concentrate and euphoria. Higher doses or prolonged use is often followed by depression and fatigue,[4] with the depth of the depression and the extent of the fatigue directly related to the extent and duration of use. From the perspective of the nonmedical user, methamphetamine has two advantages over cocaine. First, methamphetamine can be taken in pill form, while cocaine is not absorbed well when taken in oral doses. Second, the high from methamphetamine lasts substantially longer—hours rather than a fraction of an hour.[5] In the body, amphetamine has a half-life of ten to thirty hours; the half-life of methamphetamine is even longer.[6] A comparison of treatment clients suggests that compared with cocaine users, those seeking treatment for methamphetamine abuse had a shorter period of time between first use and regular use and between regular use and entry into treatment.[7] This accelerated progression of problem development is sometimes referred to as *telescoping*.

Studies have compared the subjective effects of amphetamine with those of heroin, morphine, and barbiturates, and the findings are consistent. Double-blind experiments show that nearly all subjects receiving amphetamine report the experience as pleasant, whereas most receiving heroin, morphine, or barbiturates report the experience as unpleasant.

"The amphetamine user almost always considers the excitement of the central nervous system it produces a pleasant experience, at least in the beginning, and often he has a feeling of increased efficiency, perseverance, endurance, and overall competence."[8] Thus it appears that while drug users often must learn to enjoy the effects of such drugs as heroin and marijuana,[9] no such learning process is required for amphetamine. While amphetamine may not be instantly addictive, for most users it is instantly pleasurable. Writer Frank Owen describes his first experience with methamphetamine:

> The odd thing about methamphetamine is that it doesn't get you that stoned, at least not in the conventional sense of the word. My fingers went numb; my face flushed, and my body seemed to vibrate like a plucked string, but I actually felt more sober after taking the drug than I did before, as if I had awoken from a long slumber. Unlike other drugs that I had tried before, meth didn't blur the senses but sharpened them to a machinelike focus. . . . Most drugs are about losing control or escaping to some distant region of the mind. Meth was exactly the opposite: I felt ultrasharp. Edgy and exhilarated. Ready to roll. Equal to any task. Possessed by boundless amounts of energy. A wave of grandiosity washed over me. Give me enough meth, and I was ready to conquer the world.[10]

With an effect like that, it's easy to see the appeal of methamphetamine to people working two jobs, to truck drivers, or to women who try to balance full-time work with being a homemaker and mother.

In the body nearly half of a methamphetamine dose is metabolized into amphetamine.[11] Unchanged methamphetamine is excreted through the urine. The amount excreted appears directly related to the acidity of the urine.[12] In highly acidic urine as much as 80 percent of the drug may be excreted through the urine whereas in highly alkaline urine less than 3 percent will be excreted.[13] Early treatment recommendations for amphetamine and methamphetamine overdose included raising the acidity of urine to facilitate the removal of the drug from the body.[14] More recent research, however, advises against this, noting that raising the acidity of urine may also lead to kidney failure.[15] There are anecdotal stories of desperate methamphetamine users who "recycle" by filtering their urine to extract the excreted methamphetamine, including a case from California in which a meth user was burned after the solvent he was using to extract methamphetamine from his urine caught fire.[16] Such cases are rare and it is unlikely that for most users the amount of methamphetamine retrieved through this process would be worth the trouble involved in extracting it. Such cases do, however, reflect the desperate measures some will take to continue using the drug.

As many as 10 percent of Caucasians are deficient in an enzyme, CYP2D6, that is important in metabolizing methamphetamine and amphetamines. These individuals are more sensitive to the effects of methamphetamine and may more easily develop complications from amphetamine use.[17] Methamphetamine does appear to be popular among white people, though it is unclear how much of this pattern is due to physiological differences across races, cultural patterns, or distribution networks. Whether the absence of this enzyme in Caucasians helps account for the popularity of methamphetamine among Caucasians is an open question.

Amphetamine and Brain Chemistry

CNS stimulants act upon neurotransmitters, which are chemicals that send information between brain cells. Neurotransmitters are released by brain cells (neurons), cross a gap (synapse) to receptor neurons, and stimulate those neurons, causing them to generate an electrical impulse. Having done their work, the neurotransmitters are reabsorbed by the releasing neurons in a process known as reuptake. The neurotransmitters are "recharged" and are available to again be released to stimulate the receiving neurons. In this manner messages are sent from one brain cell to another, with different neurotransmitters influencing different neurons and consequently having differing effects on mood and/or behavior. As the number of released neurotransmitters increases at any given time, so does the intensity with which the brain is stimulated.

Amphetamine targets three neurotransmitters: dopamine, serotonin, and norepinephrine. Within the brain there are neurons specific to each.

Thus, there are dopamine neurons, serotonin neurons, and norepinephrine neurons. Dopamine is naturally produced in the brain and influences
body movement, memory, attention, problem solving, core body temperature, hunger, mood, and the pleasure centers of the brain. Serotonin acts
on the brain to influence mood, sleep, sexuality, and appetite. Finally, norepinephrine plays a large role in attention and the ability to concentrate.
Of the three neurotransmitters, dopamine has received the most attention
as the neurotransmitter accounting for many of the effects of methamphetamine and other drugs. However, all three play a role and some
research suggests that norepinephrine may be even more important than
dopamine in accounting for methamphetamine's effects.[18] In addition to
its direct influence, dopamine has an impact on the individual because it
plays a role in the production of norepinephrine and serotonin. Dopamine
is also a precursor to another chemical produced in the body, epinephrine,
also known as adrenaline. Adrenaline regulates the body's short-term reaction to stress through what is known as a fight-or-flight response.

Because it has received so much research attention, more is known
about the methamphetamine-dopamine connection than about methamphetamine's effect on neurotransmitters in general. Methamphetamine
triggers the release of dopamine, which leads to the pleasurable sensations
felt by the user as the receiving dopamine neurons are flooded with stimulation. Methamphetamine also inhibits the reuptake of used dopamine.
One consequence is that over time heavy users deplete the natural supply
of dopamine by damaging the receptors involved in reuptake. The abuser
must subsequently take increasingly large doses of methamphetamine to
achieve the same stimulating effect. A second consequence is that when
the high is over, the user feels a corresponding low or depression as a
result of a depleted supply of dopamine. Users are well aware that such
feelings can quickly be countered by another dose. While the depths of
this low tend to correspond to the heights of the user's high, the long-
term reduction in dopamine levels also leads to anhedonia, the inability
to experience pleasure from simple everyday things.[19]

Some have argued that the damage to dopamine receptors is permanent, while others suggest the receptors may be able to regenerate or mend
over time.[20] Still other research suggests that methamphetamine damages

or destroys proteins that create dopamine, rather than destroying dopamine terminals.[21] What is known is that the inability to experience pleasure may last months or even years in the heaviest users. Having such feelings and knowing that another dose will make them go away greatly challenges the former user who wishes to remain drug free.

Death from methamphetamine overdose is uncommon[22] and it is difficult in many cases to pinpoint methamphetamine as the primary cause of death, a problem complicated by the fact that amphetamines are commonly used in combination with other more lethal drugs.[23] Deaths have resulted from relatively small amounts in new users, while experienced users can withstand a thousand times that amount.[24] When it occurs, death is most likely to befall inexperienced users and is often a consequence of a heart attack, suicide, or heat stroke.[25] A heart attack appears less likely with amphetamines than with cocaine[26] and some have speculated that the risk of death from amphetamine use is four times that of the general population, but is similar to the rate for treated alcoholics and heroin users.[27]

Specific Effects of Methamphetamine

Methamphetamine can produce a variety of effects, and in many cases the effects at low doses are the opposite of those at high doses. Throughout this discussion, amphetamine, methamphetamine, and methylphenidate will be used interchangeably, as their effects are nearly identical. Further, many of the effects described here have also been reported for Ecstasy and for cocaine.

Appetite

Among the earliest recognized effects of stimulant drugs was appetite suppression, and these drugs have a long history of use as weight loss medicines. Today, methamphetamine can still be legally prescribed in tablet form for cases of morbid obesity under the trade name Desoxyn. In therapeutic doses, amphetamine and methamphetamine cause a short-term loss of appetite, usually lasting about thirty days. After that, increased doses are required to produce the same effect. This pattern of escalating use to maintain continued appetite suppression can easily become a path to abuse, and this appears to be a route often followed by women. Unfortunately, the serious abuser may use several hundred times the therapeutic amounts, and weight loss over time can be substantial. In the most extreme cases, "appetite suppression may be so profound that users may find the very act of swallowing difficult."[28]

Those whose obesity is the result of poor impulse control may be particularly likely to fall into a pattern of amphetamine abuse.[29] Further, abstaining from food and sleep may exaggerate the psychotoxic effects of these drugs. At the same time, reduced food intake may increase the acidity of the urine, causing a greater percentage of the drug to be excreted unchanged and thus requiring a larger dose to obtain the same effect.[30] A suppressed appetite may produce other undesirable effects, including abscesses, nonhealing ulcers, and brittle fingernails.[31]

Though it may seem the link between stimulant use and appetite is direct, the association appears complex. For example, when people fast or reduce their food intake without using amphetamine, their appetite continues to be reduced after the fast has concluded. In the case of amphetamine abusers, however, the end of a long meth run in which food intake has been drastically reduced is followed by a brief period in which the individual has a voracious appetite and abdominal cramping.[32] Studies of monkeys given amphetamine have reported initial anorexia, but, when given high doses, the monkeys began eating three times their usual daily amount while continuing to lose weight.[33] Still other researchers have examined the effects of amphetamine on elderly patients with poor motivation syndrome and found that for these individuals the appetite was stimulated rather than depressed.[34] These are exceptional cases, but they illustrate the complex ways in which these stimulant drugs can work.

In conclusion, weight loss while using amphetamine drugs is common but not universal. The effects wear off within a month unless increasingly large doses are taken. For those whose use is initially fueled by the desire to lose weight, and who are taking the drug without medical supervision, it is easy for use to spin out of control.

Arousal

Dopamine and serotonin play a role in maintaining alertness. Nearly everyone who uses amphetamine finds that they provide an energy boost. It is not unusual for people with hectic lives to begin using methamphetamine as a pick-me-up to help them make it through that second job, or to help them take care of their families after long hours of work. For example, truckers who needed to be alert to drive long distances were among the early adopters of amphetamine.[35] If that use spins out of control, large doses may cause the user to stay awake for days at a time, and then sleep for days when the drug wears off. Overall, the user will be receiving the proper amount of sleep, but, rather than the typical seven to eight hours per night, he or she will have long hours or even days of wakefulness followed by correspondingly long periods of sleeping—an unhealthy sleep pattern.[36]

The vast majority of methamphetamine users report sleeplessness as a side effect of the drug.[37] Disrupted sleep may lead to irritability, delusional thinking, and paranoia.[38] Although psychosis may emerge from disturbed sleep patterns, it is unclear whether sleeplessness alone is enough to account for the psychotic episodes experienced by some amphetamine users (see the discussion of amphetamine-induced psychosis on pages 61–63). The sleep patterns of amphetamine users going through withdrawal have been compared with those of a control group. Subjects withdrawing from amphetamine slept longer than controls for the first six nights, but slept less per night after that. Further, those withdrawing from amphetamine showed a greater variability in their sleep patterns.[39] Little is known about the long-term health consequences of these disturbed sleep patterns, though they might be expected to further strain the body in general and the heart in particular.

Performance

If some people begin taking amphetamine to improve alertness and performance, it is reasonable to ask whether the drug works. That is, does amphetamine not only keep the user awake but also improve performance? People who use methamphetamine almost always report initial feelings of energy and optimism and a sense that they can achieve things they never could have before. It is not surprising, then, that users not only have the ability to stay awake longer but also feel their performance has improved.

Studies of the link between stimulants and performance have considered several dimensions of the issue, including cognitive functioning, academic performance, driving behavior, athletic performance, and performance by military personnel on extended operations.

Cognitive Functioning

The impact of amphetamine on cognitive functioning (e.g., immediate recall of material, problem solving, and mathematical tasks) has been the subject of considerable research. Early research in a school for troubled youth concluded that amphetamine improved the students' speed of comprehension and their academic performance,[40] though the study provided no control group and no systematic measures of performance. More recent research, paying closer attention to methodological rigor, report mixed findings.[41] Some conclude that stimulants have no effect on cognitive functioning,[42] while others find that in fatigued individuals, amphetamine can restore cognitive functioning to prefatigue levels.[43] Generally, methamphetamine users do more poorly than controls on tests of memory,[44] although they may do better on simple memory tasks and worse as the tasks become more complex.[45] However, one study found that continuous users performed best on tests of memory followed by those who had relapsed. Ironically, the worst performance was by those who had abstained for a six-month period.[46] Current methamphetamine users also perform more poorly on tests of "stop-signal response inhibition," or the ability to rapidly stop after the individual has begun to respond,[47] implying some level of cognitive impairment. Other studies suggest that in therapeutic (e.g., small) doses, methamphetamine improves cognitive performance, but that under high doses cognitive performance is impaired, and this impairment may last well after heavy use has ended.[48] Overall, studies of the link between cognitive performance and amphetamine use find either no change or improvement in performance,[49] at least when clinical doses are involved. Heavy use is another matter. Amphetamine also seems to at least partly counter detrimental cognitive effects of moderate alcohol use.[50] Further, if impairment from amphetamine does occur, it does not appear to be permanent,[51] though it is difficult to know the effects of methamphetamine alone, given that so many methamphetamine users also use other psychoactive drugs.

Academic Performance

Academic performance might be expected to improve under the influence of a drug that produces alertness, allowing students to study longer and to perceive an increased ability to focus. It is not surprising, therefore, that stimulant drugs have been popular among college students as a study aid, or to give them the energy to party longer. One-third of college students in a survey conducted in the 1960s reported using amphetamine.[52] It appears that by 2002 about a third of college students were still taking stimulants without the benefit of a prescription, with an additional 10 percent taking them with a prescription.[53] How often these drugs were taken as study aids, rather than for purely recreational purposes, is unknown. Also unknown is whether these drugs have any impact on a student's academic performance. Given the effects of the drug, students who use a stimulant are likely to feel more confident and they may believe their performance is enhanced. However, whether these perceptions have any basis in reality is an open question as there is little empirical evidence to support or refute them.

It is somewhat ironic and more than a little hypocritical that elementary and junior high students diagnosed with attention-deficit/hyperactivity disorder are encouraged, or even required, by the adults in their lives to take stimulant drugs to improve school performance, but university students face the possibility of arrest if they take unprescribed stimulants as study aids.[54]

While many students continue to use stimulants as study aids, this category of drug has also become an important part of the party scene at many universities.[55] Ironically, students report that stimulants are chosen as party drugs partly as a response to restrictive alcohol policies on campus—with illicit stimulants being easier to obtain and to conceal.

Driving Behavior

The popularity of amphetamine among long-haul truck drivers has led to the study of amphetamine's impact on driving behavior, though definitive conclusions remain elusive. One problem in assessing this relationship is that the percentage of drivers using methamphetamine is relatively small, limiting the utility of field studies. The percentage of drivers bingeing on methamphetamine is even smaller. Further, controlled studies typically use only therapeutic doses of amphetamine. Most such studies conclude there is no meaningful relationship between amphetamine use and driving behavior, except that small doses can return driving ability to baseline levels when the driver is fatigued,[56] precisely the effect desired by long-haul truckers. These same studies also suggest that when taken in combination with alcohol, amphetamine may correct for some of the impairment that follows alcohol use.[57] As with other effects, heavy amphetamine use is likely to seriously impair driving behavior. Some people have attributed the phrase "God is my copilot" to the case of a trucker high on amphetamine whose rig crashed after he turned over driving responsibilities to a nonexistent copilot.[58]

One issue raised by the research but not fully addressed is the effect of withdrawal from amphetamine on driving performance.[59] At least one study of driving-related fatalities or arrests in which methamphetamine was found in the blood of the driver noted that in most of the cases the accident resulted from drifting out of the driving lane and crashing into objects along the road—behavior more consistent with fatigue than with alertness.[60] The tendency to "crash" (i.e., fall into a deep sleep) after an amphetamine run has serious implications for users who are behind the wheel, and suggests that the fatigue experienced when coming down from stimulants poses a greater danger to drivers than does the stimulant effect of the drugs.

A Norwegian study had nearly nine hundred drivers with amphetamine in their bloodstream assessed by physicians trained in administering a clinical test of impairment.[61] It was concluded that amphetamine had a modest but important detrimental effect on impairment, and that this impairment was more pronounced in younger drivers, even if they had levels of amphetamine in their blood comparable to the levels of older drivers. Although the study included a relatively large sample and utilized established instruments administered by physicians trained in their use, study authors had no way of knowing when the amphetamine was taken or how much was taken over time. This made it impossible to distinguish the stimulating effects of amphetamine from the fatigue resulting from withdrawal, or to distinguish the effects of low doses from those of high doses.

Athletic Performance

Athletic performance is also an issue associated with amphetamine and other stimulant drugs. The effects of these drugs, including enhanced self-confidence and a perceived increase in energy, have made amphetamine particularly appealing to athletes. Concern about this issue was sufficient enough that in 1957 the American Medical Association formed a special committee to investigate the effects of amphetamine on athletic performance.[62] The committee decided to provide support for two studies. Both studies used a double-blind methodology and both used competitive college athletes in a variety of sports. One study used relatively small doses (10 mg or 20 mg) and measured the effect between thirty minutes and one hour after ingestion.[63] In this study there was no effect on the athletes' performance running on a treadmill, swimming, or running track. Most subjects receiving 10 mg could not correctly guess whether they received amphetamine or a placebo, though most correctly guessed when they received a 20 mg dose of amphetamine.

The second study was considerably more elaborate and can still be considered a benchmark in the study of stimulants and athletic performance.[64] This study used a wider range of athletic events, measured the effects after two to three hours of ingestion, when the drug's effects should peak, and gave larger doses of amphetamine adjusted to body weight. The study included nearly eight hundred measured performance trials in such events as swimming, running, and weight throwing. "In all three classes of athletes, the majority of subjects performed better under the influence of amphetamine (14 mg per 70 kg) than placebo. . . . Eighty-five percent of the weight-throwers, 73 percent of the runners, and from 67 to 93 percent of the swimmers [depending upon the event] performed better under the influence of amphetamine than placebo."[65] While the improvements were only in the 1 to 4 percent range, the study's authors noted that competitive athletes may spend months training in order to achieve a gain of 1 or 2 percent and this gain is often the difference between a gold medal and finishing without a medal. Largely based on the findings of this study, the American Medical Association recommended these drugs be banned from athletic competition.[66]

The larger issue, however, is whether gains in performance come at a cost to the athletes' health. The evidence on this is less clear, though there are good reasons to be concerned. The Food and Drug Administration asked the Rand Corporation to conduct an extensive review of the effect of ephedrine on athletic performance.[67] Ephedrine is a comparatively mild stimulant and precursor to more potent stimulants. It had been sold over the counter in pill form in truck stops and convenience stores as a dietary supplement that would aid in weight loss and be an energy booster. The review concluded that there were few methodologically sound studies of the issue, but did note a series of individual cases in which the death of young athletes was thought to have resulted from the use of ephedrine products. As a result of these cases, ephedrine was banned by the federal government in 2004 in over-the-counter tablet form. In the absence of research providing empirical evidence, one might expect the death rate from methamphetamine to be higher than that from ephedrine.

Use in the Military

Stimulant drugs have also been used in the military. Amphetamine was given liberally during World War II to U.S., Canadian, British, Japanese, and German soldiers. Some historians claim that Hitler's troops were able to march through Europe so quickly because amphetamine gave them increased energy and endurance. Japanese kamikaze pilots were said to have prepared for their missions by taking large doses of amphetamine. It is also claimed that British soldiers shared as many as eighty million amphetamine tablets with American soldiers, who may have received an additional eighty to one hundred million tablets from American Army medics. By the end of the war as many as 1.5 million U.S. soldiers returned home with some experience with amphetamine.[68] American military forces (illegally) used injectable amphetamine while in Korea and Japan in the early 1950s[69] and were officially given amphetamine in tablet form during the Korean, Vietnam, Desert Storm, and Afghan wars.[70] Beginning in 1960 the U.S. Air Force dispensed amphetamine for pilots in extended flight operations. While this practice was supposed to have ended in March 1991, following Operation Desert Storm, it was apparently used again in the war in Afghanistan.[71] In 2002 two U.S. Air Force pilots were charged with manslaughter for mistakenly bombing and killing Canadian troops in Afghanistan. As part of their legal defense, the pilots claimed their judgment had been impaired by the amphetamine they were given to counter fatigue.

A series of studies on the impact of amphetamine (or "go pills") on pilot performance during extended flight operations suggest that in the doses typically given pilots, amphetamine can improve the performance of sleep-deprived aviators to prefatigued levels. Amphetamine does not, however, improve the performance of rested pilots.[72] Though most of the research has used amphetamine in its tests, similar patterns have been observed with methamphetamine.[73]

The use of stimulants by pilots does not lead to negative side effects, so long as use is carefully monitored by a physician. Anecdotal evidence suggests there were problems of adverse side effects during the Vietnam War, but during that war amphetamine was reportedly "available like candy . . . [with] essentially no control over the dose or frequency of use."[74] After Vietnam the Air Force adopted policies to more carefully regulate the use of stimulants by pilots. When amphetamine is used within these more restrictive conditions:

> There is no evidence that aviators attempt to abuse amphetamine if the medication is occasionally made available. And there is virtually no similarity between the effects of high dosages or chronic amphetamine abuse among addicts and occasional, low-dose administration of the same drug to military pilots involved in extended operations.[75]

Others have made the point more strongly, arguing that for soldiers on active duty "in situations where sleep deprivation is unavoidable, Dexedrine could make the difference between life and death."[76]

Related research outside of the military setting supports these general conclusions, finding that methamphetamine lessens disruptions in performance by night-shift workers but does not reduce errors by day-shift workers.[77] In short, improvements in work-related performance are generally limited to those individuals who are sleep deprived or who have jobs requiring an unusual sleep schedule. These improvements, however, only return the user to normal levels of performance, and no more.

Parkinson's Disease

Among its many functions, dopamine regulates smooth body movement. A shortage of dopamine is associated with Parkinson's disease, in which the individual exhibits tremors or stiffness. Those suffering from Parkinson's may also experience mood disorders, including depression, apathy, and panic attacks. At the other end of the spectrum, an excess of dopamine is believed to cause Tourette's syndrome, in which the individual may exhibit tics and/or periodic vocal outbursts, sometimes of offensive language.

The cause of Parkinson's is not well understood, though it is generally thought to be caused by environmental factors rather than genetics.[78] Some researchers believe it may be the result of exposure to a chemical or combination of chemicals, though which chemicals still remains a mystery. The view that environmental chemicals may be responsible for Parkinson's was reinforced in the early 1980s by studies in which addicts taking MPTP, a synthetic substitute for heroin, developed permanent parkinsonism,[79] and by a study in twins that cast doubt on the genetic origins of the condition.[80]

Because extensive amphetamine use depletes brain dopamine, it has been speculated that the long-term use of amphetamine might lead to Parkinson's. However, there appears to be no connection between amphetamine abuse and the development of Parkinson's. To the contrary, in 1963 the American Medical Association recognized amphetamine for the treatment of Parkinson's, also suggesting that amphetamine was effective and without risk of addiction.[81]

In principle, those suffering from Parkinson's would benefit from being administered dopamine itself, rather than drugs that stimulate the production of dopamine. The problem with administering dopamine directly is that it is unable to cross the blood-brain barrier and cannot reach the regions of the brain experiencing a shortage of dopamine. Current therapies rely on drugs that are precursors to dopamine, that are able to cross the blood-brain barrier, and that are thought to facilitate the production of dopamine in the brain. Among these precursor chemicals, the drug L-DOPA is among the most popular drugs for reducing the tremors associated with Parkinson's. While L-DOPA may reduce Parkinson's-related tremors, it does not appear to counter feelings of depression. In therapeutic doses, about 20 percent of patients report psychiatric side effects, often similar to those of amphetamine. These effects include psychosis, depression, and hypersexual activity, though these effects are seen primarily in patients with preexisting tendencies toward these conditions.[82]

Though we might expect a direct relationship between amphetamine use and Parkinson's, this appears not to be the case because amphetamine primarily depletes dopamine that acts on the caudate nucleus, a cluster of nerves involved in cognitive functioning. Parkinson's, in contrast, is the result of depleted dopamine in the putamen, a cluster of nerves involved in motor function.[83] This still leaves open the possibility, however, of the creation of new synthetic stimulants that do create Parkinson's, much as the attempt to create synthetic heroin did in the 1980s.

Psychosis

One of the more serious effects of heavy methamphetamine use is psychosis, which can also be produced by other central nervous system stimulants, including cocaine, methylphenidate, and ephedrine. Though rare, there is at least one documented case of psychosis induced by Ecstasy.[84] Very high doses may lead to psychotic episodes that are nearly identical to paranoid schizophrenia. In Thailand, the largest per-capita consumer of amphetamine in the world, it has been estimated that over 10 percent of psychiatric hospital admissions are for methamphetamine-induced psychosis.[85]

The term *psychosis* generally refers to a constellation of symptoms that may include visual, auditory, and olfactory hallucinations; delusions of persecution; paranoia; and delusional thinking, such as the belief that one's spouse is unfaithful in the absence of any indicators to support such a belief.[86] Psychosis may also involve ideas of reference, which means the psychotic may believe that others are talking about him or her. This may even extend to the belief that a television newscast is speaking directly about the psychotic, or that a newspaper editorial was written specifically about him or her. While anyone exhibiting all of the above described symptoms would be diagnosed as having a psychotic episode, it is more useful to think of psychosis as existing along a continuum from no symptoms to full-blown psychosis, rather than viewing psychosis as an all-or-none condition.[87] The most common psychotic symptom of individuals experiencing methamphetamine-induced psychosis is the delusion that they are being persecuted. Other common symptoms include auditory hallucinations, strange beliefs, and the perceived ability to read the thoughts of others.[88] It has been argued that while paranoia is a common feature of methamphetamine psychosis, most experienced users recognize this effect and do not act on their paranoid delusions.[89]

Psychosis has been a well-documented outcome of amphetamine use. Although psychosis undoubtedly affected early users of amphetamine, for many years doctors did not recognize the connection between psychosis and amphetamine, and until the 1950s there was still debate about whether amphetamine was addictive.[90] This was partly due to the lack of any convenient and reliable test for the drug combined with the tendency of (paranoid) users to deny having used stimulants. In 1938 several cases of methamphetamine-induced psychoses were reported in the medical literature,[91] followed by a few additional cases reported in 1954.[92]

The extent of the problem was not fully appreciated until 1958 when P. H. Connell located and analyzed thirty-four published cases in which amphetamine was thought to have caused psychosis severe enough to require hospitalization. The patients generally exhibited delusions of persecution, ideas of reference, auditory and visual hallucinations, and acute terror. Upon admission their symptoms usually subsided. Recognizing the poor reliability of patient self-reports and the lack of standardized biological testing procedures, Connell devoted half of his book *Amphetamine Psychosis* to assessing the validity of various techniques for detecting amphetamine in body fluids.

A study of admissions to a New York mental hospital in the 1960s for amphetamine-related problems found that about half exhibited psychotic symptoms,[93] and psychotic symptoms have even been produced in laboratory animals. Given enough of the drug over time, psychosis can be induced by amphetamine in otherwise healthy, well-adjusted individuals.[94] One study concluded that methamphetamine users were eleven times more likely than the general population to experience clinically significant psychotic episodes, and that the likelihood of such episodes was directly related to the extent of methamphetamine abuse.[95]

Not all users develop psychotic symptoms. Psychosis is generally the result of prolonged heavy use, though there are cases in which a single large dose resulted in psychotic symptoms. Further, once psychotic symptoms emerge they may reoccur with substantially smaller doses of the drug. Psychotic symptoms may also reoccur during periods of abstinence for individuals experiencing stress.[96] The development of psychosis has also been associated with an early age of onset of methamphetamine use.[97] Even among heavy long-term users psychosis is not inevitable. Rather, some people appear to be predisposed to developing psychotic symptoms. Methamphetamine users with preexisting mental health problems may be particularly prone to developing psychosis, as are users with a family history of mental health problems.[98]

Preexisting mental problems also appear related to the duration of the psychotic episode. For healthy, well-adjusted individuals the psychotic episode generally ends as the drug leaves the system, whereas for those with preexisting mental conditions the psychosis may last much longer, even years after the effects of the drug have worn off.[99]

Ironically, while methamphetamine has been tied to psychosis, at least one study found that more than a quarter of the meth users in the study used the drug "to cope with mental illness, distress, or trauma,"[100] including one subject who used methamphetamine to self-medicate for symptoms of schizophrenia and to "feel normal."

Stereotyped Behavior

Heavy amphetamine use can also lead to what researchers have termed *stereotyped behavior*—compulsive repetitive behavior such as plucking at some object for hours, disassembling electronic devices, clocks, or motors, obsessive grooming, or picking at the skin.[101] In the United States this behavior has sometimes been called *tweaking* (a term also used to describe a meth run) while in Sweden it is referred to as "punding."[102] One manifestation of stereotyped behavior is the sensation that bugs are crawling under the user's skin. Continuous picking at these "meth bugs" can leave the user covered in open sores. In Hawaii, taking devices apart and then trying (often unsuccessfully) to reassemble them has been called "The MacGyver Syndrome" after the fictional television character known for his ability to create complex devices from everyday objects.[103] "Meth bugs" have their counterparts in other drugs, including cocaine, but the potency of methamphetamine appears to make this condition a more frequent feature of methamphetamine abuse.

Amphetamine-induced stereotyped behavior has been replicated in a variety of laboratory species including rats, mice, guinea pigs, cats, and monkeys.[104] In these animals stereotyped behavior includes compulsive licking and biting, and in some species aggression is found when animals are placed together in a cage. In humans, stereotyped behavior often precedes psychosis.[105] In general, the more complex the species the more complex the stereotyped behavior, with humans showing the most complex behavior of all species.[106] It also appears that stereotyped behavior goes away as the effects of the drug wear off.

Hyperthermia

Methamphetamine and other stimulant drugs can interfere with the body's ability to regulate its temperature, elevating it to sometimes toxic levels. As a stimulant, methamphetamine speeds up heart rate and blood pressure, raising the body's temperature, as well as the temperature of the brain. Increased body temperature places a strain on the heart and vital organs, with the liver and kidney being particularly susceptible to damage or even shutdown. Urine flow is often dramatically reduced, placing strain on the kidneys.[107] Elevated brain temperature increases the speed of dopamine release and uptake and leads to the accelerated depletion of dopamine.[108] Higher temperatures may also damage neurons, perhaps permanently.[109] Further, CNS stimulants are vasoconstrictors, constricting the flow of blood and reducing the body's ability to carry away excess heat. Finally, methamphetamine and related drugs give users a sense of heightened energy, giving them the stamina to keep active beyond their normal limits. This heightened level of physical activity further magnifies the problem of hyperthermia.

Studies using laboratory animals suggest this elevated temperature is the result of the drug's action on the brain and is not primarily the product of increased physical activity.[110] That said, increased physical activity, high ambient temperatures, stress, and even social interaction can magnify the temperature increase.[111] Perhaps it is fortunate that many methamphetamine addicts are "couch potatoes," but the same cannot be said for athletes who use stimulants to enhance performance. While methamphetamine is of obvious concern, even milder stimulants can raise body temperature to dangerous levels. In February 2003, minor league baseball pitcher Steve Bechler died of heat stroke during a team workout in Fort Lauderdale, Florida. He had been taking an over-the-counter supplement containing ephedra as a weight loss aid.[112]

Curiously, while all stimulant drugs may raise the body's temperature, and just as importantly the temperature of the brain, there are some differences across stimulant drug groups. Methamphetamine and Ecstasy tend to elevate brain temperatures in a purely dose-dependent fashion. That is, brain temperature increases correspond rather directly with increases in dose, to the point that damage to brain cells may result when temperatures rise above 104° or 105° F, though whether such damage occurs and the extent of the damage is highly variable across individuals. In contrast, cocaine and ketamine (and the narcotic heroin) initially increase brain activity and hence brain temperature, but both brain activity and temperature invert with increases in dose, and temperatures tend to remain below levels that would damage brain neurons.[113] In the case of cocaine, the vasoconstrictor properties of the drug can lead to hyperthermia-related renal failure and death, though seizures may play a larger role in the death than does hyperthermia.[114]

Death from methamphetamine overdose is not common, but when it does occur, hyperthermia is often a key contributing factor.[115] In a process nearly identical to death by heat stroke, the body's organs begin shutting down, particularly the kidneys and liver, and the heart is under stress. The likelihood of death is related to the severity and duration of hyperthermia, though the particular temperature that leads to death appears to vary from person to person and will be influenced by a variety of factors, including ambient temperature, stress, physical activity, and other drugs consumed with methamphetamine. It is also possible that some people are genetically limited in their body's ability to counter liver damage from amphetamine.[116]

Treating drug-induced hyperthermia generally involves cooling the patient with sprays of tepid water and cooling by fans, ice packs, cooling blankets, and pumping the stomach with ice water.[117] It is also important to calm agitated patients, as agitation may contribute to hyperthermia. Some physicians suggest administering chlorpromazine (a powerful tranquilizer) while others recommend benzodiazepines, a class of tranquilizers that also reduces anxiety.[118]

Meth Mouth

Among the more graphically disturbing images of the methamphetamine user is that of *meth mouth*. As depicted in the media, and in numerous antimeth campaigns, the term generally refers to a mouthful of grotesquely decayed and abscessed teeth. Just how prevalent meth mouth is among users is not known. When in-treatment methamphetamine users in Southern California were asked about problems they experienced from using meth, over half reported having "dental problems," though precisely what that meant was not defined.[119] Another study, focusing specifically on the consequences of methamphetamine use for dental hygiene, concluded that methamphetamine users were four times more likely than nonusers to exhibit dental health deterioration, a condition that again was vaguely defined.[120]

Though the issue of meth mouth has garnered much attention, it has been the subject of relatively little research. One popular explanation is that the caustic chemicals used to produce methamphetamine themselves break down the teeth's enamel, but some research discounts this explanation[121] and dental research has generally focused its attention elsewhere.

Not every meth user or meth addict develops meth mouth. It appears that meth mouth is the result of a confluence of circumstances, including (1) dryness of the mouth, (2) sugar-filled soft drinks, (3) grinding of the teeth, (4) clenching of the jaw, and (5) generally poor dental hygiene. And, while the condition has been linked to methamphetamine in the public's eyes, it has also been associated with the use of Ecstasy.[122]

Dry mouth, also known as xerostomia, is a common side effect of methamphetamine.[123] Dryness of the mouth is the result of vasoconstriction of the maxillary artery. This restricted blood flow to the mouth also reduces the output of saliva, which may weaken teeth over time. Further, this reduced output has been found to persist for as long as thirty days of abstinence.[124] It also has been speculated that methamphetamine may further damage the teeth not only by reducing the flow of saliva but also by altering saliva's characteristics, lowering the pH and thus making the saliva more acidic.[125] In addition to dryness as a result of the direct action of the drug, methamphetamine also dehydrates the body because it increases the metabolism and physical activity.[126] Reducing the water content of the body by as little as 8 percent will reduce the flow of saliva to zero.[127] At least one study examined three cases of extreme tooth decay, or gross caries, in childhood and adolescence and concluded that methamphetamine, given in the form of medication for narcolepsy and attention deficit disorder, led to a reduced saliva flow which, in turn, resulted in the extreme breakdown in the dental enamel.[128] These three cases notwithstanding, attributing meth mouth entirely to methamphetamine is complicated by the fact that most meth users also smoke tobacco and/or marijuana, both of which also lead to dry mouth.[129]

Sugar-filled carbonated soft drinks contribute to meth mouth in two ways. First, the low pH of soft drinks contributes to weakening the teeth's enamel.[130] Second, sugar contributes to the growth of bacteria. Neither of these circumstances would be a particular problem if soft drinks were consumed in moderation. Unfortunately, hard-core methamphetamine users, suffering from a serious case of dry mouth, will consume many times what an ordinary person would drink in an effort to quench their continuous thirst.

Also contributing to meth mouth is the tendency of those high on methamphetamine to grind their teeth, a behavior known as bruxism. Bruxism appears to be particularly damaging to the front teeth. Sometimes this grinding also sharpens the front teeth, a behavior known as *thegosis*. A companion behavior to bruxism is the practice of clenching the teeth together, sometimes referred to as trisma. This process has its greatest effects on the back teeth and may also lead to pain in the muscles and joints of the jaw.[131] Further, the process of jaw clenching has been observed to continue for many hours after the drug has worn off.[132] Like dry mouth, teeth grinding and jaw clenching have also been observed among Ecstasy users.[133]

Finally, all of the issues listed above are compounded by the poor dental hygiene practiced by some methamphetamine users. In some ways the problem is self-perpetuating in that as the teeth decay or are worn away they become sensitive and brushing them becomes painful. Failure to brush only hastens further decay. Poor dental hygiene alone, however, cannot explain all cases of methamphetamine-related dental problems. Howe has observed "gross dental caries" among adolescents and children who were prescribed methamphetamine for either narcolepsy or attention-deficit/hyperactivity disorder and for whom both diet and oral hygiene were considered average.[134] Further, the cases described by Howe suggest that for some individuals there may be a more direct association between the drug itself and dental caries, given that the subjects he observed were taking legally manufactured methamphetamine in clinical doses. Thus, the methamphetamine used by these subjects did not contain the residual corrosive chemicals that remain in some of the homemade product, nor could the problem be solely attributed to the excessive use of the drug or to poor hygiene.

Dental problems are not unique to methamphetamine users, having been documented in regular users of the opiates, marijuana, and cocaine.[135] Marijuana and cocaine users, though not opiate users, may experience xerostomia—the reduced flow of saliva that produces the sensation of dry mouth and that facilitates the growth of bacteria. Common among all of these categories of frequent drug users, however, is the tendency to practice poor oral hygiene. There appears to be nothing in the drugs themselves, or in the chemicals used to create or to cut the drugs, that directly accounts for the high rate of dental problems experienced by these drug users.

It is an exaggeration to say that an oral health crisis is strictly the result of using methamphetamine.[136] Those who suggest that meth mouth is a myth[137] are equally misinformed. Regular methamphetamine users often do have dental problems, problems that are the product of an unhealthy lifestyle, and that may be exacerbated by the effects of methamphetamine, such as dry mouth and a reduced appetite. However, the cases observed by Howe,[138] though rare, suggest that in some cases the drug itself may be the problem. In any event, claims concerning the enormous costs associated with treating meth mouth suggest the issue is worth further systematic study.

Effect on the Heart

Much is made of methamphetamine's effect on the brain, in particular on the release of dopamine and noradrenaline. Aside from their other effects, dopamine and noradrenaline modulate heart rate and blood pressure.[139] Through these neurotransmitters conflicting messages are sent to the body. The heart rate is increased while at the same time blood vessels are constricted. Operating at an increased rate, the heart requires additional oxygen, but constricted blood vessels reduce the flow of blood and consequently the supply of oxygen to the heart. This can lead to myocardial infarction (also known as a heart attack), or in extreme cases sudden cardiac death.[140] The main artery taking blood from the heart to the body is the aorta, and the increased blood pressure and heart rate may cause the inner walls of the aorta to tear, a condition known as acute aortic dissection. Methamphetamine use is second only to hypertension (high blood pressure) as a cause of aortic dissection[141] and, of course, methamphetamine itself is a cause of hypertension. These negative effects on the heart are amplified if the methamphetamine user is also consuming alcohol, cocaine, or opiates, a situation that is all too common.[142] Further, there is some indication that heart problems from the use of methamphetamine may occur less frequently than from the use of cocaine.[143]

In general, high doses do more damage than low doses, though for regular users a tolerance may develop that mitigates the effects of high doses on the heart, and there are variations across individuals in their physiological response to a given dose.[144] Thus, it is not possible to state that a particular dose will necessarily lead to heart-related problems. While it may be obvious that the amount of methamphetamine used is relevant, one counterintuitive finding from a study of methamphetamine's effects on animals is that the effects on the heart are greater when doses are separated by days rather than by shorter time periods.[145] Whether this holds for humans is as yet unknown.

Finally, it appears that although methamphetamine places a strain on the heart and the circulatory system, major complications do not typically befall the healthy user. Rather, heart attacks, aortic dissection, and even death appear more likely in methamphetamine users with preexisting heart conditions.[146] This also explains why heart attacks or deaths sometimes follow relatively minor doses of the drug.

Damage to the Eyes

Although rare, there are reports of a link between regular methamphetamine use and damage to the cornea of the eye. Symptoms begin with irritation of the eye, followed over time by infection. If untreated, or if unresponsive to treatment with antibiotics, the infection may progress to the point that a corneal transplant may be required.[147] These symptoms have also been observed among crack cocaine users.[148]

The mechanism through which methamphetamine might damage the cornea is unclear, and there are several possible explanations, separately or in combination, for the link.[149] First, there may be direct effects of the drug, either through ingestion or by the user's handling the drug and then rubbing his or her eyes. Methamphetamine is known to concentrate in the saliva and it is possible that it also concentrates in tears, directly exposing the eye to the drug. Further, methamphetamine tends to restrict blood vessels and through this action it may lead to excessive dryness of the eye, facilitating infection. Second, chemicals sometimes used to dilute the drug for street sales, such as lidocaine or procaine, have themselves been linked to corneal damage. Finally, it is possible that damage to the cornea results from exposure to chemicals used in the process of manufacturing the drug, or to chemicals left in the final product as residue from the production process.

The Effects of Methamphetamine on Children

How methamphetamine affects children is an emotional topic that has generated a correspondingly strong response from the public and from policy makers. It is also an issue in which objective data lag far behind the public response. There are several dimensions to the issue, including prenatal exposure, the effects of exposure to the drug on performance and cognitive functioning, and the effects of exposure to chemicals used to manufacture methamphetamine.

Prenatal Exposure to Methamphetamine

The evidence regarding methamphetamine's effects on the neonate is mixed at best. Understanding of the issue is complicated by the fact that most pregnant women who use methamphetamine also use other drugs, including alcohol, during the course of their pregnancy.[150] Alcohol is the most popular drug to use in combination with methamphetamine, and the combination of these two drugs places a burden on the heart beyond that of either drug acting alone.[151] In addition to the use of other drugs for purely recreational purposes, alcohol and/or other sedatives are often used by methamphetamine abusers to counter insomnia,[152] and the detrimental effects of alcohol on the developing fetus are well documented. Even controlling for the use of other illegal drugs, methamphetamine-exposed babies have lower birth weight, being an average of 4.5 times more likely to be small for their age. Methamphetamine (and cocaine) use by pregnant women does appear to lead to children who have lower birth weight and are generally small for their gestational age.[153] However, lower birth weight is also associated with nicotine use during pregnancy, and tobacco smoking appears to be more common among pregnant methamphetamine users than among pregnant women in general.[154] Further, compared with other pregnant women, methamphetamine-using pregnant women receive less prenatal care, have fewer visits to the doctor, and begin visiting a doctor later in their pregnancy.[155]

Studies of pregnant heroin users suggest that the shock of sudden withdrawal may restrict growth of the fetus. The recommendation that pregnant heroin users be given methadone implies that sudden withdrawal from heroin may be more damaging to the fetus than the narcotic itself.[156]

Methamphetamine use can certainly lead to dependence, and withdrawal may be accompanied by *psychological* effects, including depression, but the *physical* effects of withdrawal appear to be less severe than those of heroin. Although this issue has not been systematically studied, it is likely that withdrawal from methamphetamine has a lesser impact on the developing fetus than does withdrawal from heroin.

The extent to which the developing fetus is affected by drugs is also a function of the method of administration.[157] Drugs taken orally undergo some filtering by the liver before circulating throughout the body, thereby reducing their effect in the fetus somewhat. In contrast, "drugs taken intramuscularly, intravenously, or by inhalation do not undergo first-pass metabolism and may more readily cross the placenta following absorption from the site of administration."[158] This difference is important regarding methamphetamine, in that it can be taken intravenously, intramuscularly, snorted, smoked, or eaten, with the particular method of administration, as noted in chapter 1, varying in popularity from one region of the country to another.[159]

It is important to distinguish short-term effects of withdrawal from long-term neurological damage from the drug, given that early reports of permanent damage to the child from exposure to cocaine in the womb turned out to have been much exaggerated. While it has been speculated that the longer-lasting effects of methamphetamine might make it more damaging to the developing fetus than cocaine,[160] a comparison of cocaine-exposed and methamphetamine-exposed infants concluded that methamphetamine-exposed infants appeared less impaired in the first year, though compared with infants not exposed to any drug they were more lethargic and exhibited poorer feeding and less alertness.[161] The point at which drugs are taken during the course of a pregnancy also matters. The most critical time for the developing fetus is the first eight weeks of pregnancy.[162] Unfortunately, this is often before the woman even realizes she is pregnant. The particular short-term effects of methamphetamine on the newborn appear to be related to the trimester during which the drug was used:

> MA [methamphetamine] use during the first trimester was related to more signs of stress, particularly more gastrointestinal stress. Use in the

second trimester was associated with more lethargy. Use in the third trimester was related to poor quality of movement and greater physiological stress . . . we [also] found that MA-exposed infants were more likely to cry in response to initial stimulation and demonstrated poorer respiratory control and neural control of the vocal tract.[163]

The long-term effects of methamphetamine exposure in the womb are less clear. In one of the only longitudinal studies, the children of mothers who used methamphetamine during pregnancy in Sweden were studied at the ages of four, eight, and fourteen.[164] At age four, the extent to which a child had a disturbed or problematic social adjustment was related to alcohol and drug use before and during pregnancy, but was *not* related to birth weight, complications during pregnancy, neonatal illness, or quality of the home environment at the time of the interview. Aggressiveness at age eight was related to maternal drug use before pregnancy, regular amphetamine use during pregnancy, number of amphetamine injections during pregnancy, number of months before use stopped, attitude toward the pregnancy, and maternal alcohol use in the first eight years. At age fourteen, amphetamine-exposed youth scored lower than other students on tests of mathematics, Swedish language, and physical training. Boys were taller and heavier than the norm, and girls were shorter than the norm. While these observations over time are suggestive, the findings are complicated by the fact that 81 percent of the women in this study used alcohol during their pregnancy.

Perhaps the best summary of our knowledge about the effects of exposure to methamphetamine in the womb comes from Lester and colleagues' study of more than twenty-seven thousand newborn infants:

Current public concern about MA [methamphetamine] is reminiscent of attitudes about cocaine 20 years ago. Sensational reports are abundant, but scientific evidence about prenatal MA effects on children's development is scant. As with cocaine, effects of prenatal MA exposure depend upon the time of use during pregnancy, the quantity used, and the purity of the drug, as well as protective factors in the fetus. No distinguishing features can identify a baby as MA-exposed. What we do know is that harm will come to children if pregnant women avoid the health care system because they fear detection of their MA use or manufacture, incarceration, and placement of their children in foster care. We know that labeling children as "meth babies" or "meth orphans" can harm them. We know that risky environments can magnify the impact of drug exposure on children.[165]

Most studies of methamphetamine users focus on the adult population, which is surprising given that at least one study of addicts in treatment found that the average age of first use was eleven[166] and that regular use began at around age fourteen.[167] Other studies place the average age of initial use in the middle or late teens,[168] or in the early twenties.[169] The National Survey on Drug Use and Health for 2005 found that methamphetamine use by people twelve to seventeen years old was higher than for people age twenty-six and over (0.7 percent versus 0.4 percent), though lower than the rate for those eighteen to twenty-five (1.6 percent).[170] Younger users may also engage in more risky patterns of use. For example, stimulant users age twelve to seventeen are more likely than older users to be injection drug users.[171] Other research suggests that methamphetamine users who primarily inject the drug began doing so at an average age of nineteen.[172] Unfortunately, little is known about the youngest users, with most studies focusing on older individuals who have been using for many years.

Attention-Deficit/Hyperactivity Disorder and Methamphetamine

While the public is accustomed to hearing about the evils of methamphetamine, many people are unaware that methamphetamine can be prescribed by doctors in tablet form, though the prescriptions are nonrenewable. One of the legally recognized uses for methamphetamine is in the treatment of attention-deficit/hyperactivity disorder (ADHD). Although methamphetamine can be legally given to children in tablet form, it is not the drug to which doctors most frequently turn. Amphetamines are the most often prescribed drugs for ADHD, accounting for nearly 39 percent of the prescriptions.[173] Methamphetamine, in contrast, accounts for only 0.1 percent of the prescriptions. Among the general public, perhaps the most well-known drug prescribed for ADHD is methylphenidate (also known by the trade name Ritalin), which accounts for about 36 percent of prescriptions. Methylphenidate is a psychostimulant with effects similar to those of methamphetamine,[174] and it has been used by addicts as a substitute for methamphetamine.[175] It has also been reportedly used as a substitute for cocaine in making *speedballs,* in which heroin is mixed with a stimulant drug.[176] Research on both animals and humans suggests that the abuse potential of methylphenidate is similar to that of cocaine and amphetamine.[177]

Support for using amphetamine-type drugs to "treat" children with behavior disorders emerged early and enthusiastically. A 1937 study of children in a residence for children with behavior disorders reported dramatic improvements in both academic performance and in reducing aggressive behavior when the children were taking Benzedrine, a form of amphetamine.[178] In half of the cases the improvements were described as "spectacular." Children who were aggressive, noisy, and domineering were reported to become "more placid and easy-going" while on the drug.[179] Other researchers cited medical texts of the day, noting that

> as to addiction, the drugs to which human beings become addicted are the narcotics. There is no evidence in the entire literature of medicine that stimulants become habit forming. . . . Despite popular fears, addiction is very rare and only occurs in the severe psychopath who would have probably become addicted to some drug or other anyway. There are no withdrawal symptoms.[180]

As a group, early studies viewed amphetamine as a relatively benign drug, and one whose side effects were certainly less serious than the behavior the drug was intended to correct. Cole also gave a glowing review of amphetamines for childhood behavior disorders, all but dismissing adverse effects by noting: "Side effects, except for a little anorexia, nausea and vomiting and a very rare increase in overactivity, were nonexistent."[181] Cole also argued there was no evidence that children abused these drugs or took them recreationally. The recreational use of stimulant drugs, including methylphenidate, was something that researchers would become aware of only years later.

By 1975 researchers were still citing the benefits of stimulants on aggressive behavior in children.[182] However, positive assessments were accompanied by concerns about adverse effects from large doses, including increased aggression among those predisposed to aggression, and paranoid psychosis.

By the end of the 1990s the use of stimulant drugs to subdue overactive children, at least overactive in the minds of teachers and parents, had expanded dramatically. At the same time there emerged a small cadre of critics who not only questioned the use of stimulants to manage disruptive classroom behavior but also the validity of ADHD as a legitimate disorder.[183] Breggin observed that as many as 50 percent of children given stimulant drugs (dextroamphetamine, methamphetamine, or methylphenidate) for ADHD experienced an adverse reaction to the drug, and between 10 percent and 20 percent experienced severe adverse reactions.[184] He also suggested that children given stimulant drugs for ADHD were also at higher risk for abusing cocaine as young adults, though more recent research suggests that treating ADHD youth with stimulant drugs may reduce the likelihood of later substance abuse.[185] Data supporting either position are very weak. Leo buttressed his argument that ADHD was largely a clever marketing fiction created by drug manufacturers by noting that in the United States approximately 10 percent of children are diagnosed as ADHD, whereas in England only 0.03 percent are so diagnosed.[186] More recent data suggest the rate in the United States is closer to 7 percent and that in England it is closer to 0.1 percent or 0.2 percent—but in any event the gap between the United States and England is substantial.[187] Concern about overprescribing methylphenidate in the United States has also been fueled by the rather dramatic increase in the diagnosed number of ADHD cases. For example, from 1990 to 1995 the number of diagnosed cases rose 2.5 fold, and the rate at which methylphenidate was prescribed increased 2.6 fold.[188] According to the United Nations, the United States consumes 90 percent of the methylphenidate in the world, even though it has only 4.5 percent of the world's population.[189]

By 2006 the medical profession had begun urging caution in the use of stimulant drugs to treat ADHD. A panel assembled by the Food and Drug Administration noted that methylphenidate had led some children to suffer hallucinations and that physicians too often then prescribed an additional drug to counter the hallucinations. The hallucinations often took the form of the sensation of insects crawling under the skin, a condition strikingly similar to the meth bugs reported by some methamphetamine users. The committee recommended that strong warnings be placed on the labels of stimulants warning of potential dangers to children.[190] Later in 2006 the Substance Abuse and Mental Health Services Administration (SAMHSA) issued a report on emergency room admissions involving ADHD stimulant medication. The report noted that the nonmedical use of these medications (methylphenidate and amphetamine-dextroamphetamine) accounted for nearly half of the stimulant-related admissions to emergency rooms and was the single-most frequently cited reason for the admission.[191]

By 2008 concerns about the health effects of such stimulant drugs as methylphenidate and methamphetamine had reached yet another level. As noted earlier in this chapter, methamphetamine and other related stimulant drugs can be damaging to the heart, particularly if there are preexisting heart-related problems. In April 2008, the American Heart Association released a statement urging that children be screened for heart problems before they are given stimulants for ADHD. The recommendation was for a thorough exam, including an EKG and an extensive family history. The recommendation followed reports of nineteen sudden deaths and twenty-six other adverse heart-related problems in children between 1999 and 2003.[192]

As the use of stimulant drugs by children has expanded, both as a therapy and as a recreational drug, there has been a corresponding rise in concern about adverse effects. A disturbing trend has been to prescribe methylphenidate and other stimulant drugs as a treatment for ADHD in preschool children.[193] Stimulant drugs appear effective at reducing ADHD symptoms in preschoolers, though the effects are small and less than those observed in school-age children.[194] Also, there is evidence that when administered at an early age, stimulant drugs for ADHD may stunt physical growth.[195] The negative side effects experienced by some children exposed to these drugs are even more pronounced among preschool-age users, where as many as 30 percent are reported to experience moderate to severe adverse reactions to the drug.[196] These adverse effects include emotional outbursts, trouble sleeping, repetitive behavior and thoughts, reduced appetite, and irritability. Still unknown are the long-term effects of these drugs on children and adolescents. At present the medical community is divided on the issue of prescribing stimulants as a treatment for ADHD, with passions inflamed and hyperbolic rhetoric on each side.[197] Debating whether ADHD children given stimulant drugs are provided with an effective treatment that improves their quality of life or are simply being drugged into submission may simply be creating a false dichotomy. It is possible that some children are helped if they have been carefully diagnosed and their drug doses carefully monitored, while other (perhaps most) children are the victims of overprescribing physicians. To date, those who defend current practices regarding the use of stimulant drugs for ADHD have not provided a convincing explanation for the fact that most (perhaps 80 percent to 90 percent) of the methylphenidate in the world is consumed in the United States.

How Two Related Drugs Fit into the Picture

Along with the discussion of the physiological effects of methamphetamine, two related CNS stimulants bear mention. Ecstasy and cathinone have much in common with methamphetamine and have been the subject of considerable public concern in their own right.

Ecstasy

Ecstasy, also known as MDMA or 3,4-methylenedioxymethamphetamine, is a popular party drug. Research on treatment populations suggests that it is not unusual for methamphetamine users to also be regular users of Ecstasy.[198] In fact, some of what is sold on the street as Ecstasy is heavily laced with methamphetamine. Ecstasy has the stimulant property of methamphetamine, and adds mild hallucinatory effects comparable to those of mescaline. However, Ecstasy has more in common with methamphetamine than with mescaline.[199] The effects of Ecstasy include euphoria, loss of appetite, grinding of the teeth, and sweating. Unlike methamphetamine, Ecstasy brings out feelings of empathy for and emotional closeness to others and an enhanced appreciation for touch, sound, and movement.[200] While Ecstasy and methamphetamine share many effects in common, Ecstasy is less likely to lead to habituation because with continued and heavy use there develops a tolerance to the positive effects and an enhancement of negative effects.[201] In particular, tolerance to the empathy and emotional dimensions of the drug develops quickly and is not enhanced by increased doses or by continuously taking the drug over a long period of time. As Jansen and Theron describe it:

> Taking more MDMA may prolong stimulation, but it tends not to prolong or reproduce the empathy effect. Physical side effects, however, will increase with dose even if the mental effects have reached a plateau.[202]

Some practitioners have claimed that MDMA is a useful tool in therapy, and it was used for that purpose for over a decade, though since 1985 the U.S. Drug Enforcement Administration has ruled it has no therapeutic value and prohibits its use for any purpose.[203] Currently there are no legal manufacturers of the drug. It is, however, a popular "club drug" produced mainly in Europe and smuggled into the United States, often through Canada.

Cathinone

Another related stimulant is cathinone, derived from the khat plant *(Catha edulis)* and used extensively in portions of eastern Africa.[204] Cathinone is concentrated in the young leaves of the khat plant and is released when the leaves are chewed, much as members of some South American societies chew coca leaves for their mildly energizing effects. In its chemical structure cathinone is nearly identical to amphetamine except that a hydrogen molecule is dropped and replaced by an oxygen molecule. Cathinone produces effects nearly identical to those of amphetamine, and it has been described as a "natural amphetamine."[205] These amphetamine-like effects include increased energy and alertness, talkativeness, euphoria, insomnia, hyperthermia, anorexia, and sometimes hyperactivity. As with amphetamine, the effects of cathinone are dose-dependent; small doses have few harmful effects while large doses may produce a litany of physical and psychological problems that mimic those of amphetamine, including toxic psychosis.[206] Unlike amphetamines, however, the manner in which khat is ingested (chewing leaves) makes it more difficult to ingest large doses and this limits the concomitant damage to the user.[207] Further, in its natural form (i.e., leaves), khat chemically breaks down rather quickly, making the global transportation of these leaves impractical—at least until recently. Globalization, with its extensive and rapid distribution networks for legitimate goods, has also facilitated the transshipment of khat leaves to parts of the world where they were previously unavailable. For example, in July 2006, U.S. officials arrested forty-four people in six states and seized twenty-five tons of khat. The drug was smuggled from Africa to New York, where its estimated value was $10 million.[208] Transporting tonnage of khat from Africa to the United States would simply have been impractical just ten or twenty years earlier. By the time the shipment arrived in the United States the leaves would have lost all of their potency.

In its natural leaf form, khat is at best a minor threat. Of greater concern is a synthetic stimulant based on the chemical structure of khat. This drug, methcathinone, is to khat as methamphetamine is to ephedrine or as cocaine is to the coca leaf.[209] That is, it is similar in its effects but many times more potent. As with methamphetamine, methcathinone is relatively easy to manufacture from pseudoephedrine.[210] Many of the effects of methcathinone mirror those of methamphetamine.

CONCLUSION

Like the two-faced Roman god Janus, methamphetamine is one drug with two very different sides. In clinical (small) doses under medical supervision its effects are constructive and therapeutic. In large doses, however, it can ravage the body and warp the mind. Of course, methamphetamine is not the only drug with these features, but they are particularly pronounced in the case of methamphetamine. This dual nature of the drug has serious implications for policy and research.

Studies of the pharmacology of methamphetamine abound, but research is made more difficult if methamphetamine's effects are contradictory, depending on dosage size, duration of use, and the physical and psychological status of the user. For example, in low doses methamphetamine can calm hyperactive children, but in high doses it agitates and stimulates behavior. In low doses the drug can improve neurocognitive functioning, but in high doses it impairs such functioning. In low doses methamphetamine can improve task performance for those suffering from fatigue, though it does not improve the performance of those who are rested.[211] However, in high doses methamphetamine impairs task performance.[212] At low doses the risk of habituation appears limited,[213] but at higher doses as many as 50 percent of users will become addicted.[214] Studies of laboratory rats suggest that at high doses methamphetamine reduces dopamine levels and the number of dopamine uptake sites in the brain. At low levels no such effect is observed.[215] The effects of methamphetamine appear to be different for rats and monkeys, suggesting the drug may have a different impact across species.[216] The impact of meth on memory also presents conflicting findings. Generally, methamphetamine users do more poorly than controls on tests of memory.[217] However, one study of memory found that continuous users performed best, followed by those who quit and then relapsed. The worst performance was by those who abstained.[218]

Most controlled studies give subjects either 5 mg or 10 mg of methamphetamine, but abusers may use one hundred times that amount or more in a twenty-four-hour period.[219] In addition, laboratory studies generally administer the drug for only a few days while abusers will have used for months or even years. Further complicating matters, it appears that nicotine used in combination with methamphetamine enhances the effects of methamphetamine,[220] and smoking tobacco is common among methamphetamine users.

Studying the impact of stimulant drugs on children, particularly preschool children, should be a high priority, but such studies also present difficult challenges. Aside from concerns about experimental designs with such young subjects is the practical issue of determining long-term effects. It should not be assumed that young children will always consume therapeutic doses or that apparently harmless doses at age four have no lasting effect on the physical and emotional development of the child.

Research, whether in the laboratory or in natural settings, has told us more about the effects of methamphetamine at the extremes—clinical doses versus extreme abuse—than about that large gray area in between. It is clear that methamphetamine is not instantly addictive and may not be addictive at all in lower doses. Research has told us little about whether there is a threshold of use, above which the chances of addiction increase dramatically. It is hard to imagine how human subjects might be adequately protected in research using progressively larger doses of methamphetamine, but, absent such research knowledge, the territory between clinical and excessive doses will continue to be difficult to explore. Waldorf and colleagues have undertaken natural studies of heavy long-term cocaine users whose use did not spin out of control.[221] Locating and studying a comparable group of methamphetamine users might be a useful starting point to further understand the effects of a full range of use patterns.

The dilemma for policy makers is to make the drug as available as possible for therapeutic purposes while simultaneously protecting against overprescribing and recreational use. Unfortunately, people in general—and young people in particular—may have a difficult time understanding that a drug can be safe in small doses but quite dangerous in unrestricted use.

Methamphetamine has been in existence for more than one hundred years. There is a good general understanding of how the drug works and its physiological effects. However, there is still much to be learned. In particular, there is a relatively poor understanding of how these physiological effects translate into social behaviors, an issue to which we turn in chapter 4.

CHAPTER 4

The Social Effects of Methamphetamine

The term *epidemic,* as discussed in previous chapters, has been attached to several perceived increases in drug use in the United States, beginning with alcohol in the mid-1800s, followed by the opiates, cocaine, marijuana, and stimulants—with some drugs making repeat appearances. A drug epidemic consists of one part drug use and one part public perception. As the understanding of the drug's physiological effects evolves, so does the perception of its social effects. At any moment, it can be difficult to accurately gauge the social effects of a drug, but it is particularly hard to separate fact from fiction while society is in the throes of what is perceived to be an epidemic. What is taken as fact during the epidemic may be viewed quite differently with hindsight. For example, at one time it was thought that crack cocaine babies were so damaged they could never lead normal lives, but later thinking was that proper care and nurturing could counter many of the adverse effects of exposure to crack cocaine in the womb.

A variety of social ills has been attributed to methamphetamine as well. This chapter will sort through the various beliefs about the social effects of methamphetamine while recognizing that society's understanding of these effects is constantly evolving. Chapter 3 provided an extensive review of what is known about the physiological effects of methamphetamine; chapter 6 will illustrate the impact of methamphetamine on two midwestern counties. This chapter describes what is known about the social effects of methamphetamine, with a focus on its effects on violence, property crime, sexual behavior, and parenting.

Methamphetamine and Violence

Methamphetamine's association with violence may seem straightforward, but there are many ways in which the two may be linked. Goldstein has suggested that drugs and violence may be connected in one of three ways: psychopharmacological, systemic, and economic-compulsive.[1]

Psychopharmacological violence is the result of the actions of the drug on the brain. While the precise mechanism by which this might happen is unclear, methamphetamine might be expected to generate a perfect storm of conditions that lead to violence. The tendency of methamphetamine users to become stimulated and excited, to go long hours without sleep, to experience paranoia, and, among the heaviest users, to become psychotic might, in combination, be expected to yield bizarre and unpredictable outbursts of extreme violence. Indeed, such cases can be found, just as they can be found with alcohol and with other stimulant drugs, such as cocaine. However, such cases are atypical of methamphetamine.

Observations on the connection between alcohol and violence caution against any direct link between alcohol consumption and violence, and the same can be said for methamphetamine. Many who take the drug never engage in violence while under its influence, and even those who have been violent while high on meth are not *always* violent while high. The psychopharmacological effect of a given drug on violence is itself complex. White has identified six ways in which drugs may have a psychopharmacological effect on violence:[2]

1. *Independent effect:* The individual may have been using a drug at the time of the violent incident, but the drug had no role in the violence. Physically, that same individual may be more capable of violence when sober.

2. *Rationalizing effect:* In this situation the drug does not cause violence but is used to excuse or rationalize it.

③ *Causative effect:* In these cases the drug user may suffer from psychosis or delusions of persecution that lead to violence. In this example violence would not occur without the disturbed pattern of thinking caused by the drug. Such cases are probably rare, but they do occur.

④ *Additive effect:* The individual is at risk for violence and under ordinary circumstances is able to suppress violent urges. While under the influence of drugs, however, those violent urges surface. This pattern is sometimes seen in domestic violence cases, in which violence primarily occurs while the batterer is under the influence of alcohol or drugs.

⑤ *Synergistic effect:* In this situation the drug does not simply add to existing violent tendencies but multiplies them, and those existing tendencies are typically powerful. The histories of these individuals often include troubled childhoods and show frequent and extreme incidents of violence.

⑥ *Neutralizing effect:* While it is sometimes assumed that drug use will fuel violence, there are circumstances in which drugs may reduce or inhibit violence. We saw in chapter 3 that clinical doses of methamphetamine can reduce aggression. Similarly, marijuana is thought to mellow the user and reduce the likelihood of violence.

In addition to these psychopharmacological links between drugs and violence, White also identified what he referred to as a *contextual effect,* the effect of a criminal or drug culture in which violence is part of the social environment. In these cases the source of the problem is not the drug or its effects on the user, but the social environment or context of drug use.

White's contextual violence corresponds with Goldstein's notion of *systemic violence,* that is, violence resulting from disputes over turf or over drug payments. While this kind of violence is very real, it is a form of violence shared with many drugs bought and sold through illicit networks. In this instance, violence is more a product of the illicit market than of the drug itself. Consequently, we might expect less systemic violence in rural areas where small, independent methamphetamine laboratories (also known as "mom-and-pop" labs or "Beavis and Butt-Head labs) predominate. Methamphetamine production and distribution in rural areas often take place within friendship networks. Within these networks relatively small amounts of cash may trade hands. Instead, much of the "business" is fueled by bartering for goods or services, as when a user steals precursors for the methamphetamine cook in exchange for a portion of the final product. In urban areas where methamphetamine is distributed through more traditional cash-based drug networks, or in rural areas where "super labs" are operating on a cash basis, it can be expected that systemic violence will be more frequent.

Finally, *economic-compulsive violence* is associated with efforts to fund a drug habit (e.g., armed robbery). Here again rural-urban differences might be expected because, as stated above, in rural areas much of the methamphetamine business involves relatively small amounts of cash and a significant role for bartering. Shoplifting, petty theft, and even identity theft might be issues, but violence will be relatively infrequent. In contrast, where methamphetamine is distributed through more traditional cash-based drug markets, robbery will more frequently be turned to as a method for raising money to purchase drugs.

This tripartite framework is primarily a device to simplify a complex world in the hopes of more thoroughly understanding it. In reality, the lines between these categories are likely to be blurred. A drug deal may lead to an argument, which is fueled by the paranoia and excitement of the user. The result may be a physical confrontation, thus creating a scenario in which both systemic and psychopharmacological factors are at work. Given the characteristics of methamphetamine and the nature of its production and distribution networks, we might expect that methamphetamine would be a likely candidate for fueling a psychopharmacological link between drugs and violence, and that it would be comparable to other habituating drugs in its connection to systemic and economic-compulsive drug-related violence. As we will see, however, methamphetamine is less than a perfect example of how the psychopharmacology of a drug may explain its connection to violence. The association between methamphetamine and violence may be considered from a number of vantage points, including violence by methamphetamine users, methamphetamine users as victims of violence, and the use of animal studies to further unravel the methamphetamine-violence connection. Methamphetamine also appears to have a special connection to domestic violence.

Violence by Methamphetamine Users

There have been several perceived *epidemics* of methamphetamine and amphetamine in the past (chapter 2). In the 1940s and 1950s Japan saw such an epidemic.[3] The United States saw an epidemic of amphetamine from the 1940s through the 1960s,[4] and an epidemic of methamphetamine in the early 1960s and the early 1970s.[5] Despite these perceived epidemics in amphetamine and methamphetamine use, violence associated with the use of these drugs was scarcely mentioned and little researched. If the link between methamphetamine use and violence were strong, we would have expected a substantial public outcry and a subsequent flurry of research early in the history of the drug. Instead, violence was treated as almost incidental to the use of stimulant drugs. Referring to the scant research available in 1969, Blum concluded that "research done to date directly contradicts the claims linking amphetamine abuse either to crimes of violence, sexual crimes or to accidents."[6] Despite such disclaimers, and in the absence of systematic research, anecdotal reports and general concerns about a methamphetamine epidemic kept alive the notion of a methamphetamine-violence connection.

In the 1970s the issue began to draw serious research attention, which continues to the present day. Studies suggest a complex association between methamphetamine use and violence. While methamphetamine-related violence may be at times extreme, violence is by no means universal among methamphetamine users and it is by no means usually extreme. Some researchers suggest between one-fourth and one-third of methamphetamine users have committed acts of violence while under the influence of the drug,[7] while others suggest the association may be much weaker.[8] Even if we accept the high-end estimate that one-third of methamphetamine users have engaged in violence while high on methamphetamine, two-thirds of users have not engaged in such violence. Further, those who have ever committed a violent act while high on methamphetamine do not necessarily do so on most methamphetamine-using occasions. This is not to minimize or dismiss concerns about methamphetamine and violence, but to point out that violence is neither inevitable nor even the most likely consequence of methamphetamine use. The infrequency and inconsistency with which methamphetamine seems to produce violence complicate our ability to explain the association, while the serious consequences of methamphetamine-related violence make such an understanding imperative.

Ellinwood conducted some of the most influential early work on the methamphetamine-violence nexus, beginning with a handful of case studies. He concluded that violence associated with methamphetamine use was the result of three factors: (1) predisposing personality characteristics, (2) involvement in the drug subculture, and (3) the use of other drugs.[9] Ellinwood was initially aware of only four cases of homicide related to methamphetamine use, and after contacting six forensic psychiatrists was able to locate only nine additional cases. If we consider the popularity of the drug at the time, these numbers seem small and raise questions about the idea that methamphetamine use routinely leads to fits of homicidal rage.

Regarding predisposing personality factors, Ellinwood concluded that while paranoia was common among the regular amphetamine users, most users recognized paranoia for what it was and resisted the urge to act on those feelings. However, some users had isolated themselves physically or emotionally from trusted others, or had limited their social interactions to other equally paranoid users. They isolated themselves from people who could give them reality checks, and as a consequence they found it increasingly difficult to separate their paranoid thoughts from reality. In such cases, paranoia served to feed existing aggressive impulses. A final trigger was often the use of an unusually large dose of methamphetamine, or of repeated large doses over several hours. In other words, methamphetamine by itself did not cause violent behavior, but facilitated violence in users whose personalities made them predisposed or primed for it, a finding echoed by Bell.[10] Asnis and Smith have corroborated these observations while suggesting some specific characteristics:

Although there is conflicting evidence over the question of the importance of predisposing personality factors as a cause of violence in amphetamine abusers, a large percentage of the cases reviewed in the literature point to a high incidence of unstable social adjustment, criminal or delinquent histories, poor impulse control, or paranoid tendencies which appear to be exacerbated by the use of amphetamines.[11]

Sommers and Baskin have also concluded that while measures of social adjustment and adolescent development are important in predicting which methamphetamine users will be violent while using the drug, the single best predictor is previous violence,[12] and previous acts of violence usually predate the initiation of methamphetamine use.

Extended heavy use of methamphetamine may also lead to psychosis (see chapter 3). A frequent component of psychosis is paranoia, a fear of others and the belief that others wish to harm the user.[13] Such fears increase the likelihood of violence.[14] While psychosis has no automatic connection to violence, the features of some psychotic episodes may explain bizarre and unexpected violent acts. For example, some rare episodes of amphetamine psychosis include false recognition, in which the user:

> . . . often falsely identified strangers as family or friends. Many accosted strangers on the street and began intimate conversations. When this symptom became more fluid, everyone looked like an intimate acquaintance.[15]

It is not hard to imagine how such behavior might lead to altercations, particularly if the user is agitated and predisposed to violence. Conversely, and also rare, some users experience *prosopagnosia,* or the inability to recognize faces, in which the individual:

> . . . cannot recognize family, friends or themselves by physiognomy. Even pictures of persons present are frequently not recognized. The impairment of recognition may extend to animals.[16]

In such circumstances users might fail to recognize a friend or family member, and in their paranoia might misinterpret innocuous or helpful comments as threatening, leading to a violent response. This is not to suggest such cases are typical. To the contrary they are probably quite rare, but they may help explain those unexpected and particularly violent events associated with methamphetamine.

Ellinwood also believed that aside from these traits of the individual and the individual circumstance, the drug culture and the use of other drugs were important factors in eliciting violence from stimulant drug users. Of the three relevant factors, he saw preexisting personality characteristics as third in importance, falling behind the influence of the drug subculture and the concomitant use of other drugs. Angrist and Gershon have echoed Ellinwood's emphasis on the role of the drug subculture in creating a context for methamphetamine-related violence.[17] In this respect methamphetamine is much like other drugs purchased through illicit markets.

One of the more interesting studies of the association between methamphetamine use and violence was conducted by Dobkin and Nicosia using data from California.[18] Rather than using the self-reports of methamphetamine users, they relied on aggregate patterns of methamphetamine use and of crime. They considered how sharp limits on access to precursor chemicals affected levels of methamphetamine consumption, health, and other social consequences of methamphetamine use. They concluded that precursor limits markedly reduced methamphetamine use and associated health consequences, at least for a short while. Interestingly, they found that rather dramatic fluctuations in indicators of methamphetamine use had no association with violent crime. Robbery was the only violent crime associated with patterns of methamphetamine use, and even there the authors suggested alternative explanations. This finding is similar to that of Weisheit and Fuller who found no association between the presence of methamphetamine in a county and the county's level of violent crime.[19] Taken together, these studies suggest that even if some individuals engage in violence while using methamphetamine, an upturn in methamphetamine use does not automatically mean an upturn in general levels of violence.

Untangling the association between methamphetamine and violence is complicated by the reality that so many methamphetamine users are polydrug users.[20] Alcohol is commonly used by methamphetamine users both for its own effect and as a drug to counter the effects of methamphetamine. In particular, alcohol and sedatives may be used by experienced methamphetamine users to help them end a meth "run" and sleep.[21] In the 1960s and 1970s heroin was often the drug of choice for easing out of a meth run.[22] Sedative drugs serve as what have been called "chemical parachutes,"[23] easing the user out of the meth high and into much needed sleep.[24] The frequency with which alcohol is associated with violence is well documented, even if the underlying mechanism of that relationship is poorly understood.[25] LSD plays a role in its tendency to potentiate or amplify any methamphetamine-induced psychotic thinking. A drug commonly used to accelerate the end of a methamphetamine run is marijuana,[26] though no studies suggest marijuana has any connection to methamphetamine-related violence.

The importance of these factors—paranoia, social isolation, preexisting aggressive tendencies, the consumption of unusually large doses of the drug, living in a drug subculture, and the consumption of other drugs—may explain why violence erupts from some individuals and not others, and in some circumstances and not others. It also may explain the early observation that while violence was not common, when it occurred it was "frightening because of the unprovoked, arbitrary, and grossly psychotic quality of the acts themselves."[27] It might be expected that the greater the number of these factors present in a given situation, the greater the likelihood of violence stemming from methamphetamine use, and the greater the intensity of that violence.

> **Key Factors in the Meth–Violence Link**
>
> ➤ Paranoia
> ➤ Social isolation
> ➤ Preexisting aggressive tendencies
> ➤ Large doses of the drug
> ➤ Living in a drug culture
> ➤ Consuming other drugs

While these factors in combination may be associated with an increased likelihood of violence in many users, the effect is not universal. For a small subset of users, alcohol in combination with methamphetamine appears to reduce tendencies toward aggression, while in others methamphetamine alone appears to reduce expressions of aggression and violence.[28]

Other studies present mixed results. In a study conducted by Clark and Mankikar, geriatric patients with Poor Motivation Syndrome were given amphetamine to make them more active. Among the side effects was an increase in aggression for some (but not most) of these patients.[29] Self-report studies also have found that while methamphetamine use was associated with committing violent crimes, the best predictor of committing such crimes while using methamphetamine was whether the users had committed such crimes before they began using methamphetamine.[30] The pattern of methamphetamine use is also relevant, with daily users being most likely to engage in violent crime.[31] Cartier and colleagues considered the statistical association between methamphetamine use and self-reported violence among prison parolees. Methamphetamine was associated with reports of violence, but the link was very weak.[32] Derlet and colleagues examined methamphetamine-related emergency room admissions and concluded that about one in five admissions was agitated and the symptoms of this agitation included screaming loudly, belligerence, aggression, and hyperactivity.[33] Viewed differently, about 80 percent of the admissions exhibited no agitation or aggression. Thus, while methamphetamine may lead to aggression, there is no "one-size-fits-all" model of the link between methamphetamine and violence. Perhaps, as Ellinwood suggested, rather than causing violence in the peaceful user, methamphetamine merely amplifies preexisting violent tendencies.

Methamphetamine Users as Victims of Violence

Another approach to the study of a methamphetamine-violence link is to focus on the victims of violence. Several studies have utilized information from coroner or medical examiner records. These studies have the disadvantage of limiting the information that can be gathered, making it difficult to untangle causal patterns. Studies of coroner files have another significant shortcoming. These files do not indicate the prevalence of methamphetamine use in the community. If, for example, there are one hundred methamphetamine-related deaths, we do not know if the number of methamphetamine users in the area is two hundred or two million. If the number of users is two hundred, then methamphetamine is clearly a deadly drug. If the number of users is two million, we might reach a very different conclusion. We also do not know whether methamphetamine was instrumental or incidental in the deaths of these victims. Homicide victims, for example, are in no position to report their motivations or emotional state at the time of their death.

With these limitations in mind, studies of coroner records can still be useful. In these studies, suicides were somewhat more likely than homicides to be associated with a methamphetamine-related death, but, in most cases, deaths from overdose or medical complications substantially outnumbered those from either suicide or homicide.[34] This is important given that deaths from methamphetamine overdose are relatively rare (chapter 3), and these findings are in contrast to Bailey and Shaw's findings from San Diego County coroner files in which methamphetamine-related homicides were two and one-half times more likely than methamphetamine-related overdose deaths.[35] As discussed in chapter 3, death from methamphetamine use is generally the result of long-term use in which the heart, liver, or kidneys eventually fail, and not due to a single large dose or to short-term exposure. In contrast to the findings of Ellinwood, whose work focused on live users, studies of those who have died as a result of a methamphetamine-related cause find relatively few cases in which the deceased was also using alcohol, perhaps because deaths typically occur before the user is attempting to cut short a methamphetamine run.[36]

One study of methamphetamine-using incarcerated women found that nearly all of the women who injected methamphetamine had been sexually assaulted at some point in their lives, as had over half of women who were noninjectors of methamphetamine. The majority of those women had been sexually assaulted both in childhood and as adults, and nearly half of those women met the clinical criteria for posttraumatic stress disorder.[37] Other researchers have found that most patients who are admitted to treatment for methamphetamine abuse report a history of violent victimization, including both physical and sexual abuse.[38] These observations do not clarify the causal role of methamphetamine in sexual assault, but they are consistent with the idea that social environment may be an important factor in both victimization and in methamphetamine use.

Finally, methamphetamine may be a poor choice for a "date rape" or drug-facilitated sexual assault (DFSA) drug. The most popular date-rape drugs (e.g., alcohol, Rohypnol, GHB) have sedative effects, leading to victim unconsciousness or blackouts. Those under the influence of date-rape drugs may be only vaguely aware of their surroundings and unable to offer physical resistance. In contrast, "methamphetamine is a poor choice for a DFSA drug because it heightens alertness, may impede sexual performance, increase confidence and heighten suspicion and aggressiveness, and can make the user [victim] hyperaware of their environment."[39]

Animal Studies of Methamphetamine and Violence

Violence is a term generally applied to human behavior. When comparable behaviors are studied in animals, the commonly used term is *aggression*. Animal studies can prove useful in studying methamphetamine's effects on aggression because it is possible to control drug dose, physical environment, and social environment, and continuously monitor the animals' behavior. Further, animals are not expected to exhibit the same level of self-control as humans, more clearly revealing any connection between impulse and action.

Animal studies generally find that in most species small doses of stimulant drugs either reduce or have no impact on aggression, whereas high doses increase aggression.[40] Some studies find that aggression is likely to increase in animals with a history of aggression but not in other animals, though across studies the findings are mixed.[41] Others suggest that aggression is only exhibited in animals given the drug over time, as opposed to a single dose.[42] It has also been observed that aggressive behavior in animals is often directed inward, such as when high doses of amphetamine are administered to monkeys over time and, while under the influence, they bite themselves and poke their own eyes.[43]

Animal studies generally support the idea of a connection between amphetamine use and aggression, particularly when high doses are given over time. However, not all studies find this, reinforcing the conclusion that a simple, direct association between methamphetamine and violence is inadequate to fully understand the relationship.

Methamphetamine and Domestic Violence

Recent research has focused more attention on the specific forms of violence that might flow from methamphetamine use. What is striking is the frequent finding that the association between methamphetamine use and violence is particularly strong for domestic or partner violence.[44] The association between methamphetamine use and domestic violence has been considered from several perspectives. One approach is to examine the prior history of physical abuse by current methamphetamine users, including both adult experiences and the family environment in which they were raised. Current methamphetamine users are often found to have been raised in chaotic family environments in which domestic violence is common.[45] For many, childhood abuse is so common that as children they had believed it was normal.[46] This includes physical violence between adults and sometimes the sexual abuse of children by parents or by other adults in the home.[47] Other researchers have found that adult methamphetamine users often have a history of physical abuse.[48] That substance abuse may be associated with violence in the home is not unique to methamphetamine, but is an issue with many illicit substances, particularly when combined with alcohol.[49] In some parts of the United States both methamphetamine use and domestic violence may cross two or even three generations.[50]

Baskin-Sommers and Sommers propose an interesting explanation for the prevalence of domestic violence among methamphetamine users:

> As a result [of the longer high from methamphetamine], methamphetamine users are able to remain away from the market environment longer as they are not constantly "chasing the pipe." Consequently, methamphetamine users are more likely to return to work, school, or home settings while high. Thus, in contrast to their crack using counterparts, they are less likely to be entrenched in street networks yet more likely to engage in violent behavior at home, in the workplace, or within other more mainstream social settings.[51]

Some observers have suggested that methamphetamine-related domestic violence is a consequence of irritability that accompanies coming down from a meth high.[52] This is consistent with the observations of others who have commented that when the user crashes, or comes down quickly, there is often considerable irritability. Consider this description from the 1960s:

> Irritability is so intense that it appears to the outsider as intolerant selfish-
> ness. Arguments, to the point of yelling and occasional hitting, occur for
> what appear to the outsider to be fairly insignificant reasons. The crasher
> feels that demands made on him are inconsiderate, insufferable, and
> impossible.[53]

More recent studies emphasize the impact of methamphetamine use on children. Methamphetamine-abusing parents are reported to have a parenting style described as "polar parenting,"[54] in which the treatment of their children swings between extremes of anger and apathy. When high, the parents will either ignore the children or treat them with hostility, depending on where their attention is focused at the moment. When coming down from a high, the parents may avoid the children, to the point of locking themselves in a room to avoid all contact.

As described in chapter 3, in one of the only longitudinal studies of its kind, children who were exposed to methamphetamine in the womb were, by age eight, more likely than other children to exhibit aggressive behavior,[55] though it was not possible to separate the effects of methamphetamine from other environmental factors. Children exposed to methamphetamine while in the womb may be subject to parenting styles and a general social environment that is different from that of other children. Further, other researchers have found that as many as 80 percent of methamphetamine-using pregnant women also used alcohol and tobacco during their pregnancy.[56]

Additional studies have looked at the impact of methamphetamine-related violence on children who live in homes with adult methamphetamine users. A midwestern study of children age seven to fourteen who had been removed from their homes because of parental methamphetamine use is instructive.[57] Six of the eighteen children described aggressive behavior by adult users in the home. These six children reported that "users became 'mean' or 'aggravated,' 'fought a lot,' 'hit kids,' and just wanted to 'hit somebody.'"[58] One child in this study described his memory of the chaos and violence:

My dad beating up my mom. . . . All the time. I would hit my dad because he wouldn't get off of her. He would stand her up against the wall and started choking her. I kept on hitting him and I kicked him. . . . [One time] my mom pulled out a hammer and hit my dad in the head. And then she took it out and hit herself in the head. . . . And then my dad went outside and we locked all the doors and windows and he busted the back window out when I was there. I got a piece of glass stuck in my eye . . . my dad took me out the window. . . . And I had to get in his girlfriend's car. And my mom went out there and took a hammer and busted her windshield.[59]

Even in this group, in which children had been removed from the home because of methamphetamine use, only one third of the children reported aggression, and this included behaviors that varied widely in their seriousness. Domestic violence, like violence in general, is by no means a universal outcome of methamphetamine use, but for children the long-term consequences of modeling such behavior is particularly troubling.

The prevalence of domestic violence among methamphetamine users is particularly important when considering the rural setting, where methamphetamine appears to have made strong inroads.[60] While violence in general is less frequent in rural areas, domestic violence is equally likely in rural and urban communities,[61] at the same time that community resources for responding to domestic violence are more limited.[62] Consequently, it is important to consider the rural context when examining the association between methamphetamine and violence.

The Chicken or the Egg?

What is known about the association between methamphetamine and violence produces as many questions as answers. In most cases the effect is small and indirect, though it is possible to find individual cases in which the effects are striking. Adding alcohol to the mix, a relatively common practice, can substantially increase the likelihood of violence. Studies using laboratory animals, which should provide the clearest evidence of a direct relationship, also suggest the connection is real but complex. Studies of humans have thus far been unable to conclusively answer the "chicken-and-egg" question of which came first—violence or methamphetamine use. At present the best answer seems to be that methamphetamine facilitates or brings out violence in those with preexisting tendencies to be violent.

Methamphetamine and Property Crime

Though property crime by opiate and cocaine users has been extensively studied, particularly among inner-city street addicts, methamphetamine-fueled property crime has been largely ignored by researchers, although anecdotal reports in the media suggest it may be an issue. The type of property crime fueled by methamphetamine use will be largely influenced by the nature of the local methamphetamine market. Where methamphetamine is distributed through traditional cash-based drug markets, we might expect that meth would foster predatory theft, burglary, and robbery, in the same way as heroin and cocaine. A survey of sheriffs found that 70 percent believed that robberies and burglaries had increased in their county as a consequence of methamphetamine.[63] To the extent that methamphetamine remains less expensive than cocaine or heroin there is less pressure for users to rob and steal, but there is some pressure, nonetheless. Anecdotal evidence suggests that in addition to fueling traditional street crime, meth may also be connected to identity theft. The survey noted above also found that more than one quarter of the sheriffs believed that methamphetamine was related to an increase in identity theft in their county.[64] Awake for hours at a time and having the ability to concentrate on a single issue, the methamphetamine user is well positioned to think through the mechanics of identity theft.

Methamphetamine is almost certainly connected to property crime by those who run mom-and-pop cooking operations. The cook and those who help the cook in exchange for a portion of the final product sometimes steal the necessary precursors, either because they lack sufficient funds to buy precursors directly or because they wish to avoid the attention that might be drawn to overt purchases. While such thefts undoubtedly occur, the extent to which they are a problem and their impact on the local business community are unknown.

The study by Dobkin and Nicosia cited earlier found that substantial fluctuations in overall methamphetamine availability in California were unrelated to levels of violent crime.[65] That same study also concluded that, at the aggregate (county) level, levels of methamphetamine use and levels of property crime were unrelated.

Finally, there are many users for whom it is difficult to determine the extent to which methamphetamine causes property crime. Studies of the connection between property crime and the use of other drugs commonly find that crime precedes drug use, but that drug use can accelerate involvement in crime.[66] Once again the image emerges of drugs bringing out existing tendencies rather than creating them in the user.

Methamphetamine and Sex

One of the most written about social effects of methamphetamine is its relationship to sex. Stimulant drugs have physiological effects that should, in principle, enhance the desire for sex and the ability to perform. Optimal sexual function depends on maintaining levels of serotonin, norepinephrine, and dopamine,[67] the very neurotransmitters released by methamphetamine (chapter 3). A drug that improves self-confidence, energy, and stamina sounds like an ideal aphrodisiac. Indeed, amphetamine has been described as the most potent aphrodisiac ever created.[68] As one of the most potent of the amphetamine-type stimulant drugs, methamphetamine should also be a particularly strong sexual stimulant, and there is considerable evidence to support this supposition. Methamphetamine—more than alcohol, opiates, or cocaine—appears to enhance the sexual thoughts and behaviors of users.[69] While this is generally true, it is not universally true. As many as one-third of users report no effect on their sex drive, and a small percentage report a reduced sex drive while on methamphetamine.[70] Further, because sex is more about psychology and social context than it is about pure physiology, animal studies of the effects of methamphetamine on sex will not provide many insights into the association in human subjects.[71]

For many users, methamphetamine has an effect on both the quality and quantity of sexual behavior and sexual thoughts. Marijuana, LSD, or Ecstasy tend to heighten users' sensitivity to the sexual needs and desires of their partners.[72] Sex is a shared activity and an act of emotional closeness.

Methamphetamine's effects on sexual dynamics are quite different. Sexually aroused methamphetamine users often focus on their own pleasure, to the point that the feelings and even the very presence of their partner is secondary, or no more than instrumental in feeding their own desires.[73] As one methamphetamine user described sex while on methamphetamine: "Sex is 'programmed' while on crystal. My front lobe shuts off and the rat brain takes over."[74] Consequently, masturbation and sex with a partner may be equally satisfying. While methamphetamine may work for the user seeking anonymous sex, over time it is damaging to long-term romantic relationships.[75]

The importance of physical pleasure over emotional connectedness also accounts for the popularity of pornography among methamphetamine users who tie use of the drug to sexual stimulation. One drug enforcement officer reported that pornography was present in nearly all of the methamphetamine houses he raided. The impersonal nature of methamphetamine-fueled sex may also account for its appeal to sex workers.[76] The self-absorbed nature of methamphetamine-fueled sex also may lead to lapses in judgment, such as when methamphetamine-using parents engage in sex in front of their children, or when they allow their children to have sex.[77]

The nature and extent of methamphetamine's effect on sexual behaviors and thoughts vary across users, though the desire to improve sex is often cited as a reason for using methamphetamine.[78] The sex-related effects of methamphetamine are related to the duration and pattern of use, gender of the user, preexisting sexual urges, and the social context in which sex and methamphetamine co-occur.

Duration and Pattern of Methamphetamine Use

Early in a using career, or in a career in which the amount of methamphetamine used is limited and controlled, the drug often has dramatic positive effects on sex that approach life-changing in intensity. As one user reported:

> And then it became like a sex thing. Because I discovered quite by accident that crystal plus sex equals, oh my God. I mean, you know, you thought it was good before when you were sober. . . . It's like I didn't even think that a human body would have the capacity to create those sort of sensations.[79]

When use occurs over extended periods or during periods of heavy use, sex may become a particularly mechanical exercise. There are reports of sex marathons, sometimes lasting ten, twelve, or even eighteen hours.[80] The extended and extensive use of methamphetamine may provide the energy needed for such sessions, and the sensations may be exceptionally pleasurable, but there is often a concomitant difficulty in achieving orgasm.[81] For males this is a condition that users describe as "crystal dick,"[82] and, as a consequence, those seeking to counter such performance problems sometimes supplement methamphetamine with Viagra or a related drug.[83] For some users, stereotyped behavior (e.g., compulsive and repetitive behavior) may be expressed via the sex act, giving a compulsive quality to what should be psychologically healthy behavior.[84]

Methamphetamine's tendency to reduce bodily fluids (chapter 3) also has implications for marathon sex sessions in that the drug reduces the flow of those lubricating bodily fluids that facilitate sex, leaving the user's genitalia raw.[85] This not only is uncomfortable, but also facilitates the transmission of communicable diseases. For those whose use escalates, the focus on sex may diminish over time to be replaced by a focus on the drug itself.[86] Ellinwood suggested that an increased sex drive and an interest in polymorphous sexual activity often precede methamphetamine-induced psychosis.[87]

The method by which the drug is administered also appears related to the intensity of the link between methamphetamine and sex. Injection drug users are substantially more likely to associate sex with methamphetamine use.[88] Though the reasons for this are unclear, at least one Freudian psychologist speculated that drugs, and particularly the act of injecting drugs, may produce what he termed a *pharmacogenic orgasm,* which for some users comes to be seen as preferable to a genital orgasm.[89] Some users describe the rush that follows injection as a total body orgasm.[90] The combination of injection drug use and methamphetamine-fueled sex makes these users particularly likely to become HIV-positive, perhaps as much as three times more likely than those who inject other drugs.[91]

Gender, Sex, and Methamphetamine

Not everyone's sex drive is enhanced by methamphetamine, and differences in effects are particularly marked across gender. Among intravenous methamphetamine users, the group for which drug use and sex are most closely linked, as many as one-half of men but only about one-fifth of women report sex as their primary activity while on methamphetamine.[92] Some women have reported having their first orgasm while on methamphetamine,[93] but this response is probably not typical. Women are much less likely than men to report that methamphetamine improves their sex drive, sexual performance, and sexual pleasure.[94] At the same time, some women use methamphetamine specifically because it is a sexual stimulant.[95]

As discussed in chapter 3, both cocaine and methamphetamine are members of the same family of stimulant drugs, and their effects are in many respects similar. However, cocaine and methamphetamine have very different effects on the sex drive of women and of men. Women whose primary drug is cocaine report more negative than positive effects of the drug on sex. In contrast, women for whom methamphetamine is their primary drug report more positive than negative effects on sexual drive and satisfaction.[96]

Preexisting Sexual Urges

As with violence, methamphetamine amplifies preexisting sexual urges rather than creating them. When such urges do not already exist, methamphetamine will have little effect on sexual behavior.[97] Methamphetamine users are more likely than nonusers to engage in risky or extreme sex, including sex without condoms, sex with strangers, group sex, bisexuality, and threesomes.[98] For some users methamphetamine becomes so psychologically tied to sex that the mere act of injecting can cause an erection.[99]

Engaging in risky sex, combined with injection use of the drug, means that methamphetamine users are at greater risk than many other drug users for HIV.[100] Just as the use of alcohol in combination with methamphetamine may fuel violence, those who combine stimulants with binge drinking may be particularly likely to have multiple sex partners and to not use condoms.[101]

Though an increase in libido may be attributable to the release of neurotransmitters, the willingness to engage in risky sex may be the result of methamphetamine's tendency to make the user feel invulnerable[102] (also see chapter 3), an issue to which we return in the next section of this chapter.

Methamphetamine and Gay Sex

While methamphetamine appears to enhance the libido and reduce inhibitions for both genders, there has been particular concern about its popularity among sexually active gay men.[103] Studies have rather consistently found that methamphetamine use is associated with gay male sex that is unprotected, with strangers, with multiple partners, and is anal insertive. It appears that methamphetamine makes the user feel somewhat invincible and is consciously used by men who wish to take risks they would otherwise avoid. That is, risky sex is an intended consequence of methamphetamine use and not merely incidental to it. Methamphetamine also appears linked to the creation of "instant bottoms," or the willingness to engage in anal receptive sex.[104] To both localize and speed the absorption of methamphetamine for anal receptive sex, some users report anal insertion of methamphetamine[105] while others report "water injecting," in which methamphetamine is first dissolved in water and then injected into the anus.[106]

The association between methamphetamine use and risky sex by men who have sex with men (MSM) is one of the most studied of the social effects of methamphetamine. In the era of AIDS such behavior is potentially deadly. Methamphetamine-fueled risky gay sex has also been linked to the spread of hepatitis B.[107] Not only are men who use methamphetamine to facilitate gay sex less likely to use condoms but also when they do use condoms they are more likely to experience condom failure, increasing the risk of HIV infection.[108]

What little research exists on the link between sexual orientation and HIV suggests the focus on gay male sex may be justified. A California study of treatment-seeking methamphetamine abusers found that gay males had thirteen times as many sexual partners as heterosexual males or females. Further, 62 percent of gay males in that study reported being HIV-positive while none of the heterosexual males or females so reported.[109]

It is not just that methamphetamine use may increase the risk for HIV, particularly among gay men; the consequences of HIV infection may be exacerbated by the use of methamphetamine. Methamphetamine appears to reduce the effectiveness of antiretroviral drugs used to treat HIV,[110] and it may also accelerate the onset of HIV-related dementia[111] and other HIV-related neuropsychological functions.[112] Some researchers have suggested that such neuropsychological impairments are also associated with a poorer treatment outcome.[113] As if risky sex were not enough, methamphetamine users who inject are at even higher risk of contracting HIV. Thus, methamphetamine poses a threat to the spread and treatment of AIDS on multiple fronts.

The response of the gay community to the threat of AIDS has changed over time since AIDS was first identified in 1981. Those changes in perception and behavior have had important implications for the use of methamphetamine as a sexual stimulant by gay and bisexual men. Ostrow suggests there are four stages in the gay community's response to AIDS, and these stages correspond to the responses of researchers to the connection between gay sex and drug use. The stages are as follows:[114]

- *Stage 1 (1981–1985/86):* Not much was known about AIDS, but researchers tended to see gay sex and drug use as separate modes for transmitting the disease. Consequently, sex and drug use were studied independently.

- *Stage 2 (late 1980s and early 1990s):* Knowledge about HIV increased and the first treatment drugs were introduced. Testing for HIV became common and both risky sex and drug use connected to sex declined substantially. Safe sex was stressed and often practiced. There was also the belief that stimulant drugs might harm the immune system, a further disincentive to combining sex and stimulant drugs.

- *Stage 3 (the mid-1990s):* The term *MSM* (men who have sex with men) was coined to include both gay and bisexual men. Reports began to filter in about relapse into risky sexual behavior, and researchers began to consider both drug use and risky sex as possibly the result of a common underlying personality trait. At the same time improvements in the treatment of HIV infection emboldened some gay males to engage in "barebacking"—intentional unprotected anal sex with strangers.[115] During this period some observers reported the rise of "safe sex burnout" in which gay men were resigned to eventually getting AIDS and were tired of taking precautions. For some gay men, particularly young men who grew up after the discovery of AIDS, there was a romanticized notion of pre-AIDS sex that was worry free and "no holes [sic] barred."[116] Methamphetamine was a vehicle that allowed them to physically and psychologically return to a time of worry-free MSM sex. Ironically, while methamphetamine use has reportedly fueled self-centered sex in which the partner is little more than a tool for the user's pleasure, some users report that they seek out barebacking as a way to feel emotionally connected to their partner.[117]

- *Stage 4 (2000 and beyond):* This is the post-AIDS era in which researchers and health care providers take a holistic approach that includes the behaviors of individuals as well as a focus on the community as a whole. Barebacking and resistance to always practicing safe sex continue to be problems, and there is a growing tendency toward safe sex burnout and relapse to unsafe sexual behaviors. There is a concern that risky sex will become even more common as treatment for HIV improves, providing a false sense of security. Those who are HIV-negative may underestimate the seriousness of infection and even those who are already HIV-positive may be at risk if they feel they have nothing to lose by barebacking when, in fact, they may be exposed to even more virulent and drug-resistant forms of HIV. Further complicating matters in this post-AIDS era is that willing partners for barebacking and no-holds-barred sex with strangers can be found easily through the Internet.[118]

Methamphetamine plays a role in facilitating unsafe sex, but it is not the only drug to do so. Indeed, it is not the most popular drug linked to unsafe sex. That distinction belongs to alcohol.[119] However, for those who respond to methamphetamine as a sexual stimulant the association can be quite powerful. Such individuals often have a difficult time separating sex and meth use in their minds. It may be difficult for them to even consider sex without methamphetamine. As one researcher described it:

> So strong is the association that many of our participants reported they could not have sex unless they were high on meth. The fear of no longer being sexual was identified as a major barrier to giving up meth.[120]

Understanding the link between methamphetamine use and risky gay sex is further complicated by the reality that multiple drugs and alcohol are often used in combination before an episode of risky sex. While poly-drug use is common among all categories of methamphetamine users, combining methamphetamine with other illegal drugs is particularly prevalent among gay males, and this may be true of as many as 95 percent of these methamphetamine users.[121] The greater the number of drugs used, the greater the likelihood of unprotected anal intercourse[122] and the more likely that sex will be without a condom.[123] It also appears that for many gay males, methamphetamine use is sporadic and linked specifically to sex.[124] Consequently, these users would not meet the basic criteria for methamphetamine addiction.[125] However, when a patient's or client's patterns of use cross the line into addiction, treatment must address both methamphetamine use and sex.[126] One of the things that distinguishes Twelve Step methamphetamine programs from those that focus on other drugs is the inclusion of sex as an issue for discussion. As one subject reported, "'I went to AA and NA but couldn't relate as well as I do to those in CMA [Crystal Meth Anonymous] . . . [because of] the way sex and drug use are intertwined."[127] Researchers have even suggested that for this group tri-morbidity (drug use, sex, and mental health) may be an issue.[128]

Methodological Issues in the Gay Sex–Methamphetamine Relationship

Several curious issues surround our understanding of the link between methamphetamine and gay sex, issues that merit further study. First, many of the studies have been conducted in cities in which methamphetamine has not been an issue in the heterosexual community (e.g., New York, Chicago, Miami). Time will tell if the problem remains limited to the gay community in those cities. If methamphetamine becomes a popular drug in the general population, will it become so having spread out from the gay community, or will it be introduced and spread through existing structures for distributing other street drugs?

Second, while much has been made of the impact of methamphetamine on rural communities (see chapter 6), none of the research considers methamphetamine use among rural gays. Although it is possible that methamphetamine use and risky sex by rural gays is simply not an issue, it seems unlikely that it would be only an urban phenomenon. A more likely explanation is that a study of rural gays presents particularly difficult research challenges, such as the absence of gay clubs and related venues where substantial numbers of potential research subjects congregate. One avenue for accessing the rural gay population may be the Internet, which is used by some gay men to locate partners in their area. The Internet has been successfully used to draw a large national sample of MSM[129] and may prove a useful tool for studying the meth–sex connection among rural gays.

Third, subjects in these studies are typically recruited from gay clubs, bars, or other public places where men may be seeking out sex with other men, including strangers. Before the advent of the Internet, such venues were among the few safe (i.e., safe from attacks by homophobes) places for gay men to meet other gay men. In many ways, gay bars served as community centers for the gay community.[130] Ironically, some observers suggest that those MSM in clubs who are most actively seeking out partners for risky sex may be least likely to participate in research.[131] While men who use gay clubs to locate sex partners are important subjects because of their high risk for HIV and other STDs, they may represent the fringe of the gay community and thus paint a distorted picture of the drugs–sex connection among gays as a group. For example, studies of alcohol abuse by MSM have found rates of abuse by those attending gay clubs to be much higher than for those MSM in the general population.[132] Gay social venues (bars, dance clubs, bathhouses), where gay and bisexual men gather to socialize and meet potential sex partners, may, by their very nature, foster an association between recreational drug use and unsafe sex.[133]

Fourth, it is curious that while there are numerous studies of methamphetamine and gay/bisexual male sex, there have been no studies of methamphetamine and lesbian sex. When women and sex are considered, it is generally within the context of heterosexual sex. While lesbian sex is less risky, the subject of methamphetamine's effects on lesbian sex would seem to merit study and might further our understanding of the methamphetamine–sex association.

Fifth, conspicuously absent from the research on methamphetamine and risky gay/bisexual sex is any mention of methamphetamine-fueled violence. This is particularly surprising given that meth-fueled gay sex is often described by participants as aggressive. As one subject described it, "Using [meth] was a psychological breakthrough for me. I saw my masculine aggressive side. I discovered I could be the sexual being I never thought I could be." Another said, "[It made me] emotionally blocked out, inhumanly ruthless—crystal is a great conscience remover."[134] Other subjects report using methamphetamine to facilitate episodes of sadomasochism.[135] The apparent absence of violence in these circumstances would appear to present an opportunity to better understand the methamphetamine-violence association in general.

Amphetamines have been linked to violence and to heightened sexual activity, but they do not appear to be commonly associated with sexual assault,[136] except perhaps for the sexual abuse of children discussed above. One study detailing the various drugs used in sexual assaults concluded that amphetamines were present in only 4 percent of the cases.[137] Without knowing the prevalence of amphetamine use in the population from which these cases were drawn, it is difficult to reach a firm conclusion about the extent to which methamphetamine is linked to sexual assault. However, on the basis of the numbers presented, it is difficult to argue that the problem is pervasive. For a drug that has been used since the early 1900s, and for which there is substantial evidence of a link to sex, and aggressive risky sex in particular, the absence of methamphetamine-fueled sexual violence in both the popular press and the academic research is interesting.

Methamphetamine and Parenting

If methamphetamine-stimulated gay sex is among the most studied of the social effects of methamphetamine, the effects of methamphetamine on parenting may be among the least studied of the drug's social effects.

However, the problem of methamphetamine's effects on parenting may be substantial. A California study of women in drug treatment for methamphetamine abuse found that one-third had lost parental rights to at least one child, and that fewer than half were living with their children at the time of treatment admission.[138]

Most states have protocols for handling children whose parents have been arrested for using or manufacturing methamphetamine. Cases of "drug-endangered children" (a popular phrase used to describe this situation) have garnered considerable attention in the media. However, methamphetamine use by parents is not an automatic trigger for removing children from the home, nor should it be. Methamphetamine users, particularly casual or recreational users, are not automatically unfit parents. Further, if removing the children means placing them in foster care, their circumstances will not necessarily improve. It may even be that removing infants exposed to methamphetamine in the womb from the home is a mistake in that such exposure probably does less harm to the emotional development of the child than does being moved from one foster care setting to the next.[139]

A very different situation presents itself when children are placed in danger because of parental use or manufacturing of methamphetamine in the home. For example, children should be considered in danger if they are playing on carpet contaminated with toxic chemicals used in methamphetamine production, if they are allowed to play in areas where they may be punctured by contaminated needles or glassware, or if they have traces of methamphetamine on their clothing or on their bodies.[140] These circumstances often trigger removing children from the home. Such precautions are necessary and prudent, though the extent to which toxic exposure of children is a problem has not been well documented. Efforts to limit access to precursor chemicals appear to have substantially diminished domestic production, or at least small-scale production in the home. This, in turn, limits the frequency with which children are exposed to toxic chemicals used in methamphetamine production.

The sparse research on methamphetamine's effects on parenting may partly reflect the difficult research challenges the issue presents. These issues include the following:

❶ It is neither practical nor ethical to be an unobtrusive observer of parenting while the adult is high on methamphetamine.

❷ Methamphetamine-using parents in treatment may not be able to look back and accurately depict their own parenting behaviors, and those currently using the drug may be even less able to paint an accurate picture.

❸ Even when the parents have a true understanding of their parenting behaviors while high, they are under considerable social pressure to present themselves as competent and caring parents. There is probably no greater social stigma associated with bad parenting than with being a drug user.

❹ The children themselves may not be in a position to fully appreciate their circumstances, particularly if they do not have experience with healthy functioning families as a basis for comparison. For example, one study inquired about the childhood experiences of methamphetamine users and concluded that abuse was so common that many of the users assumed they had grown up in normal conditions.[141] One childhood household was described in these words:

> . . . you just grow up and you don't know any better. You just know your family does drugs. And there's like, nothing you can do about it . . . you're so used to hollering and screaming. . . . You're used to everything that you grew up around. . . . All the people I knew were drug addicts.[142]

Further, many children are reluctant to say things that may get their parents into trouble.

With these methodological limitations in mind, it is possible to form a general picture by piecing together what little research exists and using anecdotal evidence to fill in the gaps. A broad look suggests that counties with high rates of methamphetamine use and of methamphetamine laboratory seizures also have high rates of reported child abuse and neglect.[143]

The creation of drug courts in some communities has been seen as a response to the problem of child abuse and neglect by methamphetamine-abusing parents.[144] Studies of methamphetamine addicts in treatment and of child welfare cases suggest an association between methamphetamine use and the abuse and neglect of children, though these reports often do not distinguish among neglect, physical abuse, and sexual abuse.[145] Where distinctions among these three forms of maltreatment are made, neglect is the form most often mentioned.[146]

Not all methamphetamine-abusing parents are guilty of neglect, but some become self-absorbed to the point that the needs of their children are not met. Abusers may not be hungry and so they don't think to fix meals for their children. They are not sleepy and so don't consider that it's bedtime for their children or that their children will need to get up in the morning for school. They may become so fixed on the experience of using that they don't bother taking care of basic hygiene, and so don't think to do so for the children either. Such everyday activities as doing the laundry or cleaning the house may be pushed aside by the compulsive methamphetamine user, leaving the children to live in filth. As one observer noted, "The drug is so addictive, parents lose sight of everything else, including the children."[147] In these situations older children may be compelled to take on the role of parent and caretaker of younger siblings.[148]

As noted earlier, the physical and emotional ups and downs that accompany a methamphetamine run may result in polar parenting, in which the parent has mood swings that range from extreme anger to extreme apathy. In addition, the irritability that often accompanies coming down from a methamphetamine high may lead parents to avoid their children.[149]

Taken together, the effects of the drug and chaotic lifestyle that often accompanies drug use can be emotionally traumatic for the children of methamphetamine users. One study of children removed from the homes of methamphetamine-using parents concluded that many of these children had significant mental health problems. "Most children described difficult family relationships at home, including losing trust in the parent, worrying about the parent's well-being, and feeling abandoned and neglected by the parent. In addition, children reported few social resources for coping with emotional pain or understanding what was happening at home."[150]

Child neglect and maltreatment by methamphetamine-abusing parents are of grave concern. However, neglect, abuse, and poor parenting practices have been associated with the abuse of other illicit drugs, and of alcohol. A review of cases in which child protective services intervened because infants were exposed to drugs suggests that later child abuse is unrelated to the particular type of drug involved in the initial investigation.[151] As one reviewer concluded, "In fact, child maltreatment is one of the primary documented psychosocial outcomes of substance abuse among pregnant women, and one which frequently results in out-of-home placement."[152] In many cases drug-abusing parents have dysfunctional family histories. "Parental death, desertion, divorce, marital disharmony, poor parental role modeling, and parental substance abuse have been identified as characteristics of the families of origin of chemically dependent individuals."[153] Whether methamphetamine's contribution to child maltreatment is greater than that of other drugs is an open question, though it does appear that women whose primary drug of abuse is methamphetamine are more likely than those whose primary drug is alcohol or opiates to be involved in the child welfare system.[154] Aside from abuse, many addicted parents simply lack good parenting skills.[155] Having not had good parenting modeled for them when they were children, many adult addicts simply do not know how to parent. Further, addicted women often report symptoms of depression which, in turn, have been associated with inadequate parenting.[156]

A final and much understudied issue related to parenting and methamphetamine abuse is the intergenerational use of methamphetamine. There is limited systematic research on this topic, but it has received attention in the media (e.g., the HBO special *Crank: Made in America*). In the absence of systematic research, it is not possible to say whether intergenerational use of methamphetamine is more common than is true for other drugs. Still, it is an issue too important to neglect.

There is much to be learned about the effects of methamphetamine on parenting. Studies of serious abusers and of those in treatment may not reflect the parenting behavior of sporadic or occasional users. Not surprisingly, one is hard pressed to find research suggesting methamphetamine has a positive effect on parenting, though some women report first taking the drug to give them the energy to keep up with household chores and to clean up after the kids.[157] Given the importance of the issue and its implications for future generations, it is unfortunate that the effects of methamphetamine on parenting have received so little research attention.

CONCLUSION

Studies of the association between methamphetamine and violence and between methamphetamine and sex reveal what is likely a real but complex connection in which the psychopharmacological action of the drug is for most users a secondary factor. Writing in 1969, Blum made observations about the association between drugs and violence that still ring true today, and appear equally relevant to the issue of methamphetamine and sexual behavior. Noting a string of myths about the role of drugs in violence, Blum concluded:

> . . . one belief has it that drugs *cause* behavior and another that drug effects are highly predictable. These are incorrect. Psychoactive drugs can only modify bodily processes and capabilities already present; thus while drugs may contribute to conduct—and strongly so—they are not, at least not yet, capable of adding unique dimensions to performance nor of compelling any particular type of performance . . . drugs do not *compel* any particular social conduct, be it humor or murder.[158]

Less complex is the association between methamphetamine abuse and parenting. The abuse of methamphetamine may lead to the physical or sexual abuse of children, either by a parent, adult relative, or other adults who come and go in the house. More typical, however, is the tendency of methamphetamine-abusing parents to neglect their children. Absorbed in their own world, the serious abusers of methamphetamine may simply not be fully aware of the needs of their children.

The next chapter will cover the illicit production of meth in the United States, including how it is made, the health risks associated with meth cooking, and the efforts to stop meth manufacturing.

CHAPTER 5

Cooking Methamphetamine

While methamphetamine has been around for nearly a century, the recent rise of domestic methamphetamine laboratories has added a sense of urgency to responding to the problem. First, methamphetamine laboratories pose environmental and health risks that transcend the effects of the drug on the user. Apartment residents may be killed or injured by a meth lab explosion in the adjoining apartment, children in homes where meth is cooked may be exposed to toxic chemicals and to meth itself, hotel guests may be injured by toxic chemical residue from the previous tenant's meth lab, children may be burned or seriously injured by the meth trash dumped along the roadways near their homes, and emergency responders may be sickened when they enter a lab site. Thus, meth labs pose a type of threat to innocent citizens that simple drug use does not.

Second, most illegal drug distribution and use occur in the shadows, well out of sight of the majority of citizens who do not use drugs. For the most part those outside of the drug culture may be unaware of its extent, or even of its presence in their community. In contrast, methamphetamine labs and waste from these labs provide concrete and undeniable evidence of a community's drug problem. Some government Web sites even use the number of meth labs seized as a measure of the extent of a community's methamphetamine problem and of progress in combating methamphetamine. An urgent response is called for when the problem is undeniable.

Finally, when drugs (e.g., cocaine, heroin) originate in a foreign country, it is easy to define the drug problem as one that is ultimately the creation of producers in the source country, and thus a foreign problem. When the drug is produced here at home (literally at home in many cases), denial of domestic responsibility is more difficult. When both manufacturing and consumption occur here at home, production becomes a problem that we own and for which we have a direct obligation to respond.

For the drug manufacturer, methamphetamine production has several advantages over the production of such plant-based drugs as cocaine and heroin. Producing methamphetamine in domestic labs means that production can be very close to the point of sale.[1] The domestic methamphetamine producer does not have to worry about crossing borders or losing shipments at sea. Thus, methamphetamine producers lose less of their product to interdiction or accidents. A short distance between the producer and consumer also dramatically reduces the number of hands through which the product must pass before it reaches the consumer, substantially reducing the cost to the final consumer and dramatically increasing profits for the producer. Cocaine, for example, is very cheap in South America, but must pass through many hands before it reaches the final consumer in North America. As Reuter notes, "Fully 99 percent of the price of the drug, when sold on the streets in the United States, is accounted for by payments to people who distribute it."[2] This, in turn, requires an exceptional level of organization and the ability to be a good manager/CEO.[3] Finally, producing methamphetamine requires fewer precursors than does producing heroin.[4]

The building blocks of plant-based drugs are often plants that are indigenous to specific regions, have particular growing seasons, require a substantial amount of physical space in which to grow, and are subject to the vagaries of weather. Further, plants simply require time to grow. This not only limits the amount that can be produced in a given year but also means that the grower is exposed to risk of eradication by law enforcement, insects, thieves, and weather for the duration of the growing season. In contrast, meth cooks can produce the final product in any weather, in a few hours, and in a limited space, and, if they suspect imminent arrest, they can quickly dispose of their equipment and materials.

Finally, those who would manufacture methamphetamine can start with very small operations and grow (or shrink) their business as the market allows. What may start out as a "hobby" may easily be turned into a business. Startup costs and technical expertise required for small operations are minor, but the successful small-time meth cook can easily grow the business, both in size and in complexity. Thus, in the United States, synthetically manufacturing methamphetamine gives the drug a host of distinct business advantages over cocaine or heroin.

What Is a "Meth Lab"?

Another issue in the study of methamphetamine laboratories and their operators is simply defining what constitutes a methamphetamine lab. The problem of deciding what is a lab is reflected in a report issued by the Community Epidemiology Work Group on the abuse of stimulants.[5] Drawing on data from the Drug Enforcement Administration (DEA) and the El Paso Intelligence Center (EPIC), the group reported that for 2004, 301 methamphetamine laboratories were seized in Illinois and 614 in Missouri. Later, in the same report, and citing the same sources, the group reported "clandestine lab incidents," a broader term including labs, dump sites, and chemicals. By this broader measure 926 "labs" were seized in Illinois during 2004, and 2,707 were seized in Missouri. For the sixteen states cited in both sections of the report there were 2,278 methamphetamine labs and 7,013 lab incidents.[6] Clearly, the definition used will have a dramatic impact on the reported size of the problem. The DEA has produced a 122-page document providing guidelines for cleaning up clandestine methamphetamine laboratories,[7] but the document does not provide a definition of a lab. The National Drug Intelligence Center (NDIC) provides the following broad definition: "A methamphetamine laboratory is an illicit operation that has the apparatus and chemicals needed to produce the powerful stimulant methamphetamine."[8] Would a car stopped with boxes of pills containing ephedrine and a cooler intended for holding anhydrous ammonia be considered a lab? Clearly, there is considerable flexibility in what may be defined as a lab.

Ralph Weisheit, one of the authors of this book, interviewed narcotics officers who worked in three separate midwestern drug task forces that focused on methamphetamine. Task force members were asked what constituted a methamphetamine laboratory. While the answer may be clear in the case of a fully functioning methamphetamine laboratory, many of the reported laboratories did not fit this description. In determining what constituted a methamphetamine lab, there was general agreement within a task force, but there were variations across task forces. One task force counted meth trash where hazardous materials were present as a lab, even if the material was limited to one bottle in which chemical reactions had occurred. Members of another task force were reluctant to categorize trash as a lab unless at least three essential ingredients were present. The difficulty is in categorizing "partial labs" or situations in the gray area between precursors and full-blown labs. As another example, one fire chief reported being called to a house where fumes were rising from a cistern in the yard. Meth cooks were dumping meth waste into the cistern, and chemical reactions in that waste generated the fumes. Was this a meth lab? Further complicating a full understanding of the issue is the fact that national figures of laboratory seizures are often based on lab seizures involving the DEA and thus are often different from those reported by individual states. Within individual states not all laboratory seizures are reported to a central registry, such as the state police. For example, the state police may elect to count only those labs in which state police officers took part in the raid, omitting from the count any lab found solely by local authorities. Alternately, the state police may count locally seized labs, but local officials may fail to report their seizures to the state police.

An awareness of problems in counting methamphetamine labs should not detract us from the reality that labs do exist and they do pose problems. Accurate counts are of more concern to officials seeking to document their antidrug activities. The larger point is simply that precise counts do not exist, even of seized labs let alone all labs, and that the reported number of seized labs may be inflated or deflated depending on the definition used or the agencies involved. Whatever the true number of methamphetamine labs, the problems created by those labs are very real.

However, methamphetamine can be produced in a variety of ways, and the particular problems labs present depend in part on the method used. Our attention turns now to a description of those methods.

Illicit Production in the United States

As discussed in chapter 2, amphetamine was first synthesized in 1887 and methamphetamine in 1919. In the early years these drugs were readily available through legal channels or through diversion from legal channels, and there were few incentives for illicit manufacturing. The history of illicit manufacturing worldwide is unknown, but in the United States it is thought to have begun in California in the early 1960s. Amid concerns about overprescribing by doctors and diversion to the illegal market, Abbott Laboratories withdrew injectable Desoxyn (the trade name for legally manufactured methamphetamine) and Burroughs Wellcome withdrew injectable Methedrine (another trade name for legally manufactured methamphetamine), leaving "intravenous methamphetamine users without a product which could be readily injected. Demand was created for an inexpensive water-soluble powder product."[9] As a result of this unmet demand, the first illicit methamphetamine laboratories emerged in San Francisco in 1962 or 1963, perhaps with the help of some legitimate chemists.[10]

By 1967 San Francisco had become a center for the manufacture of methamphetamine. Small labs proliferated and a crackdown by police pushed larger labs from the city to surrounding rural areas.[11] The 1970s and early 1980s witnessed the publication of several manuals providing instruction in the manufacture of methamphetamine.[12] During the 1980s virtually all of the substances sold on the street as amphetamines contained methamphetamine, and nearly all of the methamphetamine sold on the street was illicitly manufactured, rather than diverted from legitimate pharmaceutical production.[13] Eventually, methamphetamine production made its way along the entire West Coast from San Diego to Washington State. From there production moved eastward so that today methamphetamine labs have been found in every state.

Ingredients used in a small meth lab.

While it is true that hundreds, perhaps thousands, of recipes for methamphetamine can be found on the Internet, it appears that most meth cooks learn their skills from other meth cooks. The Internet and books with technical descriptions of the cooking process may be useful for cooks who wish to hone their skills, but that is probably not how the majority of cooks begin. Thus, knowledge about cooking meth spreads in much the same way that communicable diseases spread—through social networks.[14] This is particularly true of smaller operations—known by such street names as "mom-and-pop," "Beavis and Butt-Head," or "kitchen" labs. In rural areas, for example, it is not unusual for one rural county to have a large number of meth labs while an adjoining rural county has few or none. The county with many labs is often one in which a knowledgeable cook moves into the community and teaches others in exchange for their help with such things as providing the necessary chemicals. Thus, small methamphetamine labs are often based on friendship networks in which a cook works with others, eventually teaching them, and they, in turn, eventually teach others in their friendship network. In this way knowledge about cooking meth can spread geometrically.

For many cooks (though not all), cooking meth has the features of an art, in that they may endlessly experiment to find the perfect recipe. Such cooks have often been arrested with detailed records of their experiments and take pride in the quality of their product. As Frank Owen observed in *No Speed Limit:*

> Different from regular drug dealers who express their status through ostentatious displays of guns, cars, and jewelry, a meth cook's standing is determined solely by his ability to produce Grade A dope. Like a chef in a four-star restaurant, meth cooks often employ helpers who, in exchange for meth, do the menial preparatory work. One person's job might be to buy the cold pills. Another is sent out to get the batteries. Yet others rub their fingers raw punching pills from blister packs.[15]

For many cooks, it is not simply the finished product that drives their activity but the satisfaction in the very process of cooking—much as marijuana growers have been found to become infatuated with the process of cultivating and cross-breeding varieties of marijuana.[16] As Owen described it:

> But more than a cheap high, meth is attractive because of the outlaw lifestyle that surrounds the manufacturing of the drug. Talk to practically any meth cook in the Ozarks and they'll tell you pretty much the same thing: The ritual of gathering the ingredients and cooking the drug gets them just as excited as the drug itself. "I got higher off the cooking than I did off the dope," says Stanley Harris.[17]

From the standpoint of controlling the methamphetamine problem, arrested cooks who are obsessed with the details of manufacturing meth present an interesting dilemma. Does putting them in jail or prison provide them with a "classroom" full of "students" eager to learn the trade, and thus serve to spread knowledge about cooking meth? Does it put them in contact with others with whom they can swap recipes? Does it provide them with contacts that enable their local operation to expand to other communities in their region? And, if they are not imprisoned, how can they be kept from spreading their knowledge in a society that values free speech?

Consider the case of the trained chemist who uses the pseudonym "Uncle Fester" to write the book *Secrets of Methamphetamine Manufacture*, which in 2005 went into its seventh edition.[18] The book provides information on a variety of manufacturing methods, along with tips on obtaining chemicals in a way that will not arouse the suspicion of authorities. The book also describes how to brew the precursors P2P (also known as phenylacetone or phenyl-2-propanone) and ephedrine, thus skirting laws designed to limit access to P2P and to ephedrine via cold and allergy medicines. Uncle Fester has also written books on making explosives at home, manufacturing LSD, and making toxic materials for guerrilla warfare, and techniques for defeating bulletproof vests. The First Amendment to the U.S. Constitution protects such writings as long as they are explicitly marketed as educational materials and not as calls to engage in criminal activity.

The spread of knowledge about methamphetamine production is not only an issue concerning cooks who are jail or prison inmates. Similar questions can be asked about putting those enamored by the process of cooking together with methamphetamine users in group treatment settings:

> The other thing that came up frequently was how the meth addicts spend much of their time in treatment learning new techniques to manufacture the drug. Proponents of self-help groups and 12-step programs often cite the sense of comradeship that such programs engender among drug users. . . . But community isn't necessarily a good thing when it comes to kicking meth. Self-help groups can easily turn into chemistry classes.[19]

Those who wish to control methamphetamine production are thus confronted with a host of issues beyond those related to simple distribution.

The Process of Making Methamphetamine

There are a variety of ways to manufacture methamphetamine, many of them outlined in Uncle Fester's book. Some methods require several days of round-the-clock work by a team of cooks, while others require only a few hours and a single cook. Some labs are suited for large-scale production, what the DEA describes as "super labs" capable of producing ten pounds or more of methamphetamine in a twenty-four-hour period. Other recipes are best suited for small-scale production.

Two common methods for manufacturing methamphetamine are the amalgam or P2P method and the ephedrine/pseudoephedrine reduction method. Several variations are available for each method. The P2P method uses P2P and methylamine (a derivative of ammonia) as the primary precursor chemicals[20] and produces a tell-tale odor similar to that of stale cat urine. This method may also utilize hydrochloric acid, formic acid, and/or mercury, among other chemicals.

The P2P method of methamphetamine manufacture is by far the more time consuming and demanding of the two. For example, one recipe involves a cooking process that requires special laboratory equipment, spans three days (after manufacturing one's own P2P), requires constant monitoring and modulation of the mixture's temperature, and must be stirred every thirty minutes. The very complexity of this process may make it appealing to trained chemists and others who relish the process of making meth as much as the effects of the final product, but it will have comparatively little appeal to untrained methamphetamine cooks eager to get their final product quickly. Further, the methamphetamine produced in this manner is often of a lower quality than that produced by the ephedrine/pseudoephedrine method.[21]

In February 1980, P2P became a Schedule II controlled substance and methylamine is now on the DEA's watch list. As P2P became more difficult to obtain, the ephedrine/pseudoephedrine reduction method became more popular, first appearing in clandestine laboratories in 1982, although the technique was understood well before that.[22] The National Drug Intelligence Center reports that the ephedrine/pseudoephedrine reduction

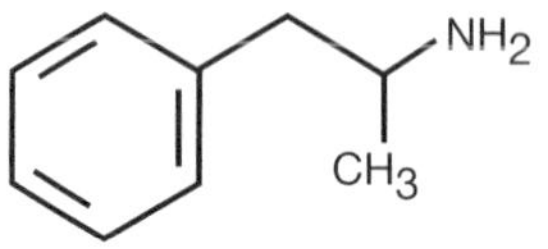

Amphetamine

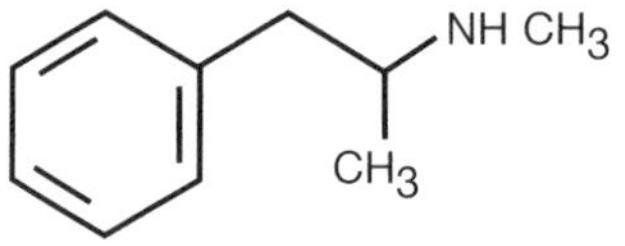

Methamphetamine

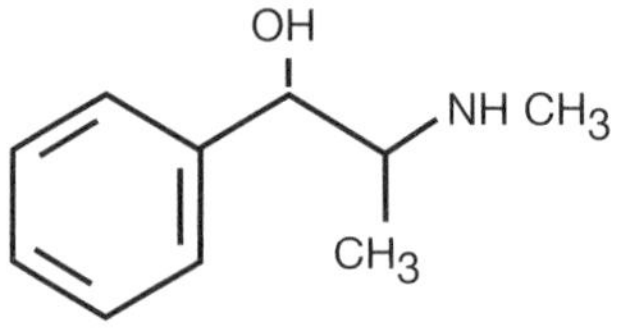

Ephedrine

method, which is simple to do and based on relatively inexpensive household products, is now the predominant method for manufacturing meth in both large and small labs.[23] Not only is the method easier than the P2P method but also the final product is more potent. It is called a reduction method because it involves removing an oxygen molecule, as can be seen by comparing the formula for ephedrine with that for methamphetamine. As the illustration shows, the only thing that differentiates ephedrine from methamphetamine is a single oxygen molecule.

Ephedrine: $C_{10}H_{15}NO$
Methamphetamine: $C_{10}H_{15}N$

Within the general ephedrine/pseudoephedrine reduction method are two primary ways of converting ephedrine or pseudoephedrine to methamphetamine (along with several other less familiar ways): the red phosphorous or Red-P method and the Nazi or Birch method.

The Red-P method utilizes ephedrine/pseudoephedrine and red phosphorous, as is found in the striking pads of matchbooks and in road flares. Depending on the recipe, red phosphorous is combined with iodine and/or hydriodic acid. It is also possible to replace red phosphorous, which is a restricted chemical, with hydrophosphorous acid, another restricted substance. However, those who have difficulty locating hydrophosphorous acid can find instructions for several ways of making it themselves. The Red-P method yields relatively high-quality methamphetamine.

Another ephedrine/pseudoephedrine reduction method utilizes anhydrous ammonia, lithium (typically extracted from lithium batteries), sodium hydroxide (lye), and toluene (paint thinner or camping fuel). Some researchers believe this so-called Nazi method got its name because it was used by the Nazis during World War II, but others dispute this idea, suggesting the name came from the Nazi symbols on the letterhead of the paper an early cook used to record the recipe.[24] The method is also referred to as the Birch reduction method, after the Australian chemist Arthur John Birch who first published his discovery of this method in 1944. Whatever the source of the name, the Nazi/Birch method has become particularly popular because of its simplicity, requiring substantially less technical knowledge than the P2P method, and because of the potency of the final product.

Efforts to End Illicit Production

Trying to stop the production and trafficking in illicit drugs is like trying to grab a balloon—squeeze in one place and it bulges out in another. One solution sometimes leads to new problems. Methamphetamine production is no different. As already noted, illicit methamphetamine production in California was triggered by the decision of drug manufacturers to voluntarily withdraw legally manufactured methamphetamine. What followed was a series of efforts by the federal government to end methamphetamine production. These efforts have had an impact, but they have also generated unintended consequences. Four federal laws provide good illustrations of these efforts and of the consequences:

1. Drug Abuse Control Amendments of 1965 (Public Law 89–74)
2. Controlled Substances Act of 1970 (Public Law 91–513)
3. Chemical Diversion and Trafficking Act of 1988 (Public Law 100–690)
4. Combat Methamphetamine Epidemic Act of 2005 (Public Law 109–177)

The Drug Abuse Control Amendments of 1965 modified the Federal Food, Drug, and Cosmetic Act to include barbiturates and amphetamines, including methamphetamine. The act limited the frequency with which prescriptions for methamphetamine could be renewed and required manufacturers to keep detailed records. The intent was to limit the diversion of these drugs away from legitimate therapeutic uses. Doctors could still prescribe these drugs, but their production and distribution were now more carefully monitored. Legitimate production was indeed reduced, and the law did limit the availability of legally manufactured methamphetamine tablets (and the eventual ban on injectable methamphetamine) for recreational purposes. However, it also spawned the rise of illicit production, as well as the smuggling of the restricted drugs from Mexico.[25]

The Controlled Substances Act of 1970 gave the DEA the authority to place drugs in one of five "schedules." Substances listed under Schedule I were deemed to be of no medical or therapeutic value and thus banned for all but research purposes, with the DEA deciding which types of research were legitimate. The act made it illegal to possess methamphetamine without a prescription and gave the DEA the authority to regulate legal production. The law had the effect of further reducing legal access to methamphetamine and, consequently, increased the profits to be made by those illicitly manufacturing meth. As might be expected, the effect was to substantially increase illicit production.

The Chemical Diversion and Trafficking Act of 1988 (CDTA) regulated bulk shipments of ephedrine and pseudoephedrine, but did not apply to over-the-counter medicines that contained these substances. "Within a month following enactment of the CDTA and the controls it placed upon ephedrine powder, the first encounter in the United States with ephedrine tablets at a clandestine methamphetamine laboratory seizure occurred. Traffickers had quickly realized that noncontrolled ephedrine tablets could be purchased easily in large quantities for subsequent conversion to methamphetamine."[26] Unfortunately, Mexico had no such controls on bulk shipments of powdered ephedrine and during the 1990s methamphetamine production in Mexico flourished. Mexican traffickers imported hundreds of tons of ephedrine powder from India, China, Pakistan, and the Czech Republic through circuitous routes via such countries as the United Arab Emirates, Switzerland, Guatemala, Germany, and the Netherlands. In an eighteen-month period beginning in 1994, more than two hundred tons of powdered ephedrine destined for Mexico were seized, enough to make one hundred forty tons of methamphetamine.[27] In all likelihood this was only a fraction of the amount actually sent to Mexico.

The Combat Methamphetamine Epidemic Act of 2005 sought to end domestic methamphetamine production via the Nazi method by restricting access to over-the-counter medications containing ephedrine and pseudoephedrine. The long-term consequences of this act are as yet unknown, but the short-term effects seem clear. Limiting the amount of these medications that can be purchased (no more than 9 grams per month) and requiring the buyer to provide a photo ID and to sign for the purchase do seem to have reduced the number of methamphetamine labs, as reflected in the fact that fewer labs have been seized—particularly those mom-and-pop labs that depended on their local drugstores to provide the ephedrine required to manufacture meth. Interestingly, however, while the number of seizures did go down, not all labs were eliminated.

In many ways, precursor regulation is a good example of states serving as laboratories for drug policy. Oklahoma's much touted success in regulating ephedrine was quickly followed by other states and eventually by the federal government.[28] In 2005 alone, thirty-five states enacted legislation to restrict the sale of ephedrine and pseudoephedrine, with another six states enacting legislation in 2006.[29] These laws generally regulate the packaging and display of ephedrine products and restrict who can buy and sell such products and the amount that can be sold within a specific time frame.

States also have adopted tough penalties for the illegal possession and transportation of anhydrous ammonia. In twenty-one states it is a felony to possess anhydrous ammonia for the purpose of making methamphetamine, and in fifteen states it is a felony to possess or transport anhydrous ammonia in unapproved containers. In some states possession and transportation are separate felonies.[30] This, in turn, has led to a lucrative market in stolen anhydrous ammonia. In Kentucky, for example, it has been reported that while the retail price of anhydrous ammonia is about one dollar per gallon, the price for stolen anhydrous ammonia can be as high as four hundred dollars per gallon. Such legislation has also led to the illicit synthesis of anhydrous ammonia.[31]

The effect of precursor regulation on overall levels of methamphetamine consumption is much debated. Cunningham and Liu have argued for the effectiveness of these measures, noting that methamphetamine-related hospital admissions have gone down following restrictions on legal access to precursors.[32] Reuter and Caulkins doubt these claims, noting that other measures suggest no effect of these regulations.[33] For example, following precursor regulation the price of methamphetamine went down, when there should have been shortages of the drug that drove prices up. Similarly, there were no sharp reductions in the reported use of methamphetamine by newly admitted jail inmates.

Interviews with methamphetamine users and cooks in Arkansas and Kentucky found that local production did decline after restrictions on the sales of pseudoephedrine, to be at least partially replaced by imported methamphetamine. Interestingly, the cooks in this study did stop cooking, but they attributed the stoppage to concerns about arrest, family pressures, and health concerns—not to the difficulty in obtaining pills.[34]

In perhaps the most detailed study to date, Dobkin and Nicosia considered the impact of a major disruption in the supply of precursors on a variety of methamphetamine-related indicators.[35] In the months immediately following this disruption, the price of methamphetamine rose from thirty dollars to one hundred dollars a gram, purity dropped from 90 percent to less than 20 percent, hospital admissions declined by 50 percent, treatment admissions declined by 35 percent, felony arrests for methamphetamine possession fell by 50 percent, misdemeanor arrests for methamphetamine possession fell by 25 percent, and the percent of arrestees testing positive for methamphetamine declined by 55 percent. All of these changes occurred with no evidence that users were switching to other drugs. Unfortunately, the impact of this major precursor disruption was short-lived as new sources of precursors were identified. "Price returned to pre-intervention levels within four months while purity, hospital admissions, drug treatment admissions and drug arrests recovered to near pre-intervention levels over eighteen months."[36]

If precursor regulation has had an unclear effect on overall levels of methamphetamine consumption, the effects of these regulations on production patterns seem clearer. It appears that various efforts to regulate methamphetamine production through restrictions on precursors have had the unintended consequence of centralizing production and enriching powerful drug trafficking organizations. It seems likely that an increasingly centralized production and distribution system will also increasingly be associated with violence to protect the enormous profits involved. In their description of mom-and-pop operations in Arkansas and Kentucky, Sexton and his colleagues observe:

> Participants reported independent production of small amounts of MA
> [methamphetamine], often in one ounce lots, with quality varying widely
> based on the competence of cookers. None of the participants indicated
> involvement in criminal gangs or organized drug trafficking. Rather, they
> produced MA for personal use, gift giving, barter with friends and
> acquaintances, and some local sales. Thus, most MA was distributed and
> consumed within local social networks and immediate communities.[37]

One drug enforcement officer was asked in an interview by Weisheit
about the difference between methamphetamine and other drugs. His
experience was in the Midwest and mostly involved a large number of
mom-and-pop operations:

> One of the things you don't see with other cases—we operate on a grant
> and fine and seizure money—with cocaine and marijuana cases, it's not
> unusual to go in and nab $3,000, $5,000, $20,000 in drug proceeds. With
> meth cases, it's zero; they have no money. There are very few meth deal-
> ers, as you would consider drug dealers. Most people considered drug
> dealers set up a house, people come by, a guy sells the drugs and keeps the
> money. Say he buys a pound of drugs for $10,000, then sells an ounce for
> $1,200. So, he's making about $19,000, and he puts $9,000 in his pocket,
> and he goes to buy another pound. That doesn't happen with meth. Now
> they're trading precursors, pills, stuff like that. Very few people make any
> money selling meth. Most of the people involved are addicts; that's the
> reason they got into manufacturing. One, they're not very good with their
> money. They don't work. A lot of the guys who sell marijuana and cocaine
> also have jobs, so that job pays their bills, and everything else is just play
> money. These people don't work, so they have to pay their rent, lights, gas,
> phone, whatever. So any money that they do have is going towards that.
> Plus, being a meth addict doesn't lend itself very well to keeping track of
> money. When you talk about crack, a lot of dealers aren't users. They don't
> even drink; they're in it solely for money. One of the first things I taught
> [other drug officers] about meth was that cocaine, marijuana, and all that,

was all about money. Meth cooks are all about getting more meth. It's all about manufacturing meth for them to use. They'll sell a little bit to pay the bills and get more ingredients, but as far as profits, there really are none. That's the biggest difference I see between meth and other drugs.

Replacing these localized production networks with national or international criminal networks is likely to present a very different set of problems for the community, for police, and for the users of methamphetamine themselves. For example, Mexico has been a major supplier of methamphetamine to consumers in the United States since the 1990s, and the demise of small independent methamphetamine labs has the potential to enable Mexican drug traffickers to dominate the U.S. methamphetamine market. There are some signs of this happening. According to a report by the National Drug Intelligence Center:

> As methamphetamine production in small-scale laboratories has decreased nationally since 2004, Mexican criminal groups have expanded direct distribution of methamphetamine, even in many smaller communities. For example, in Midwestern states such as Iowa, Missouri, Illinois, and Ohio, where methamphetamine laboratory seizures have decreased significantly—in some states by more than 55 percent—Mexican criminal groups have gained control over most distribution of the drug. In fact, the Midwest High Intensity Drug Trafficking Area (HIDTA) reports that in cities such as Des Moines and Sioux City, where methamphetamine production and distribution previously were controlled by local independent traffickers, Mexican criminal groups, primarily distributing ice methamphetamine, have supplanted independent traffickers. Law enforcement reporting confirms a similar trend throughout much of the Great Lakes, Mid-Atlantic, Florida/Caribbean, Southeast, and West Central Regions. These groups pose an increased challenge to local law enforcement because they are often Mexico-based, well-organized, and experienced drug distributors that have been successful in blending into somewhat insular Hispanic communities or among Hispanic workers employed in the agricultural, landscaping, construction, and meatpacking industries.[38]

The concern is that the small-scale operators are being replaced. Whereas mom-and-pop labs mainly cooked for themselves and for friends and relatively small amounts of cash changed hands, in large-scale operations profit is the driving motive, the amount of money involved is substantial, and the potential for violence is considerable. As recently as 1994, Jenkins could state with some confidence:

> The dominant mode of use tends to reflect the tastes and traditions of local subcultures. In view of the highly regional nature of manufacture and distribution, suppliers do not find it difficult to accommodate these local tastes. Fashions that emerge in one city or region can become dominant in that area without making much impact elsewhere. *In short, there is no such thing as a national market in methamphetamine* (emphasis added).[39]

By 2003 a national market appeared to be emerging, with the DEA estimating that "Mexico-based groups control 70 percent to 90 percent of methamphetamine production and distribution in the United States."[40]

An ominous consequence of a shift from local mom-and-pop operations to super labs with a national market is the reported marketing of candy-flavored methamphetamine.[41] Candy-flavored methamphetamine is apparently designed to appeal to the very young. While mom-and-pop labs may have allowed young people—mainly family and friends—access to methamphetamine, there were no strong financial incentives for aggressively marketing their product to youth. In contrast, when methamphetamine production becomes a business run by people with no stake in the well-being of the local community, there are strong incentives for expanding the customer base. The young are a particularly appealing target (just as they are for many legal industries, including alcohol and tobacco) in that they have the potential to be customers for years to come. Some observers have argued that candy-flavored methamphetamine is a myth,[42] but the possibility has moved two U.S. senators to introduce the "Saving Kids from Dangerous Drugs Act of 2007." One provision of the act would

> double the maximum penalties applicable to drug crimes if a criminal defendant manufactured, offered, distributed, or possessed with intent to

distribute a controlled substance that is flavored, colored, packaged, or otherwise altered in a way that is designed to make the substance more appealing to a person under the age of 21.[43]

Regulations on precursors did not create the methamphetamine problem, nor did they create major trafficking organizations, but they did change the nature of the industry surrounding methamphetamine production and the manner by which methamphetamine users had access to the drug. Further, the future may hold as yet undiscovered recipes for producing methamphetamine, which will call forth a new round of restrictions on precursor chemicals.

International Production

The misuse of methamphetamine is an international problem. It should come as no surprise, then, that production is also a global issue. The United Nations routinely monitors drug use and production around the world, including the use and production of methamphetamine.[44] The United Nations estimated that in 2005 the global production of methamphetamine was 290 metric tons (1 metric ton is equivalent to 2,200 pounds), and that production levels had stabilized in recent years. It was also estimated that over 95 percent of amphetamine-type stimulant (ATS) laboratories dismantled worldwide were producing methamphetamine, as opposed to amphetamine or Ecstasy, and that about half of all illicit stimulant drugs seized worldwide was methamphetamine. Although the United States is thought to be home to only about one-fifth of all of the methamphetamine users in the world, fully 95 percent of all dismantled labs in the world were dismantled in the United States. In addition, "seizures of ephedrine and pseudo-ephedrine in the USA accounted for 76 percent of global methamphetamine precursor seizures."[45] All of this suggests that production in other countries may be out of control.

Authorities seized enough ephedrine and pseudoephedrine in 2005 to produce 28 metric tons of methamphetamine. Curiously, the seizure of precursor chemicals declined in 2005, even as estimated methamphetamine production remained stable—suggesting that the amount of precursors seized was so small compared to what was available as to have little impact on production levels. There was also an increase in the seizure of pre-precursors, the chemicals used to manufacture precursors.

The UN report suggests that most illicitly manufactured methamphetamine supplies only the country in which it was produced or nearby countries. This is not the case, however, for precursor chemicals, which appear to be traded in a global illicit market. Pseudoephedrine, for example, is thought to be manufactured in Asia and sent to North America via the Democratic Republic of the Congo.[46] And as noted above, Mexican trafficking organizations have had access to powdered ephedrine from a variety of source countries from around the world.

There have been numerous agreements to monitor and regulate the international movement of precursor chemicals, including ephedrine and pseudoephedrine. Most notable, perhaps, is the 1988 United Nations Convention Against Illicit Traffic in Narcotic Drugs and Psychotropic Substances.[47] The convention calls for signatory states not only to cooperate in controlling illicit drug manufacturing and distribution but also to establish offenses relevant to the illegal use of precursor chemicals (including ephedrine and pseudoephedrine). However, as the U.S. Department of State has observed, the convention is not binding nor are agreements among countries necessarily formal.[48] But such drugs as ephedrine have legitimate pharmaceutical uses, and the convention excludes pharmaceutical preparations—a significant loophole favoring traffickers. In addition, the pharmaceutical industry is large in many countries, and pharmaceutical companies often have considerable political influence. Even within the United States, a country known for its aggressive efforts to control drug trafficking, pharmaceutical companies have strongly resisted efforts to regulate the distribution of preparations containing ephedrine.[49]

Given that most methamphetamine production is for regional consumption, that methamphetamine is relatively easy to produce, and that global methamphetamine consumption is probably equal to or greater than the consumption of cocaine and heroin combined, it is not surprising that the list of producer countries is long. One of the world's major production regions is the Golden Triangle, an area of Asia that includes

Myanmar (formerly Burma), Laos, Vietnam, and Thailand. This region, perhaps best known for opium production, has a long history of producing amphetamine-type stimulants, including methamphetamine. In recent years, however, production has expanded dramatically,[50] and local use rates have followed suit. Thailand, for example, traditionally has had a serious problem with opium and heroin addiction, but in recent years most addicts in treatment are there for methamphetamine addiction, an addiction fueled by the desire to work long hours.

Much of the methamphetamine production in the Golden Triangle takes place in Myanmar, which shares a border with China, Laos, and Thailand. Production in the region is fueled by vast fields of ma huang (*Ephedra sinica,* the plant from which ephedrine is derived) in nearby China, making China the world's largest producer of ephedrine.[51] Profits can be enormous, providing a powerful incentive to producers. A single methamphetamine pill produced in Myanmar may cost as little as three cents (in U.S. dollars) but can fetch between forty-six and sixty-five cents on the streets of Bangkok, Thailand, which is among the leading countries in the world for per capita methamphetamine consumption.[52]

China's role in the production of methamphetamine goes beyond the cultivation of ma huang. While Myanmar may play a key role in the production of methamphetamine in the Golden Triangle, China's influence can be seen throughout Asia. More than one-half of the methamphetamine seized in Japan is thought to have originated in China, and nearly one-third of the methamphetamine seized throughout Asia has been attributed to production in China.[53] And, as has so often happened with other drugs in other countries, China's involvement in the production of methamphetamine and methamphetamine precursors has led to a growing problem of methamphetamine use by the Chinese, some of which is the result of Chinese-produced ephedrine being shipped to Myanmar where it is converted to methamphetamine, and then shipped back to China for consumption.[54]

In addition to the Golden Triangle and China, much of the Asian region has been affected by methamphetamine. Production has been a problem in the Philippines, India (another major producer of ephedrine and pseudoephedrine), Hong Kong, and North Korea, though in many

Asian countries methamphetamine production primarily feeds local demand.

Methamphetamine production remains a problem, but apparently has stabilized in Oceania (Australia, New Zealand, and the many islands that make up Polynesia, Melanesia, and Micronesia), perhaps as a result of more systematic efforts to monitor and limit access to precursors. In this region methamphetamine imported from China may be compensating for reduced domestic production.[55] There is also evidence that methamphetamine became increasingly popular in Australia beginning in 2000, when there was a "heroin drought,"[56] once again revealing the peculiar relationship between the use of heroin and the use of methamphetamine, as noted in chapters 2 and 3.

In Europe, methamphetamine production is a comparatively minor problem, though the trend is for increasing production.[57] However, there are pockets of Europe in which methamphetamine production has become a particular problem, including the Czech Republic, the Republic of Moldova, and Slovakia.[58] While the number of methamphetamine labs in Europe appears to be increasing, most are mom-and-pop labs, limiting total production levels.[59]

Finally, methamphetamine production appears to have taken root in South Africa, where there are reports of an increasing number of laboratory seizures. There are also reports of seizures of ephedrine and pseudoephedrine originating in China.[60] However, production in the rest of Africa appears limited, as is production in South America. The ease with which methamphetamine can be produced, however, cautions against assuming these areas will not soon develop problems of their own.

Health Risks from Manufacturing Methamphetamine

Aside from the potential health risks from *using* methamphetamine are the potentially deadly consequences of *manufacturing* methamphetamine. Legally manufactured drugs, including methamphetamine, are created in highly controlled laboratory settings in which the process is overseen by skilled chemists. Neither a controlled laboratory nor a skilled chemist necessarily exists in the illicit manufacture of methamphetamine.

Methamphetamine labs, particularly mom-and-pop labs, are often set up by individuals with no background in chemistry or in proper laboratory procedures. Combine this circumstance with the highly volatile chemicals used to manufacture methamphetamine, add a heat source and a sleep-deprived cook, and the potential for accidents and even explosions is substantial. There are several respects in which cooking meth may damage health. First is the handling of toxic materials. Second, the process of cooking itself may cause health problems. Finally, health problems may be caused by the aftermath of cooking methamphetamine.

It is often said that methamphetamine can be made with everyday household items, such as lye and camping fuel. While this is true, some of those items are particularly harmful to the human body. Some materials—such as sodium, magnesium, and potassium—can ignite or explode when exposed to air or water.[61] Others—such as anhydrous ammonia, phosphorus, and lithium—are not only harmful but are also "everyday" only in the strictest sense of the word. Let's take just a few, beginning with anhydrous ammonia.

Anhydrous Ammonia

Anhydrous ammonia, a key ingredient in the Nazi or Birch method of methamphetamine production, is widely used in farming communities, where the chemical is a source of nitrogen fertilizer. Anhydrous ammonia is also used as an industrial refrigerant. It is one of the top twenty chemicals produced in the United States.[62] In its natural state, anhydrous ammonia is a gas. When used as a fertilizer, it is stored under pressure, turning it into a liquid. Liquid anhydrous ammonia is injected into the ground where it expands into a gas, absorbs moisture from the surrounding ground, and remains in the ground in the form of nitrogen. To keep it as a liquid for storage and transport, it must be stored under considerable pressure. The internal pressure of an anhydrous ammonia tank increases as the ambient temperature increases. For example, if the external temperature is 60° F, the internal pressure is 93 psi (pounds per square inch). However, if the external temperature is 100° F, the pressure inside the tank may reach 200 psi. By comparison, a standard automobile tire is usually inflated to 34 psi. The issue of pressure is relevant to methamphetamine production. If thieves who steal anhydrous ammonia transport it in a container that cannot withstand the pressure, the container will burst or even explode, with potentially deadly consequences. Not only must the carrier be able to withstand the pressure but also the material of which the carrier is constructed makes a difference. For example, anhydrous ammonia is corrosive to copper, brass, bronze, and zinc, and, consequently, will eat away at the metal in the valves of propane tanks (as used in outdoor barbecues), causing them to eventually fail and release the chemical. As these tanks are often used by anhydrous ammonia thieves, a risk is posed to both the thief and to others who might later use the tanks for legitimate purposes.

The word *anhydrous* means "without water." Anhydrous ammonia is considered hydroscopic, meaning that it seeks water from the nearest source. In the case of humans, the skin, eyes, nose, throat, and lungs are loaded with moisture, and, if they come into contact with the chemical, the water they contain is instantly removed, leading to serious burns. "When large amounts are inhaled, the throat swells and victims suffocate. Exposure to vapors or liquid can also cause blindness. . . . The chemical freezes on contact at room temperature. It will cause burns similar to, but more severe than, those caused by dry ice."[63] The chemical will burn its way into the body, killing cells it contacts unless diluted with water, which is why some states require those who legally handle anhydrous to keep water nearby. "When anhydrous ammonia is released from compression in a storage tank (200 psi) to the atmosphere (0 psi), the temperature drops from 100°F to -28°F. At this temperature, ammonia will freeze-burn the skin on contact. Clothing is actually frozen to the skin. Another risk is that ammonia when released will quickly expand from the point of release. A sudden rupture can shoot ammonia 10 to 20 feet from the point of release."[64]

Given its volatile nature and its extensive use in agriculture, it is not surprising that states have rather elaborate regulations regarding the safe handling of anhydrous ammonia. It is not legally available to the general public and can be purchased legally only by those with a special license. Thus, for most methamphetamine cooks it must be obtained through illegal channels. It is also not surprising that farmers, distributors, and law enforcement have made serious attempts to frustrate thieves by locking anhydrous ammonia tanks, storing them in enclosed facilities, and mounting surveillance cameras in lots where multiple tanks are stored. Some states even require locks.

If anhydrous ammonia is so easily released into the air, what are the implications for the environment in which the meth cook operates? When meth is cooked outdoors, the wind can carry away and dissipate the ammonia. In an enclosed house or apartment, however, the situation may be very different. Martyny and colleagues undertook a series of studies to simulate real-world conditions under which methamphetamine is produced.[65] In one study, three abandoned houses were outfitted with environmental monitors, and methamphetamine was then manufactured using the Nazi method. Anhydrous ammonia was detected in the air within five minutes after the cooking began, and within sixteen minutes all of the monitors were overloaded. The Occupational Safety and Health Administration (OSHA) recommends exposure to no more than 50 ppm (parts per million) of anhydrous ammonia averaged over an eight-hour period. The National Institute for Occupational Safety and Health (NIOSH) recommends no more than 35 ppm over the course of one hour and suggests that anhydrous ammonia levels over 300 ppm are immediately dangerous to life and health.[66] In the Martyny study, anhydrous ammonia exposure ranged from 130 ppm to 437 ppm as an average over time, with peak levels near 2,000 ppm during the initial cook and remaining at more than 500 ppm in areas distant from the cook. These levels are not necessarily fatal, but they are sufficient to cause respiratory problems. And, while it is clear that anhydrous ammonia is released into the air at noxious levels, less clear are the long-term consequences of this exposure. The risk of harm can be dramatically reduced if the anhydrous ammonia is handled in a well-ventilated area; but, to avoid detection of the noxious odors generated by a meth lab, meth cooks often attempt to seal the rooms in which they manufacture the drug.

There is ongoing research to develop additives that would render the anhydrous ammonia useless for methamphetamine production. Other research focuses on adding a dye to anhydrous ammonia, thus staining anything that comes into contact with it, including containers used to steal the chemical. But such efforts to control the illegitimate use of anhydrous ammonia must be conducted within the context of its legitimate agricultural and industrial applications. Anhydrous ammonia remains one of the most widely used fertilizers in agriculture. Farmers depend on the relatively inexpensive chemical to boost crop yields. Actions that would increase the price farmers pay for anhydrous ammonia will cut into their already thin profit margins. Thus, the various mechanical and chemical fixes designed to thwart anhydrous ammonia thieves must not only be effective deterrents but also must add little to the cost of the chemical.

Flammable Solvents

Another health hazard from cooking methamphetamine comes from using flammable solvents, such as camping fuel or acetone (as found in nail polish remover). By themselves, these products are not particularly dangerous, but they can become so when meth cooks heat their mixtures with open flames. When this happens, the risk of fire or explosions is substantial. In addition to burns from the resulting fire, laboratory explosions may spray shards of glass and caustic chemicals through the air, including sulfuric acid, anhydrous ammonia, and hydrochloric acid.[67] Thus, in addition to burns from the fire itself, the patients must be decontaminated and treated for chemical burns.[68]

One study carefully compared burn patients from meth lab explosions with other patients suffering similar total body surface area (BSA) burns. Methamphetamine-related burn patients were far more likely to die, either directly from their burns or from exposure to chemicals present at the explosion.[69] Others have found that compared with other burn patients, methamphetamine-related burn patients were three times more likely to sustain inhalation injuries and had longer hospital stays, higher death rates, more days on a ventilator, more graft loss, and triple the level of hospital charges.[70] One burn center reported having to chisel melted plastic from the face of a patient who had lined the walls of her lab with it.[71] Relatively few of those treated for methamphetamine-related burns have private insurance, and many have no government assistance to cover the costs of medical treatment, putting a financial strain on hospitals.[72]

To complicate matters, methamphetamine-related burn patients tend to be substantially more agitated, making it difficult to immobilize them

Meth trash is a toxic byproduct of the manufacturing process.

and increasing the failure rate of grafts. Under ordinary circumstances skin grafts fail about 33 percent of the time, but for meth patients the failure rate is 50 percent, due mainly to their agitated state.[73] It has been reported that nearly half of methamphetamine-related burn patients needed to be sedated to control their agitation.[74] Methamphetamine-related burn patients have also been relatively uncooperative in follow-up medical treatment:

> On the basis of our experience, there is a poor follow-up in this group of patients and when our coordinator tried to contact each patient for their clinic visit; either they had given false information, transferred residence, or ceased contact with the hospital. One possible explanation for the poor follow-up is fear of prosecution.[75]

Not surprisingly, those suffering from methamphetamine-related injuries who admit themselves to the emergency room are often reluctant to reveal the source of the burn, instead attributing it to other kinds of accidents.

Phosphine Gas

Phosphine gas is produced when methamphetamine is manufactured using the red phosphorous (Red-P) method. In its pure form it is odorless and colorless, but when discovered at methamphetamine lab sites it may have an odor reflecting the presence of contaminants. Phosphine gas is created when iodine is combined with red phosphorus under conditions that a trained chemist should know to avoid. In particular, phosphine gas may be created when red phosphorous is heated in the presence of acids.[76] Phosphine gas is highly toxic and is used in agriculture as a grain fumigant to protect grains in storage or in shipment from insects and rodents. Low-level exposure can result in "headache, fatigue or weakness, thirst, pain or pressure in the diaphragm or chest, dyspnea or shortness of breath, nausea, vomiting, convulsions and coma. Some references also report vertigo, irritation of the lungs, coughing and a feeling of coldness."[77] The toxins tend to collect in areas of the body that demand oxygen, including the brain, lungs, kidney, heart, and liver. Higher doses can cause death, a fate that has befallen some methamphetamine cooks.[78] The presence of the gas may also pose a hazard to law enforcement and emergency response personnel who enter an active lab site. In one case a forensic specialist entered a lab site that had been ventilated until phosphine gas was no longer detectable. She still developed the symptoms of phosphine gas poisoning, symptoms that persisted for months.[79]

Lead Poisoning

Lead poisoning is another health risk generated by the untrained meth cook. In this case the risk comes not from the cooking process itself, but from a final product that has been contaminated with lead. Cut off from legitimate supplies of P2P, some meth cooks have resorted to synthesizing their own supplies of P2P. One recipe for doing this involves combining lead acetate with other chemicals to produce P2P. The careless or ill-informed cook can easily produce methamphetamine that contains a considerable amount of residual lead. In one case the cook created a product that was 60 percent lead.[80] The extent to which lead poisoning is an issue in methamphetamine production is unknown. Methamphetamine cooks entering the emergency department or visiting a doctor are not likely to volunteer information about their illegal activity. And, because the symptoms of lead poisoning mimic a variety of other problems, physicians may not immediately think of a lead-poisoning diagnosis. To further complicate matters, the symptoms of lead poisoning are variable and nonspecific, depending on the level of exposure and the individual, and they may include any or all of the following: weakness, headaches, abdominal pain, chills, sweats, nausea, weight loss, lower back and leg pains, diarrhea, constipation, seizures, and even coma. Acute lead poisoning has been linked to methamphetamine production.[81]

Iodine

Finally, iodine is released during the manufacture of methamphetamine when the red phosphorous method of production is used. In some cases iodine has stained the walls of the room in which methamphetamine was prepared. Iodine is a naturally occurring element that the body requires for good health. A level of iodine is required for the proper functioning of the thyroid gland. Every cell in the body depends on the hormones produced by the thyroid gland and only the thyroid gland can absorb iodine, which is then converted into the hormones that regulate the body's metabolism.[82] For most people the concern is whether they are taking in too little iodine and as a consequence will have too few of the hormones to properly regulate their body's physical functions. It is possible, however, to take in too much iodine. Ironically, too much iodine can affect the thyroid gland much like too little iodine. When presented with too much iodine, the thyroid gland will experience a decrease in blood flow and will subsequently produce too few hormones.[83]

When most people think of iodine, they think of nutrition, as in the consumption of iodized salt. Like anhydrous ammonia, iodine also has agricultural applications. It is used as a disinfectant for farm animals, including sanitizing the teats of milk cows. As with anhydrous ammonia, the agricultural applications of iodine facilitate rural methamphetamine production, and diversion of iodine from agricultural supplies is a concern.

Methamphetamine cooks generally prefer iodine in a crystal form, which is highly potent. The U.S. Department of Justice warns that in this form iodine can be dangerous:

> If iodine comes in contact with the skin it can result in painful irritation and chemical burns. Contact with the eyes can cause redness, burns, and permanent damage. Inhalation of iodine gas can lead to respiratory problems or even death. Iodine has sufficient vapor pressure to allow toxic levels of iodine gas to build up in a closed container. . . . Although iodine alone is not flammable, it is a strong oxidizer that can ignite or cause explosions when mixed with other combustibles or reducing agents such as alkali metals, ammonia, and phosphorous.[84]

Whether practicing methamphetamine cooks are exposed to sufficient levels of iodine and over a sufficient period of time to seriously damage their health remains an open question. It appears that when handled properly, levels of iodine released during the process of manufacturing methamphetamine are measurable but not toxic.[85] Direct exposure to the crystals, or the improper handling of them, is quite another matter. It is for this reason that some states have added iodine to the list of regulated precursor chemicals.

Contaminated Laboratory Sites

The chemical contamination of methamphetamine laboratory sites has raised concerns about the health and safety of those who enter the sites, in addition to the meth cooks themselves. For example, when methamphetamine is prepared in a hotel room, hotel staff and subsequent occupants may be exposed to the chemicals. It is not unusual for children to be present when methamphetamine is prepared in a home, and later occupants may have reason to be concerned about chemical contamination of the carpet and walls. Concerns have been raised about the health and safety of emergency responders. Police have reported respiratory and eye irritation, sore throat, cough, and headaches after entering meth lab sites. There have even been reports of symptoms from simply transporting arrested meth cooks from the cook site. Fires or explosions account for as many as 10 percent of cases in which adverse health consequences from methamphetamine laboratory chemicals are reported,[86] and some have reported that 20 percent to 30 percent of methamphetamine labs are discovered because of fires or explosions.[87] When fires or explosions occur during a methamphetamine cook, firefighters may be exposed to both the chemicals used in manufacturing and to toxic fumes generated by the fires. And, in moving through smoke-filled buildings, they may also be exposed to contaminated needles left behind. Other researchers have found that methamphetamine laboratory investigators experience a reduction in their lung capacity comparable to that of continuing smokers, even though most do not smoke.[88]

While it has been known for decades that chemicals are released in the cooking process, the nature and extent of contamination were highly speculative until the National Jewish Medical and Research Center conducted a series of studies in the early and mid-2000s.[89] These studies are remarkable in their attention to detail and in their consideration of multiple cooking techniques and the range of settings in which cooking occurs. The studies tested for both airborne and surface chemical residue from the three most popular methods for cooking methamphetamine: P2P, Red-P, and Nazi. The researchers tested for chemical residue during, immediately after, and many hours after cooking in settings that included a police laboratory, abandoned houses, abandoned hotels, mobile homes, and apartments. The findings of these chemical analyses were supplemented by surveying police officers who had investigated meth labs about perceived health effects of their work. Some of the highest levels of chemical release were associated with the red phosphorous (Red-P) method of cooking. This method caused the release of phosphine, hydrogen chloride, and iodine at levels that often exceeded those recommended by agencies responsible for occupational safety. Cooking based on anhydrous ammonia (the Nazi method) released high levels of both anhydrous ammonia and hydrochloric acid. Finally, the P2P method released phosphorous, iodine, and hydrogen chloride, but at relatively low levels—levels considered acceptable by standards of occupational safety. As might be expected, for all methods of cooking, concentrations were highest during the various stages of cooking, with some chemicals reaching dangerous levels. Airborne chemicals dissipated rather quickly with ventilation, but iodine remained on surface areas near the cook site for months. The level of chemical release varied from one cooking trial to the next, suggesting that the manner in which the chemicals are handled and mixed influences the level of chemical release into the environment.

Another finding that characterized every method of manufacturing the drug was that methamphetamine was found in the air and on surface areas (e.g., carpets, walls, ceiling fans, tabletops) throughout the building in which the methamphetamine was cooked. When methamphetamine is manufactured in a home laboratory, a portion of it is released as an aerosol. Also surprising was the ease with which the methamphetamine "dust" was spread. Shoes, for example, tracked meth from the apartment in which it was made into the hallway, and "police officers handling suspects or children at the scene, for very short periods of time, can become contaminated with methamphetamine. It is possible, therefore, for these

In kitchen labs, toxic chemicals are often kept near food in the home.

individuals to carry this material away from the scene and to their own families."[90] The Centers for Disease Control has identified cases in which methamphetamine-related injuries were reported by police officers, emergency medical technicians, firefighters, and hospital employees.[91]

Taken together, this series of studies by the National Jewish Medical and Research Center makes a compelling case for short- and long-term contamination of methamphetamine lab sites. What these studies were not designed to do, and what they could not do, was determine the long-term health effects of exposure to these chemicals at the levels and duration of exposure typically observed in the process of making methamphetamine. The percentage of methamphetamine laboratory officers with injuries from chemical contamination may be as low as 3.4 percent, and these tend to be relatively minor injuries. However, such findings are based on self-reports and not on systematic medical examinations, and are therefore of questionable accuracy.[92] While there have been reports of minor health symptoms experienced by first responders, perhaps the best way to determine the long-term health effects of manufacturing methamphetamine would be to monitor the health of former methamphetamine cooks. These are the individuals who are most exposed to the chemicals in question, and an understanding of the long-term impact of cooking on their health would provide a "worst-case scenario" of exposure to airborne and surface chemicals released in the process of making methamphetamine. While studies of the long-term health effects on methamphetamine cooks would be of obvious value, such studies have not been done.

The chemical found in the air and on surface areas at all methamphetamine cook sites is methamphetamine itself, but the doses received from crawling on the carpet or running one's hands across a contaminated tabletop are likely to be very small compared with the typical dose taken for recreational purposes. As we have noted elsewhere (chapter 3), in small doses methamphetamine is probably not harmful—after all it is given in pure form (under monitored conditions) to some children with attention-deficit/hyperactivity disorder and to some adults suffering from narcolepsy or who are morbidly obese. Other chemicals that remain at the site are likely to do considerably more long-term damage. The presence of these other chemicals alone is grounds for caution when entering an area that has been used as a methamphetamine production site.

Decontaminating a methamphetamine lab site can be expensive given that methamphetamine and other chemicals may permeate carpet, drapes, furniture, bedding, and other porous materials, and may be deposited on both vertical and horizontal smooth surfaces. In addition to the chemicals used in methamphetamine production, the poor ventilation that characterizes many production sites often leads to high levels of mold and mildew, which are expensive to remove.[93]

Decontamination may involve removing porous materials, neutralizing corrosives, industrial steam cleaning and pressure washers, detergent washes, and the use of chemical neutralizers and cover-ups to hide odors that remain.[94] In general, authorities will be responsible for removing the methamphetamine laboratory itself and the chemicals used in the laboratory, but they are not responsible for decontaminating the site. In every state, the property owner is responsible for decontamination, and this is generally true even if the owner unknowingly purchases previously contaminated property. The state of Washington, for example, was one of the first states to legislate on this issue. Under Washington law, the property owner is responsible for cleanup costs regardless of the owner's innocence, and cleanup must be done by a contractor certified by the state specifically to decontaminate methamphetamine labs.[95] It is often the case that insurance will not cover the cost of decontamination. Homeowners who are unable to pay the cost of decontamination sometimes decide it is easier to simply abandon the building.[96] After a site has been thoroughly decontaminated, there is no evidence that the site presents future health risks.[97] Despite this, some states require that future owners be notified that the site was at one time contaminated.[98]

Even if properly decontaminated methamphetamine laboratory sites are safe, the public is likely to be wary of such locations. The DEA has created the National Clandestine Laboratory Register to inform the public about the location of known methamphetamine laboratories, similar to the sex offender registries posted by many states.[99] The registry is available at www.dea.gov/seizures/index.html. A map of the United States at this Web site allows visitors to click on any state to see a listing of meth lab sites identified since 2004. The site provides the name of the county, city, street address, and date on which the lab was seized. The implicit message behind the registry is that the property is dangerous. Only time will tell whether this registry protects the public or merely makes the property impossible to sell while driving down the value of surrounding property.

Meth Trash

Methamphetamine laboratories also have the potential to exact substantial environmental damage after the cooking itself has been completed. It is claimed that each pound of methamphetamine produced yields five to six pounds of toxic waste.[100] That waste must go somewhere, and meth cooks have no incentive to dispose of those materials in an environmentally safe way. In most cases it is unlikely they know of the hazards, or care. It is not simply the effects of the chemicals in isolation, but the possibility of continuing chemical reactions if mixed chemicals are disturbed. Picking up a discarded container in which chemicals had been mixed may reactivate a chemical reaction and release noxious or even toxic fumes—a hazard for citizens engaged in highway cleanup or for highway and utility crews. Children playing in their yards have been contaminated by chemicals discarded by their parents.[101]

> Liquid wastes may be thrown out the window, poured down the toilet or sink drain, buried or burned. In rural areas, contamination to soil and groundwater can threaten private drinking water wells and septic tank systems.[102]

Though they are probably unaware of it, arrested methamphetamine cooks not only face criminal charges for manufacturing methamphetamine but also their criminal penalties may be enhanced for violating environmental laws regulating the storage, handling, and disposal of hazardous waste.[103]

Meth Labs and Children

For as long as there have been illegal drugs children have been exposed to them through their parents, other adults, siblings, or peers. Methamphetamine is different, however, because in addition to all of the things that go along with the presence of drugs in the home, children are exposed to the chemicals and dangers associated with producing the drug. Infants crawl on contaminated carpets and then put their fingers in their mouths, thus being exposed both through the skin and through the mouth. Children have been admitted to the emergency room after ingesting lye carelessly left in their reach by drug-addled parents.[104] Others have been admitted to emergency rooms with burns on their arms after falling from their bicycles onto dirt in the yard—dirt upon which their parents had dumped meth chemicals. Still others have been injured or died in methamphetamine-related fires and explosions.[105] Children taken from homes where methamphetamine was made often test positive for methamphetamine on their skin, clothing, toys, and even in their urine.

States have responded to the problem of meth labs and children in two different ways. First, in many states there are now enhanced penalties for anyone who manufactures methamphetamine in the presence of children. Second, protocols have been developed to facilitate a coordinated response by police and social service workers.

Some states have enacted laws with penalties specifically targeting adults who manufacture methamphetamine in the presence of children. In Illinois, for example, manufacturing less than 15 grams of methamphetamine is a Class 1 felony, for which the punishment is imprisonment for four to fifteen years. Manufacturing methamphetamine in the presence of children (or other protected groups) means the individual may also be charged with "aggravated participation in the manufacture of methamphetamine" if that manufacturing takes place in

> a structure or vehicle where a child under the age of 18, a person with a disability, or a person 60 years of age or older who is incapable of adequately providing for his or her own health and personal care resides, is present, or is endangered by the manufacture of methamphetamine.[106]

That crime is considered a Class X felony, for which the penalty is six to thirty years and a fine of up to $100,000.

Other states have modified their laws to define manufacturing of methamphetamine in the presence of children as a form of child abuse. Michigan, for example, includes exposure to methamphetamine production as child neglect, and Iowa law defines methamphetamine production in the presence of minors as child endangerment.[107] In Arizona and New Mexico child abuse has been legally defined to include allowing a child to be present where equipment or chemicals for methamphetamine production are stored, and Oregon includes exposing children to drug paraphernalia.[108]

Another trend has been the development of protocols for responding to drug-endangered children. Police responding to methamphetamine laboratory incidents are often ill-prepared to deal with children at the scene. Police are trained to find and arrest offenders, not to change diapers or determine the immediate medical needs of children found at meth labs. Drug-endangered children protocols emerged in response to various needs of these children. These protocols outline the roles to be played by various agencies when children are discovered at a methamphetamine laboratory site. The specific agencies involved will vary from one jurisdiction to another, as does the geographic reach of these protocols. In some states these protocols are statewide while in others they apply to a county.

The first drug-endangered children protocol was developed in the spring of 1997 in Butte County, California. During the Christmas holiday of 1996, three children died in a fire caused by an exploding methamphetamine laboratory. In response, a local narcotics task force officer named Sue Webber-Brown initiated the establishment of a protocol that would identify the duties of various agencies when children were discovered at the scene of a methamphetamine laboratory.[109]

Since that first drug-endangered children protocol in 1997, the concept has spread across the country, and there is now a national organization—the National Alliance for Drug Endangered Children—to facilitate information sharing and training.[110] All protocols recognize the value of interagency cooperation, though the particular agencies involved may vary from jurisdiction to jurisdiction. In general, participating agencies include police, child protective services, public health, emergency medical technicians, local hospitals, and, in some jurisdictions, the local school system. Prior to the era of home-cooked methamphetamine, children found in drug houses were often incidental to the criminal case against adults. Under many drug-endangered protocols there is a simultaneous effort to protect the child and build a stronger legal case against the adults. Thus, forensic interviews with the children will be conducted at the scene and again several days later. At these interviews questions focus on the health and well-being of the child as well as any criminal behavior by adults. For example, the Michigan protocol includes the following directions for interviewing children:[111]

1 If possible, given specific circumstances, conduct forensic interview of child at the scene to ascertain:

   a. last meal eaten and who prepared it

   b. last bathing and by whom

   c. how child feels physically and mentally

   d. child aware if anyone in home smokes? If yes, what do they smoke?

   e. Anything in house that bothers the child?

   f. Other siblings living in the house who aren't home right now?

2 A second forensic interview in a child-friendly setting should occur within 48 hours of discovery of children within a drug endangered environment.

In many cases there will also be medical protocols developed specifically for children found in the vicinity of methamphetamine production (e.g., Michigan Drug Endangered Children [DEC] Medical Protocol).[112] Medical protocols provide a relatively detailed list of the various medical tests and assessments that are to be performed by medical staff on children exposed to methamphetamine labs.

Thus, state and local governments have taken aggressive action to protect children exposed to the chemicals and by-products of methamphetamine production.

CONCLUSION

America has a long history of drug panics as "new" drugs gain popularity. Until the recent rise of methamphetamine, these panics have generally focused on what the drug did to the user and how the user's lifestyle affected family, friends, and the community. Claims that "this drug is different and presents a new danger" are usually overblown. Methamphetamine, however, can legitimately claim to be different and to pose a new danger, at least in the sense that it presents the added risk of harm from the manufacturing process itself.

Is methamphetamine safe to cook? Yes—if done by a trained chemist, with the proper equipment, with raw materials of known purity, in a laboratory designed to capture toxic fumes, and where waste materials are disposed of safely. Unfortunately, almost none of these conditions exist in the real world of illicit methamphetamine manufacturing.

There is widespread concern, even panic, over the toxic effects of methamphetamine labs on emergency responders, children in the vicinity of a lab, and the environment. In the absence of solid evidence regarding the long-term health effects of methamphetamine labs, serious precautions are justified, but there is a dearth of hard evidence. More research is needed, perhaps with former methamphetamine cooks themselves as the most obvious subjects for research. The creation of a national registry of locations where methamphetamine labs have been discovered sends a message that such locations are permanently hazardous. It seems unlikely that a methamphetamine manufacturing site that has been properly cleaned will present a permanent hazard, but this merits further research.

The proliferation of methamphetamine labs in the United States undercuts the notion that our drug problem can be laid in the lap of foreign drug producers. Ultimately it is a reminder that drug abuse of all varieties is our problem and ultimately must be tackled here at home.

Chapter 6 examines how methamphetamine has impacted two rural counties in Illinois.

Methamphetamine in Rural Communities

Methamphetamine use and production have become major problems in the Midwest, including Illinois. Although the precise extent of the problem in Illinois cannot be known, several indicators suggest cause for alarm. The amount of methamphetamine seized and submitted to Illinois State Police laboratories rose from 3,433 grams in 1994 to 19,576 grams in 2001—a nearly six-fold increase—and rural counties accounted for 57 percent of all methamphetamine seized.[1] Similarly, drug treatment admissions for methamphetamine rose from 97 in 1994 to 1,528 in 2001—a nearly sixteen-fold increase—with admissions from rural areas accounting for 71 percent of all admissions in the state.[2] Finally, the number of methamphetamine laboratories seized in Illinois rose from 24 in 1997 to 971 in 2003 and 751 in 2006. As with other indicators, rural areas have led the way in methamphetamine laboratory seizures.[3]

Although illicit drugs are not particularly new to rural areas, the speed with which methamphetamine has spread and the extent to which it has become a problem suggest that methamphetamine may be more disruptive to Illinois communities than other drugs in recent history. In addition to problems related to its use, methamphetamine creates a host of problems related to its local production. To better understand methamphetamine's impact on rural communities, Ralph Weisheit, one of the authors of this book, undertook an ethnographic study of the drug's impact on two adjoining Illinois counties in 2004.

The Setting

Edgar and Clark counties are located in east central Illinois. The two counties are adjoining, with Edgar County to the north of Clark. (See map 6.1.) The populations of Edgar and Clark counties are just over 19,000 people and about 17,000 people, respectively. Just over half of each county's population lives outside communities of 2,500 or more.[4] The population in each county has declined since the early 1900s, when Edgar County had 28,000 residents and Clark County had 24,000 residents, though each county's population has remained relatively stable in the last decade.

Of people over twenty-five years of age, about 80 percent in each county have a high school diploma or more, a figure comparable to that for the state of Illinois as a whole. In Edgar County approximately 97 percent of the population is white, and in Clark County 99 percent of the population is white.

In Clark County per capita annual income is about 66 percent that of the state as a whole and in Edgar County per capita income is about 71 percent that of the state as a whole. At 4.1 percent and 5.2 percent, respectively, unemployment in Edgar and Clark counties is lower than the state average of 6.1 percent. Thus, people in both counties are working, but wages are comparatively low. Each county has light manufacturing as its primary employer, though Edgar County also has a significant number

Map 6.1

Illinois Counties

of government employees. The number of people involved in agriculture is relatively small, but agriculture is a sizeable business. There are 1,369 farms in the two counties, averaging about 450 acres each. These farms cover approximately 86 percent of the land area of the two counties. Most of the farmland in Edgar and Clark counties is used to grow corn and soybeans, crops for which anhydrous ammonia is used as a liquid fertilizer— a fertilizer that is also a key ingredient in the area's most commonly used recipe for methamphetamine.

Although Edgar and Clark are two distinct counties, it makes sense to study them together. Not only are they physically adjoining but they also share a variety of social services. For example, the Human Resources Center (HRC), a nonprofit agency, has its primary office in Edgar County, but it also serves Clark County. HRC provides outpatient substance abuse therapy, mental health counseling, rehabilitation services for adults with developmental disabilities, residential services, and respite care for those with developmental disabilities. The two counties also share the services of one full-time and one part-time public defender, and communication among various agencies across the two counties is fairly common.

A two-lane state highway runs north-south through the two counties, and an east-west interstate highway runs through Clark County. To the east of Edgar and Clark counties is the Indiana border and Vigo County, Indiana. Vigo County has routinely been identified as the county in Indiana with the largest number of seized methamphetamine laboratories.[5] To the west of Edgar and Clark counties is Coles County, Illinois. Coles County has the distinction of being one of the Illinois counties that routinely has the largest number of seized methamphetamine laboratories.[6] While Edgar and Clark counties are bordered on the east and west by counties with high levels of methamphetamine production and use, and both counties are accessible by major highways, by all accounts the methamphetamine problem in Edgar and Clark counties is generally self-contained. That is, most of the methamphetamine produced in the county is used there; and, conversely, most of the methamphetamine used in the county has been produced there. Unlike reports from California, where methamphetamine distribution networks transport the drug from Mexico or from large U.S. labs to local drug markets, at the time of the study there were few indications of methamphetamine distribution networks linking users in Edgar and Clark counties to producers in other parts of the country. Some locals did cross county lines to steal precursors, and some people from surrounding counties did enter Edgar and Clark counties to steal precursors or to cook methamphetamine in portable labs, but primary production and use remained local.

Although methamphetamine had probably been in both counties in limited amounts for decades, in recent years the drug had come to be seen as a problem of near crisis proportions, and the local production of methamphetamine appeared to be a relatively recent phenomenon. In both counties the first signs of methamphetamine production were seen in 1998, and by 2004 the problem appeared to have increased geometrically.

Reports from a variety of local sources suggest there was little in the way of a "methamphetamine business" in either county, at least not a highly organized business driven by cash transactions. Rather, methamphetamine production and use appeared to primarily rely on bartering and trading services for drugs among acquaintances. For example, a cook would agree to provide methamphetamine to several associates in exchange for each associate's stealing or otherwise obtaining necessary precursors (e.g., anhydrous ammonia, cold pills, lithium batteries, camping fuel). In other cases the cook would agree to teach others to cook in exchange for the precursors needed to conduct the "class," with a share of the drugs serving as the cook's payment. The absence of a cash economy in methamphetamine, or at least the presence of a very small cash economy, meant that few of the cooks or users were becoming wealthy from methamphetamine. Authorities conducting methamphetamine investigations generally found few assets of value worth seizing. On the positive side, there were also few indications of violence linked to the business of methamphetamine distribution, though a double murder in early 2004 may have been connected to a drug transaction involving outsiders.

In Edgar and Clark counties, methamphetamine was not simply different from other drugs pharmacologically; the profile of the meth user was different from that of other drug users. The chief judge from Clark County described these differences, a description echoed by others who were interviewed:

I have noticed that we get more groups of people arrested. With other drug cases over the years you tended to get more single individuals arrested. Somebody is stopped in a motor vehicle and drugs are discovered, or perhaps you have a single drug buy. But with methamphetamine it's not uncommon to have three or four or five people arrested at once. The reason seems to be that oftentimes people are manufacturing meth and using meth as a group. And they are either caught in the process of manufacturing it, or they are caught in the process of being together doing something with it.

Definitely I have noticed that females represent a higher number of those picked up. We have more females in custody now than we used to. It is not unusual to have both husband and wife picked up or boyfriend and girlfriend. But females are a significant part of the caseload with methamphetamine.

Another thing is that a significant number of our methamphetamine cases also involve gun charges. I won't say that it is a high percentage, but in years past we very infrequently had a gun charge accompanying a drug charge. If somebody was picked up for cannabis or picked up for cocaine, it was usually just that. There was no tie-in with firearms. With methamphetamine we have had a number of cases where firearms have been involved. We have had one or two cases where there have been shootouts, shootings, where methamphetamine was involved. We have had several cases where guns were simply in possession of the person charged with methamphetamine. We had one particular individual who was arrested twice with methamphetamine and twice with guns, about a week apart. . . .

We have had very few juveniles in court where there was any indication of methamphetamine. That's not to say methamphetamine is not being used by the kids, but it has not shown up in the court's cases. It has not shown up in juvenile cases. I'm not sure we've had any more than one or two cases, if that, where there was some direct evidence that juveniles were involved with methamphetamine. Our methamphetamine problem, at least as far as the court cases go, is pretty much an adult problem. And again, another characteristic which is distinctive about methamphetamine is the ages. It used to be that most of the drug cases were fairly young people. They were people in their teens, twenties, or maybe even some in their early thirties. Those were the age groups that were really affected. With methamphetamine we get all ages. We've had people in their sixties. It's quite common to have people in their forties and fifties. It is definitely a drug that cuts across all age groups.

Another observation is that it is much more likely that the defendants in methamphetamine cases are not working and are not functioning within the framework of society. Typically in a high percentage of our drug cases if somebody was arrested for possession of drugs they were people who were working and were otherwise leading, at least in an outward sense, a pretty normal lifestyle. Drug use did not necessarily prevent them from working. It did not necessarily prevent them from retaining their role in the family, but with methamphetamine you see a much greater number of people who simply are not working and haven't worked. It is very characteristic to see people who have not been working for several years, or they have a lousy employment history. A history in which they may list five or six places of employment but you can't pin down when they worked, how long they worked, whether they worked full-time. In effect, the impression is left that they weren't working much at all. . . . In fact, it is fair to say that if the presentence report shows they are consuming a high level of methamphetamine, they are almost never working regularly.

In terms of the accuracy of official police counts of seized methamphetamine labs, one difference between the two counties is that Clark County is part of a drug task force run by the Illinois State Police. Edgar County authorities work cooperatively with a number of other enforcement agencies, but they are not part of a state police task force. This distinction was important because statewide counts of seized meth labs were compiled by the Illinois State Police. Counties that were not part of an Illinois State Police task force found it difficult to have laboratory seizures by local police included in statewide reports. As one officer in Edgar County lamented:

Yeah, we're nonexistent. We're working on that and I've got Dale Righter [a state senator] trying to come up with one location where we can send information so that we can start getting counted. We just didn't know where to send it. Nobody would tell us where to send it. Nobody had any idea. . . . We weren't part of a task force and therefore we weren't getting any numbers there. We were working our tails off, but they said, "You don't want to be part of our team." We did, but they didn't have any room for us.

Underreporting of laboratory seizures was not just a problem for Edgar County. A map of task forces throughout Illinois showed that the most rural southern counties, where methamphetamine production was likely to be higher, were also least likely to be part of a state police task force and therefore were least likely to have lab seizures fully counted in state totals. This meant that the dramatic increase in the number of labs reported by the Illinois State Police (from 24 in 1997 to nearly 1,000 in 2003) probably *seriously undercounted* the number of labs actually found by police in Illinois. Of course, a full accounting of all laboratories seized by the police would still have missed the many labs never detected.

The Impact of Methamphetamine

By all accounts the impact of methamphetamine on Edgar and Clark counties was substantial and cut across many aspects of life in these two counties. To give a sense of methamphetamine's impact, people from many agencies and walks of life were interviewed. As entry point to the formal system, the criminal justice system is in many ways the miner's canary of social problems. For this reason the description of meth's impact begins with accounts from those working in the criminal justice system.

Sheriffs Feel the Strain

Among the first in the criminal justice system to respond to the methamphetamine problem were the police, and among the first people interviewed was a sheriff's deputy in Edgar County. He had worked as a police officer in Paris, the county seat, but eventually joined the sheriff's office to focus primarily on methamphetamine. As he observed, the problem arose quite rapidly:

In 1998 we [the Paris police department] had our first meth lab in [the town of] Isabel. It [Isabel] probably has twenty-five people who live there. Until then, no one in the area really worked much methamphetamine. It had always been cocaine or cannabis and some LSD. . . . He [a meth cook] got sent away for ten or twelve years. It was one of our first. That was the only lab we got that year, but [the guy] said he taught six or seven people in our county how to make methamphetamine. After that, the next year, we probably had seven or eight labs. It was getting to be more of a problem than we had thought. That's when we got our task force together, what we consider our task force, a lot of officers who gave part-time to meth enforcement. We started noticing a lot more meth arrests. I started getting away from the criminal stuff and started just working the drug stuff. Then in 2001 we decided maybe we needed to put someone on this full-time. That's when I came to work for the sheriff's department.

The first year [that he worked for the sheriff] we had somewhere around fifty or sixty arrests. This last year we decided we were going to start documenting how many calls came in that had to do with methamphetamine—people who call or come in, because we had a tip line. We ended up with 365 complaints or calls on methamphetamine-related concerns, whether it be anhydrous or labs or whatever. Out of that we had 145 arrests this last year, all meth related, which is the highest we've had so far. We had 366 felony arrests in the county, and of those, 145 were for meth-related charges [40 percent], whether it be for anhydrous or whatever. They really picked up.

Aside from the demands placed on police personnel, the sheriff's office in each county had to deal with the increased burden of housing jail inmates. In most of rural America, jails have been substantially underutilized; in the past counties rented their excess cell space to larger jurisdictions, including the federal government.[7] The rise of methamphetamine, however, changed all that, leading to jail crowding and ballooning jail budgets in counties that already suffered from small tax bases. The sheriff of Edgar County explained:

Edgar County Sheriff: It's dug into our budget, immensely.

Interviewer: In what ways?

Edgar County Sheriff: Well, with the overflow of prisoners because of meth, I'd say 80 to 85 percent of the prisoners we have in here are drug-related and most of them are meth. Very few are as simple as marijuana. Very few are heroin or LSD or the other drugs that are out there now, because it's the poor man's drug. It's got our jail overcrowded, which eats up our food budget. It eats up the medical budget. Everything is affected here.

Interviewer: So they are coming in with more medical problems than other inmates?

Edgar County Sheriff: They are coming in with a lot more medical problems. . . . Honest to God, you'd be amazed at the change in somebody after they've been in jail for just thirty days, let alone sixty or ninety days. They are a totally different person. The first couple of weeks when they are here they are combative and their mood swings are so great. And then, all of a sudden, something just clicks and they become a nice person again, back to a real person, I call it. The true person comes back out in them . . . but something drives them or compels them when they get out to go back to the meth world.

Interviewer: And a lot do go back?

Edgar County Sheriff: Oh, it's unbelievable. The number of people we've taken to prison here, it's driven up our prison transportation costs and the miles on the cars we have. In fact, it's eating up the budget. We have to feed these guys, we have to give them medical attention, and the county doesn't have enough money. I think every one of my cars but two have over 100,000. I've got one with 196,000 miles on it. I've got two cars, one with 30,000 and one with 50,000. Those are my two newest vehicles. It's just unbelievable. And with gas prices all of a sudden jumping up . . . because of the drug problem it's eaten up the budget. We don't have enough men for this size of county. But our guys do a pretty good job of patrolling the entire county. We don't have enough officers on duty, usually in the days two per shift, maybe three or four. But there are not enough officers to cover the problem of drugs. We've only got one drug officer and he's completely overworked. The rest of us kick in to help him. Likewise if he has any downtime, which is very rare, he will kick in and help us with our other daily duties.

Interviewer: What is your jail capacity?

Edgar County Sheriff: Twenty-eight is the legal jail standard. I think today we have thirty-four in here and we've had up to fifty-four. It's not like they are treated inhumanely. In our particular jail we have TV in each of the cells, except for one isolation cell. We give them a smoke break once a day. We don't provide the cigarettes; the family brings in cigarettes, but that seems to keep them calm. The overcrowding is—we don't have a bunk, but we do have mattresses for everyone on the floor, or a double mattress. I'd hate to turn them loose. I think in the past, before I was here, they would just filter out the lesser crime people, you know, someone who was in here for illegal consumption or something, they would just turn them loose. We haven't had to yet, and we haven't had to house them in any other county, as of yet. It was really bad when we were up to fifty-four, but that was our peak one day. Our average is at thirty, so a couple over what used to be the legal limit, and so we're complying.

The sheriff in Clark County had an equally grim assessment. He, too, suggested that the impact of methamphetamine has rippled through his agency:

Clark County Sheriff: Just in a nutshell, it is completely tapping all the money we have as far as the operation of the jail. We have eighteen beds. Today, I've got thirty-five inmates, and now this is a guess because I didn't check the total when I came down, but I think that all of them but five or six are in there for meth-related charges.

Interviewer: Either use or stealing things to support a habit?

Clark County Sheriff: No, directly meth. Whether it be methamphetamine itself, the precursors, the anhydrous, just directly related to meth. Not necessarily burglary or anything that we know is a residual fallout from that, just the specific drug or manufacturing chemicals themselves.

Interviewer: Do you get into a bind where you can't put somebody in jail because there is just no room?

Clark County Sheriff: I try to be cognizant of what people I hold, and the bad part of that is that out of that thirty-five, I've got two people who are sentenced to jail. The rest are awaiting trial, which is a very stressful time for everybody: them, staff, just everybody. I don't really know how to answer that. It is to the point where it's just organized chaos every day.

Interviewer: And I take it that it is burning up a lot of patrol officer time also.

Clark County Sheriff: It is because we have to have extra staff for the problems in jail. We have to direct somebody off the road who should be out either serving papers or answering calls, but we have to take them off the road to bring them into the jail to work. I work a lot of the jail time myself. I do a lot of the transports, you know, going to different counties picking different people up for different things. There is a definite lack of manpower. It is a constant all the time. We have to put stuff on the back burner because we don't have people to do it. When I first started in 1982, our shifts at that time were seven days in a row. You worked seven you were off two. If I had three or four calls for service in those seven days, that was a busy week. And now I've got six patrol deputies, one full-time drug investigator, and one full-time criminal investigator who are completely overrun. The six patrol deputies are now averaging anywhere from eight to fifteen calls a shift. That's days, evenings, an assist shift, and at midnight. That's four shifts a day and we are averaging about a dozen calls per shift. Some days are worse than that and some days are less, but that's basically the average.

While the workload and staffing for the Clark County sheriff's department grew exponentially from 1982 to 2004, the population of the county was virtually unchanged from 1980 to 2002.[8] The sheriff went on to explain how methamphetamine had affected his office's workload:

Interviewer: I know you can't know this exactly, but of those calls how many would not happen if meth weren't around?

Clark County Sheriff: Half. That's a guess, but it won't be far off. You have erratic behavior that we get calls about that are directly related to meth. You have people out in areas that ordinarily they would not be in. It's a suspicious vehicle call. Or, a call that we go and check where a lab has been or possibly one is in the process of being used then. All those things are directly related to meth. . . . domestic problems because of the paranoid aspect of meth use. You have people who, over a period of time, it suddenly dawns on them what's going on around them. They call about it. That's directly related to meth. Knock on wood, our thefts and burglaries are probably at a low, but occasionally we have a significant number of ATV [all-terrain vehicle] thefts, not necessarily residential burglaries, but I think that we can probably track the ones we get solved back to meth, because of the money. They have to get money to get the ingredients to make the meth. They buy it outright. It is a daily problem that we never used to have. . . .

The meth inmate has a tremendous amount of health problems, physical problems. As a sheriff's office, we are mandated to take care of their medical problems if they don't have the resources to do it. So that means that 90 percent of the time we have to pay for their medical. We are having big instances of meth people, if they have been on it awhile, having their teeth rotting so we have to get their teeth pulled. Well, they are so abscessed that we have to do two weeks' worth of high-dollar antibiotics to get the poison out of their system before they can ever extract the tooth. The lithium, when it gets in their system from the meth, pretty well eats the calcium up in their body, as does the rest of the chemicals they put in—anhydrous ammonia, lye, starter fluid, or muriatic acid. Your body just starts to rot from the inside out. Well, any of their physical problems that they have like that we have to take care of. Last year, budget year '03 for me, I had $30,000 in my inmate medical. I spent over $60,000. I've got no recourse other than to pay for those bills because I am mandated by law to do it. And I've got no recourse to recoup that money from any of the inmates that we take. A meth inmate undoubtedly sucks the life out of your budget—medically and for housing if I've got to ship them off to another facility if I get way too overcrowded.

If I've got that many inmates it sucks the life out of my payroll budget because I've got to hire a correctional officer to come back. I've got to hire part-time people to come in with staffing as far as the number of staff per inmate. I've got one full-time correctional officer on twenty-four hours a day. But when you have twenty-five to thirty-five people it takes a minimum of two, sometimes three, people to take care of their clothing needs, their meals, and everything else that goes along with it, because there is a tremendous amount of laundry with thirty-five people that has to be done on a daily basis, too. That's blankets, tops, bottoms, shoes, towels, and washcloths. And all the expenses that go along with that. Yeah, there is a big difference.

Dramatic Increase in Court Cases

The pressures placed on local police and sheriffs rippled through the rest of the criminal justice system. Prosecutors and public defenders had to deal with these cases, as did judges and probation officers.

The Edgar County prosecutor cited court figures showing that felony court cases in Edgar County rose from 126 in 1998 (the year of the first meth-lab seizure in the county) to 328 in 2003—an increase of more than two-and-a-half times. While he believed that much of the increase resulted from an increase in meth cases, the data were not stored in such a way that counts of meth cases could be separated from other felony charges. Although there was a tremendous increase in felony charges, not only from methamphetamine but also as a result of increased penalties for many crimes, his office had had one full-time and one part-time prosecutor for the past twenty years. Similarly, the dramatic increase in cases did not result in a meaningful increase in staff for the public defender's office.

The chief judge from Clark County, who had a substantial amount of experience with methamphetamine cases, compared the impact of methamphetamine on the judicial system with the impact of other drug cases:

Let me just try to identify different patterns I see with methamphetamine than I've seen with other drugs through the years. First, we have a much higher percentage of bond revocations and probation revocations. In other words, if meth users are released on bond, a significant number of them have their bond revoked because they are picked up again while they are awaiting trial. We have a very high percentage who simply do not survive probation. They fail to comply with the conditions of probation and they end up having their probation revoked. In some cases they are put back on probation on the same or different terms. In some cases they go to the Department of Corrections. But the rate of our probation revocations has increased dramatically. I wouldn't be surprised if we don't have just about as many probation revocations as we do original cases pending at any given time, in part because probation revocations may apply to any cases that have been disposed of over the past two to three years. We certainly have seen that. In other words, the meth users are hooked on it, and they don't quit using it just because they are awaiting trial or because they are on probation. Some do comply with the terms of probation but an awful lot are revoked. So that's one thing that's different.

The volumes obviously are great. I would have never imagined three years ago that we would have had this kind of change in our caseload. I would say that 90 percent of the drug cases that are filed are in one way or another related to methamphetamine. It is either the possession of precursors, theft of anhydrous ammonia, or the illegal transportation of anhydrous ammonia, or it's possession of meth or the manufacture of meth. That's probably 90 percent of our drug cases.

Not surprisingly, probation officers in each county reported a substantial increase in their workload because of methamphetamine. The chief probation officer in each county estimated that over half of the county's probation caseload consisted of methamphetamine-related cases. Echoing the comments of other criminal justice officials, they emphasized the number of new cases, the frequency of repeat offending, and the difficult time facing addicts trying to quit.

Criminal justice officials were unanimous in their belief that methamphetamine had become a serious problem in Edgar and Clark counties. Most also believed the problem was likely to either become worse or to stabilize at a high level. There was also a general sense that the problems created by methamphetamine were different and more intractable than those of other drugs.

Emergency Responders Face Greater Risks

Criminal justice was not the only aspect of life in Edgar and Clark counties affected by methamphetamine. Methamphetamine and methamphetamine labs also had a substantial impact on emergency medical services and fire services. The Paris, Illinois, fire department was the only professional fire department in Edgar County, and Clark County had no full-time professional fire departments. The Paris Fire Department not only covered the town of Paris but also trained and coordinated one hundred volunteers who worked in various small communities outside Paris. The fire chief made clear that methamphetamine was a major concern to his department—because of the potential for fires from exploding labs, because of hazardous materials at the site of fires, and because of chemical contamination of the air and groundwater. Further, the fire department had several close calls, as described by the fire chief:

> We've had meth labs catch fire. . . . explosions. . . . in a home. We were lucky enough that I was fairly close to it when the call came in. The drug task force nexteled [called] me on the two-way [radio] and gave me a tip going in about the potential. We had three more explosions upon our arrival. We were able to pull back once we determined there was nobody in there. We had thermal cameras we could use that protected my guys. As we got into it there were needles, syringes all over the floor. My guys could have crawled into them, and it would have exposed them to bad things. And all the material that was in there. There were several places where there were off-gassers [evaporation of chemicals into the air] still sitting. A lot of precursors used, trash-wise. So it's dangerous in there for my troops when we go in there. . . . the unknowns. . . . For this one we had a tip, but that doesn't always happen. We had our first phosphorous lab. That concerns me immensely. There again going in we had a tip from the drug task force. They were on the scene. So phosphorous is our next big scare. So it's predominantly meth. You never know where you are going to find it. We've found it in trunks of cars. We've caught them making it in

the backs of pickups out here on county roads. So it's a big factor in the fire service. . . .

Meth has become a part of our job, but unwillingly. It is now an exposure risk out there that we have to be trained to deal with. Trying to keep the guys up on it training-wise, and on all of the other stuff—that is our job, and still find the money, overtime funds. It's very, very difficult for volunteers to take this additional training. . . . And the other factor that nobody's thinking about is with meth labs that are ongoing. Gathering the materials to form a meth lab is an even bigger detriment that nobody thinks about at all. Number one, anhydrous ammonia. We've had several incidents where a local fertilizer company on the west edge of the city has a bunch of nurse tanks [large tanks used by farmers in their fields that can hold around 1,000 gallons of anhydrous ammonia] in place. They [meth cooks] go in and steal the anhydrous, or attempt to, out of these nurse tanks, and maybe don't get a valve shut off. We've gotten calls at two o'clock in the morning where a plant with an air handling system on the roof is pulling anhydrous ammonia fumes into the plant. So that creates another potential problem. . . . We've had more than one call of that nature. We've also had calls from residents in neighborhoods in the middle of the night. They will smell an odor because something didn't get shut off. We've tried working with the fertilizer plants. I know law enforcement has tried putting cameras on them to monitor. They put watches on them, stakeouts, trying to work that, but you can do all that you want. There are tanks on the farm complex when the farmer goes out here and leaves them at the end of the field in the middle of nowhere. We've had one instance where a full nurse tank was stolen off the farm site, and they buried it or camouflaged it. You can make a lot of meth when you are talking about a ton-and-a-half nurse tank. There were a couple of incidents where someone took a cordless drill and tried to drill through the bottom of a tank—a thirty-thousand-gallon bulk tank.

We've had an incident here where we pull up on a house fire about 7:30 in the morning. The two female occupants and one of the girl's little brothers was there. The father was in jail already for meth. They're tweaking on meth and we're fighting this house fire and one of my firemen falls off the roof and breaks both legs. He's gone for four and one-half months on work comp. That's costly, too. So there are a lot of ramifications here that nobody stops to think about. . . . As another good example, I got called out one Sunday evening to a meth site with off-gassers in a cistern out behind the house. And it had a little round hole where an old well and old hand pump used to go down through it. We've got steam coming out of it, or off-gassing. And they called the fire department. We go down there and sure enough they've taken all their meth by-products and dumped them in the cistern. Now we have contamination of groundwater and everything else, and the fumes in the neighborhood. When the law enforcement went in and looked up in the attic areas there were so many nooks and crannies, they found like twenty-six different off-gassing materials, at twenty-six different sites in this home. It's a large two-story home. Four kids were residing in the home, but they were living in the living room only. They sleep in the living room; they eat in the living room. They stay in the living room. They are exposed to all these fumes and the meth. They were using the rest of the house for meth production.

I've brought EPA [Environmental Protection Agency] in on a couple of meth sites where, for probably months, they have produced meth and thrown the debris into a holler. That holler is a natural water runoff in rain and goes right into a creek, a small creek that goes into a bigger creek. We are creating a nightmare here in America, in the central part of the nation that we are really going to have to get a handle on.

We had two guys on a quad runner [ATV] from Indiana, we got called out on, who got to a nurse tank with a five-gallon bucket. They got anhydrous in an open five-gallon bucket. Put it between them and took off on the quad runner. A cop was called. He's chasing them in a squad car and the anhydrous is splashing all over; it's eating the shirts off of these guys.

Obviously the kinds of problems reported by this fire chief also affected emergency ambulance services. The director of the local emergency medical service (EMS) estimated that about 15 percent of calls were for methamphetamine-related illnesses. Further, the presence of methamphetamine production in the county had an impact on the way his service responded to calls.

Interviewer: Have you found that meth affects how you enter a house?

EMS Administrator: Oh yeah. Back when meth first came around, it's been four or five years ago, we jumped in the ambulance and everybody was good old people and we weren't afraid of anything. We went and handled the problem. Well, I happened to be one of the first ones who ran into a problem because a guy was high on meth and I went up the stairs of the apartment and I went into the apartment. I walk in and he jumps out from behind the door. He's actually shooting me with the TV remote, you know, going bang, bang, bang. That was the first run-in that we had EMS-wise with meth. So then we came back and we said, "Hey, we need to do something here." So, being a deputy [he also worked as a sheriff's deputy], I know where a lot of the problem houses are and so I have my guard up, and of course I tell my people. "Hey, be careful if you go here, go here, or go here. Don't enter without the police at nighttime." We've revamped and have a whole new outlook because those people don't know their actions. They don't know their power. We are just there to help. We are innocent persons here. We don't want to run in there and sacrifice ourselves. Yes, we have changed our policy and procedures. At nighttime the police don't let us go anywhere without their help. At nighttime they go, and they know, and they will call us a lot of times and tell us, "Hey, watch out they are cooking there" or whatever the case may be.

The problems, and potential problems, from methamphetamine also changed the training of emergency medical technicians in the county:

EMS Administrator: We've done a lot of medical continuing education on the signs and symptoms [of methamphetamine use]. We've done a lot of education on what to look for when you are in a house, signs that they could be using. We've done a lot of classes on odors. If you smell this odor, don't go in, get out of there. Stuff like that. We've done a lot of training on self-defense, show the paramedics where to hit somebody to get away from them. Stuff like that.

Interviewer: And self-defense used to be something you didn't worry a lot about?

EMS Administrator: We never had self-defense training. Ever. We went through the era of cocaine. We never had it. But this is a drug that is unique. It is by itself, in a separate class. There is nothing we can do for them [meth users]. There are no medicines that work. It's meth. And their high lasts about two to three hours, and they have to have some more or they start coming down. I've run into people who have been awake for seven days straight. And they look terrible. But they just can't sleep. I've run into people who have been asleep for three days. You can't wake them up. You think it's a medical condition. You take them to the hospital and test them and it's meth. It's huge. It's a huge thing.

Further, because most of those meth-related emergency calls were for people with little or no money, the problem created a substantial expense for the taxpayer:

EMS Administrator: [Methamphetamine] in this community is driving the medical costs up, which reflects on the state because they [meth users] don't pay their bills. A lot of them have public aid. That drives costs up for the state of Illinois. We are having to go get them because meth makes their heart rate go up. They think their heart is going to jump out of their chest. We go out and, of course, all of the medicines we carry don't work when you are high on meth. And so we run them in and once they are down off their high, they are released and they go about their way and do it again. We are also seeing it impacting the children because they are bringing the stuff into the house. It's impacting the children as far as making them sick. When their children get sick, they don't know what to do so they call an ambulance and we go down and take them in. A lot of times when they are cooking this stuff, they have children in the house, which is not a good thing because of the by-products—one breath at a certain stage can kill you. We are seeing a huge impact as far as call volumes here; of course, they are going up, and that's not always good because it costs everybody. It costs the taxpayer, because we are tax supported. It costs the state because they [meth users] usually have state aid. It's a huge impact.

The director of emergency services from the local hospital (which serves both counties), who was also a regional medical director for the EMS system in that region of Illinois, also expressed great concern about the impact of methamphetamine on the community. Unfortunately, hard data about methamphetamine and emergency room admissions did not exist because the attending physician could not be certain if methamphetamine was present unless a patient explicitly volunteered that information. However, the director of emergency services did note signs of methamphetamine use among some of the admissions. While he was concerned about the effects of methamphetamine on the user and on children present when meth was cooked, he was much more concerned about the toxic materials used to produce meth and the toxic by-products of the process. Referring to a military installation nearby, he commented:

> Just fifteen miles as the crow flies is one of the world's largest repositories of VX nerve agent. I'm more worried about meth labs in our county than I am the 2.5 million pounds of VX nerve agent. And I've toured the facility. We are within their range of what they call a maximal and credible event, of being exposed to it. And a drop less than a tenth of a pinhead will kill us. I'm less worried about that than I am some of the labs that are around here. We've been trained [to respond to a VX crisis]. We have a portable shower. We have five hundred M1 kits for antidotes. We have a half-a-million-dollar detoxification shower. We have all been trained on treatment of VX exposure. There are radios. There is everything else you could possibly imagine from the army and the federal government. But there is not that kind of preparation for methamphetamine labs. I'm not as worried about that [nerve gas] as I am about people driving around in their cars with meth labs.

In short, emergency responders expressed concern about dealing with people under the influence of methamphetamine, but they were even more concerned about the toxic by-products of methamphetamine production.

Social Service Agencies Respond

Another group, those providing social services, was concerned about treating methamphetamine addicts and dealing with the social problems that accompany methamphetamine use. The primary social service agency responding directly to methamphetamine issues is the Human Resources Center (HRC) of Edgar and Clark Counties. Among its many services, HRC in 2004 provided outpatient drug treatment. In response to the large number of methamphetamine clients, HRC developed a special high-intensity outpatient treatment program. The program emphasized drug testing three to four times a week and group sessions three times a week. Like most social service agencies, HRC had experienced budget cuts, but had given methamphetamine treatment a high priority. In addition to outpatient treatment, HRC provided pretreatment programming for jailed inmates with methamphetamine problems. HRC received no financial support from the state for these programs but was committed to providing them as a service to both the offenders and the community. HRC also provided staff time in support of the Coalition Against Methamphetamine Abuse (CAMA), a local community organization that arose in response to the growing number of methamphetamine cases (see the discussion below). In the study, the director of HRC noted several avenues by which methamphetamine abusers might come to the agency's attention:

> Sometimes, [meth patients come to our attention] through our normal provision of service for outpatient mental health. We may have someone who is in need of services because of a crisis intervention. We are called to go to the emergency room because someone is suicidal, or has exhibited other behaviors that suggest they need mental health intervention. Frequently they end up being clients where we start working with them, either as an individual, in a group, or both. In the process of evaluating them we will uncover other problems, such as substance abuse problems. Often there is a connection to methamphetamine, where they have been brought to our attention due to a mental health crisis or need, but they end up being a dually diagnosed client. More frequently with a meth abuser or addict, they have been identified by law enforcement. They have been arrested. They may have spent some time in jail. Typically, while they are waiting sentencing or other outcome of their illegal activity, they come to us for substance abuse service.

As director of an agency that interacts with a variety of organizations and community groups, he tended to see the larger picture concerning meth's impact:

It's a very insidious destroyer of resources within the county. Not only does it rob individuals of their ability to stay gainfully employed and avoid incarceration, and properly parent and conduct themselves as reasonable human beings, it's clearly overtaxed law enforcement. It has overcrowded the jails. It has found its way into our schools. [A survey taken at the high school showed 16 percent of the students had tried methamphetamine at some point in time.] That's an alarming number. That's a pretty high number for a drug as devastating and as addictive as methamphetamine. Among that 16 percent you have high school athletes, an increasing number of females, and really not a response from the school administration that would suggest they can stay on top of the problem. It is overwhelming their ability to deal with the numbers, to identify the numbers, and then to provide a response that would be favorable. We see enough of that to know that there are a lot of lives being destroyed by meth.

And the economic impact, if you look at the cost for medical care in the jails for the meth abuser, also with the increased utilization of other primary medical care from the public in general, these individuals typically don't have the ability to pay for these services and don't have insurance for these services, and that takes its toll. When we provide services to the meth addict, we are frequently waiving all fees because they just don't have the means to pay. We hope over thirty, sixty, ninety days at some point they will, but most times they don't. Talk to the employers; it is difficult for them in this area to maintain a workforce of a quality they are looking for and frequently they are frustrated with the number who test dirty for drugs. So, economically, educationally, and socially I think it is about as bad as I have seen it in a community. I don't think it's necessarily worse today than when I first came four years ago, but there is a lot more attention being drawn to it. What's changed is that it seems that younger and younger people are using it, and more females are using it than what we saw four years ago. Plus, our clinical director has pointed out that of our people receiving treatment for substance abuse problems we have more IV users than we've had before. And so then you worry about hepatitis, AIDS, and everything else becoming a bigger threat because of the more prevalent use of hypodermic needles. To me that becomes a general health threat to the community that's been on the rise. We don't necessarily have the sophistication of a large urban area to monitor that and keep track of AIDS cases and hepatitis. The health department does all it can do, but it all just gets below the radar screen.

The counselor who directed the local sexual assault program had prior experience providing substance abuse treatment and was among those who started CAMA. In her view, the connection between methamphetamine and sexual abuse was relatively strong:

Interviewer: Do you see an impact of meth on what you do now?

Counselor: Oh, absolutely. Because I'm interested in meth, it doesn't matter what kind of work I do. I always watch for the connection. About every quarter I go through my most current two hundred cases and track if they are meth affected or not. By meth affected I look at, is that person using or have they used meth? Was the person who abused them under the influence of meth or a known user? Are they the children of folks who were using while they were abused? So that the connection doesn't necessarily mean that they are the user. And that's what I look at. The lowest percentage, on my personal caseload, looking at the most current two hundred, has been 62 percent affected. The highest has been 84 percent. And it's usually closer to the higher than to the lower. . . . It's just pervasive. And I believe that if we tracked it in domestic violence we'd see the same thing.

One of the saddest cases for me, and there are a lot, that connects the two issues [meth and sexual abuse], is a little girl who came here. When she first came here she was eight or nine. Her grandmother brought her in. Her grandmother was very upset, very upset. The afternoon before she had looked out her kitchen window and saw two young fellows, who she decided were probably ten to twelve years old, ramming tree branches up her granddaughter's vagina. Holding her down and forcing them up. So she runs down screaming, scares them, and they take off. Nobody knows who the kids are so they're gone. She brings the little girl in here immediately. Later that night the little girl's parents were arrested. There was a drug bust for meth in their home and she had to "assume the position" [face the wall with her hands raised in order to be frisked by police]. To this day when she comes here the trauma focus isn't on what those boys did to her; it's on Mom and Dad being arrested and being in prison, and things like that. First, her parents weren't there to take care of her to prevent the abuse. Second, the response from the community was devastating, being called a druggie's kid, being looked at differently because "my mom and dad were headlines in the newspaper, and not for good things."

And she's not atypical. I had another one who's a little older than her who told me she used the white stuff on the coffee table because it makes her parents feel better and be happier and she thought it would her, too. Six boys had raped her. So she took that white stuff on the counter and used it. I see a strong connection [between meth and sexual abuse]. Now, along with that, so that it doesn't look totally focused on meth, there is just as much alcohol in the cases we see. A lot of marijuana involved. Certainly a rise in acid and a little bit of a rise in heroin. But for the most part, the two drugs that stand out in sexual assault cases are meth and alcohol.

Another impact of methamphetamine was on foster care in the community. A case manager for a private agency providing foster care services noted:

I would say it has affected foster care in the [rise in the] number of cases that we see and the effects it has had on kids. By that I mean the initial effects that you see. For a lot of kids who come from these homes not only is drug abuse an issue, but there is often environmental neglect because the parents get to a point where they don't care about what the house looks like, if there is food in the house, or things like that. I think that we are going to see a lot of effects later on in these kids who are coming from the meth homes. I think there is a lot we don't know about the effects on the children.

Her agency did not deal with all foster care cases in the area but was assigned cases on a rotating basis. Although the number of foster care cases handled by her agency was not particularly large by urban standards, the proportion of those cases that directly resulted from methamphetamine was substantial. Before the interview, she went through her agency's current case files:

> Well, I looked at our stats and it looks like right now about half the cases we have are in care due to meth. Right now, as of July 1, we have fifty-three children in care through our agency, and twenty-five of those came into care due to meth use. So it's about half. And in a lot of other cases, meth may not have been the reason why they came to care. It could have been physical abuse. It could have been neglect. In a lot of other cases we do find that there is meth use; after we get more into it, we find it was also an issue. But those that I have figured came into care specifically because of parental meth use.

And, echoing the comments of others in the study, she noted that meth-using parents had a particularly difficult time ending their drug use. This complicated, delayed, and sometimes precluded returning those children to their parents.

> *Interviewer:* And how are these meth cases different from other cases you have?
>
> *Foster Care Case Manager:* I would say they are different in the treatment options we have right now for parents. We refer them for counseling and although the counseling agencies in our counties are doing everything they can, as we have seen from CAMA, people who are on meth need a different kind of treatment than other drug people. I think that's been frustrating. There seems to be a lot more relapse—and I don't know any particular numbers, on the number that relapse—but it seems to be very high. And a lot of our parents might go to a residential treatment facility and be there for 60 days or whatever, but then they get out and a lot of them have relapse issues.

Interviews were also conducted with administrators in the Illinois Department of Human Services (DHS) in both Edgar and Clark counties. In each county, DHS provides food stamps, rental assistance, temporary cash assistance, and a variety of related social services. Administrators in each county believed that methamphetamine had a substantial impact on their office, though the extent of that impact was difficult to determine. Clients, or potential clients, were not required to reveal their drug use or to be drug tested and were understandably reluctant to share such information with the agency. When asked whether methamphetamine had an impact on his office, one Edgar County administrator replied:

> Very much so. We started seeing more and more people come through the door a couple of years ago. No visible means of support. When you looked at them, they didn't look like they were well. They had a wrung-out appearance. They always needed medical assistance. Their children who were with them always looked in need of care and attention. They always looked like little urchins, like you want to take them home and give them a bath and put some clothes on them. When we do medical and food stamp applications, we can refer individuals out into the community for other services we think they might need—rental assistance, the WIC [Women, Infants, Children] program for women and infants for nutrition. The client is not required to follow up on those if they engage in those two programs, the medical program or the food stamp program. If they apply for or receive the TANF [Temporary Assistance for Needy Families] program, which is a cash assistance program for families, they are required to take those referrals, and make contact with the agency. We all work together to eliminate barriers they might have to getting back out into the workforce. The clientele know that and you will see these people who you know probably need the money, but they would never apply for cash assistance because there was this string attached that they knew about. The string [is] that we would refer them to other social service agencies, medical providers, or whatever it might be. And they were afraid that their methamphetamine addiction would come out. I really think that. Consequently, we saw all these people coming in with no visible means who just looked terrible. But you could never get them to ask for

cash assistance where you could refer them to someone who could help them and make that referral stick.

When asked what proportion of his office's clients were affected by methamphetamine in some way, the administrator was uncertain, but after the interview he asked five of his caseworkers for their opinion. Their responses ranged from one in two cases to one in thirty, with an average of one in twenty cases having some connection to methamphetamine—using by the applicant, selling/manufacturing, or having kids in the home where meth was cooked. Such figures were, of course, guesses and not to be taken as precise measures, but they did reflect the perception that methamphetamine had a substantial impact on DHS caseload.

The DHS administrator in Clark County also believed her office was substantially impacted by methamphetamine, and this was particularly evident in the children with whom her office had contact:

> We have had a lot of families come in here who are aunts, uncles, grand-parents, who are suddenly custodians of children whose parents have been arrested and have been incarcerated. So we have noticed from that perspective that the children are being uprooted to other family members or even friends because their parents' meth addiction has gotten them incarcerated.

This sampling of social service providers reflected both the nature and the extent to which methamphetamine had affected these agencies, as well as the social fabric of their communities. Of particular note was the reported impact on kids, a theme that was repeated by school officials.

Schools Struggle with Direct and Indirect Effects

An assistant principal at a junior high school and the principal at a high school in Edgar County were interviewed about methamphetamine and its impact on their students and on school officials. The assistant junior high school principal recounted how he had attempted to find out how much his students knew about methamphetamine. This was before there were efforts to educate the public about methamphetamine in Edgar and

Clark counties and before methamphetamine became an issue receiving local newspaper coverage:

> We put up the word *meth* in a class. We said draw a picture of what you think meth is. I had four kids draw pictures of labs. That happened several years ago and that opened our eyes. . . . I'm talking a sixth grade class. Little kids. Sixth graders. Just draw a picture of meth. What do you think meth is? Is it a tree? Is it a truck? I got all kinds of pictures and they were pretty clueless. But I had four kids draw pictures of labs. So they knew what meth was, because it was happening in their homes.

The junior high school initiated an education program to teach young people about methamphetamine. However, the school discovered that meth education required not only education about the drug and its effects but also education about the hazards of *meth trash*. Another source reported that the local health department had also felt it necessary to include education about meth trash in its standard school presentation on hygiene and safety around the home.

Although his junior high students now had an awareness of methamphetamine, either from direct experience or from education programs, the assistant principal did not believe meth use was particularly common among his students. Instead, they were affected by meth use by those around them in the home:

> *Interviewer:* Have you seen any impact of meth in the job you are doing?
>
> *Junior High Assistant Principal:* Oh yeah. In my school? Yes, certainly. My impacts come in a residual fashion. Do I have students here who are possibly directly involved in methamphetamine? We are pretty optimistic that they are not using or pushing. But they are around it because older siblings and/or older peers and/or parents are involved in it in some way. It has a tremendous effect on the kids here.
>
> *Interviewer:* In what way?
>
> *Junior High Assistant Principal:* The ripple effect is truancy, kids who are not fed well, not cared for, not nurtured. Kids whose parents have other

directions or motives in their life. I can tell when a kid has been around a lab in that he has that, I call it, "the thousand-mile stare." Not because he's been using but because he is tired. Because his parents are up all the time. They don't sleep. That causes conflicts with interpersonal relationship with kids. The kid comes to school, he's hungry. He comes to school, he's tired. He comes to school, he's ill-prepared. He comes to school, he smells bad. You take those four elements. Basic elements. Somebody is going to say something to him and because he is hungry, and because he is tired, and because he is ill-prepared, his fuse is probably going to be burned down a little. We get conflict. It comes in a variety of packages.

The principal at the high school reported that methamphetamine's effects on his school were more direct. At this level, student use was perceived as a greater problem than use by adults in the home. While some students in the high school were clearly involved in the use of methamphetamine, the extent of use was difficult to gauge. By any account, levels of use fell short of what might be called an epidemic. Still, there were pockets of use among the high school students. When asked if meth had an impact on his school, the principal replied:

Most definitely. We have a program in which we have students who are in extracurricular activities drug tested. It is a random test and we have seen an effect of methamphetamine in our school. Not as widespread as maybe we would think, when it comes to the testing, but we have seen an effect. That's the type of information that I have to be careful giving out, but I will say we've had a presence of it in the school that we know of. When students self-report, when we do a survey, over half of our students will say they know somebody, or they have seen methamphetamine, either in their house or in the community, or they know somebody who is using. They will report they believe that up to 25 percent of the student body has used methamphetamine, and . . . the number one problem they see with drugs and alcohol in this community is with methamphetamine. They all say that is the number one problem. They report that probably the number one abused drug is alcohol, but they will say the biggest problem is methamphetamine.

In a small community high school where "everybody knows everybody," school officials must be particularly careful about interpreting surveys asking students if they know of other students who have used meth. Still, it was undeniable that student awareness and concern about the issue was high, and it was reasonable to have concerns about use spreading among high-school-age students.

While recognizing the potential for problems with methamphetamine use among his high school students, the principal was more concerned about the indirect effect of methamphetamine on younger students. Echoing the junior high assistant principal, the senior high principal worried about the effect of parental use on their young children:

> I think the biggest impact that I've seen is not necessarily at this level, but when I was an elementary principal. This is my third year at the high school, and I think at the beginning of my last year as a principal [at the elementary school] was the first year we started noticing we had a problem with methamphetamine, and you could begin to see patterns with those kids. You read the names in the newspaper now and you see their kids in our school and you can tell the effect on those kids. A lot of those kids are really struggling. Highly at risk for behavior problems, academic problems, and I think we are seeing quite a bit of that in our school system. Not necessarily at the high school level as much as other levels, but I think it permeates the entire system within the community.

Thus, methamphetamine had an impact on the schools in the area, but the impact was different for younger and older students. For the youngest students, methamphetamine's impact was indirect, through the disruption of a stable and nurturing home environment. This environment sometimes left the children with disrupted sleep patterns, irregular eating schedules, and a lack of love and nurturing. Students at the high school level reportedly experienced fewer negative effects from parental methamphetamine use. High school students were in a better position to escape unhealthy home environments and were at an age where they had begun spending more time with peers. For high school students, the concern focused more on their direct use of methamphetamine. Although levels of use by high school students and by the public in general could not be known with any certainty, it appeared likely from arrest patterns and from the reports of school officials that methamphetamine use had been a greater problem among adults than among the community's youth.

Drug Testing Poses Dilemmas for Businesses

It was obvious that some businesses were directly affected by methamphetamine production. Farm supply stores, for example, were victims of anhydrous ammonia theft. Local shops were concerned about the theft of such precursors as cold tablets, starter fluid, and lithium batteries. While such thefts were a problem, the true extent to which they happened could not be known. For example, the typical theft of anhydrous ammonia involved only a few gallons from a nurse tank that may have held thousands of gallons. Similarly, retail stores may have had difficulty determining just how much missing stock was the result of theft. Even if the levels of theft could have somehow been precisely known, it was impossible to know how much of the stolen merchandise was used to produce methamphetamine, given that all of these precursors had legitimate uses.

One aspect of this study considered the perceived effect of methamphetamine on the workforce. Representatives from three light manufacturing companies were interviewed. Two of those interviewed were human relations (HR) directors and the third was a plant manager. In each case the problems with employee drug use appeared limited, no doubt because the companies drug-tested applicants and current employees for cause or all employees on a random schedule. Each of these interviewed individuals had made a point of becoming educated regarding the signs of meth use and each saw some indication of use by employees, but they thought the extent of the problem was quite limited. A larger concern was the ability to fill vacant positions if drug screens ruled out too many applicants. As the plant manager observed:

> We went through a spell last year when we were just trying to hire one particular position; with business being down we are not really in a hiring mode. It took us four tries before we could get someone to pass the drug screen. I'm not confident that these were all from meth, but it certainly

signifies a problem if you have that many who fail.

An HR director observed the dilemma that companies face. If companies screen, they may have trouble filling vacant positions; but, if they don't, they may hire drug abusers whose use causes safety concerns in the plant:

> *Interviewer:* Is there a problem finding enough employees who aren't testing positive?
>
> **HR Director:** It definitely is. There is a shortage of labor in this area, and any company that is drug screening is probably screening out a quarter to 30 percent of the otherwise acceptable candidates that are available.

While these three firms drug-tested applicants, and current employees under certain circumstances, a larger issue concerned companies that did not drug-test. It was likely that such companies had more than their share of drug abusers—raising questions of workplace safety and liability:

> *Interviewer:* And the companies that aren't screening?
>
> **HR Director:** They are getting people who are working under the influence of drugs, and I know a lot of people from here who were let go because they tested positive on our drug screening and are working for other factories here in town, and it is very unlikely they have stopped using drugs, particularly methamphetamine because of the level of addiction it causes.
>
> *Interviewer:* What are some of the reasons why a company would not test?
>
> **HR Director:** Either they don't understand the impact on the workplace and the coworkers of methamphetamine and other drugs, or they are afraid that if they tested aggressively for drugs they would lose a sizeable proportion of their workers.
>
> *Interviewer:* Has anyone suggested that?
>
> **HR Director:** I've heard a lot of people suggest that. I've heard a lot of people in human resources and other management positions say that they

would not be able to staff their plants if they tested for drugs.

Interviewer: So they are in a bind. If they test, they don't fill their staffing needs. If they don't test, they fill positions with people who were rejected by other places.

HR Director: Yes. I've gone through factories here where I've seen ex-employees from our company who were let go because of a positive drug screen. I realize they need to work, but the risk is so substantial that we have chosen not to accept that.

Anhydrous Theft and Meth Trash Plague Farmers

Finally, interviews were conducted with the directors of each county's local Farm Bureau office. The Illinois State Farm Bureau is a member organization with ninety-six county-level offices. The Farm Bureau promotes successful farming by, among other things, providing farmers with education on issues affecting them and lobbying regarding laws and regulations that affect farmers. Methamphetamine production was a concern of the Illinois Farm Bureau. In the spring of 2004, the bureau's quarterly newsletter, *Partners,* devoted the entire front page and most of an inside page to the issue of methamphetamine in the farm community.

As expected, the Edgar and Clark county Farm Bureau directors expressed concern about the problem of methamphetamine and its consequences for the farm community. As the director in Edgar County said:

> From the ag standpoint the biggest issue is the anhydrous. It is a problem for the fertilizer companies because it is being stolen right off their grounds. It's happening out in the fields. When the farmers pick up the tanks and they need to spray, it is not uncommon for them to leave the tanks out in the fields overnight if they are not done with them or if they haven't gotten them back to the plant. The anhydrous is being stolen right out of the tanks in the field, from their property, and right off the lots where the tanks are, generally in the middle of the night.

Aside from the issue of stolen anhydrous, farmland is by its nature sparsely settled, making it appealing for meth cooks who wish to do their work uninterrupted. Thus, abandoned or infrequently visited sheds and even open fields can attract meth cooks, who leave behind a trail of hazardous chemicals:

Edgar County Farm Bureau Director: The other problem is the meth labs themselves. Two very common places are old farmhouses out in the country that have been kind of abandoned. That's a big problem, and right out in the middle of the fields. There have been a lot of labs discovered as farmers are in harvest. They find the remains of them in the field. Some other counties in central Illinois, they were having big problems. In one county, they [meth cooks] had a meth lab out in the middle of a field and had put up metal posts around it. Of course, a combine going through a cornfield, with all that tall corn you are not going to see that until you come right up on it and hit those metal posts. It just tears up the equipment.

Interviewer: So they hide it in the high corn?

Edgar County Farm Bureau Director: Yes. Even right now I'd say with the corn as tall as it is now [only a couple of feet high at the time of the interview].

Interviewer: So farmers need to be educated about hazardous materials around labs, too.

Edgar County Farm Bureau Director: Yes. I guess, if anything, that is something they wouldn't know much about—what to look for, the remains of a lab, and what to do if they come across one. That's very common to have them out in fields and in abandoned buildings. I know several people from my parents' hometown in central Illinois who have found them in their rental homes, and in sheds that are not near their home. As far as what can really be done to stop it, that's still the big question.

The Farm Bureau director in Clark County echoed those concerns:

Interviewer: Have there been issues of trash and other stuff from meth labs? Is that something farmers need to keep an eye on, people dumping?

Clark County Farm Bureau Director: I think so. It is my understanding that meth can be absorbed right through the skin and so you have to be extremely careful. Trash left along the fields or even a cooler might have anhydrous in it, and they [farmers] might open it up and it could cause them to be burned by it. I know for example, myself. I have a farm in Richland County and I went down and found a siphon tube on the farm. Somewhere around my operation there was meth being made, or at least anhydrous was being siphoned off. And that's the bad thing. Some of these farmers might go out and check their fields and some of these meth labs might be out where they don't expect them to be. . . . Farmers, when they are in the field working or mowing, if they see something in their way they might just jump out, pick it up, and throw it away. Which could be dangerous. If something contains anhydrous or meth residue, it could hurt them.

Every Taxpayer Is Affected by Meth in Some Way

In addition to the direct impact of methamphetamine on agencies, schools, and businesses, it is important to note that every taxpayer in Edgar and Clark counties was affected by methamphetamine. Throughout the study a concerned citizen in Clark County was kind enough to provide materials he had been assembling regarding the effect of methamphetamine on local taxes.[9] In particular, he was concerned about the tax burden created by the need for additional police, emergency services, health care, and jail space. As this study was being conducted, Clark County was moving forward with plans for a much larger and more modern jail. This concerned citizen agreed with the need for increased jail capacity, but he worried about the effects on local taxes from both the construction cost (over $8 million) for a new jail and annual operating costs. The reality was that even if a jail was not built, local taxpayers were all affected by the demands on the current jail and sheriff's budget that resulted from a substantial increase in meth cases. If this drain on local taxes continued in the absence of strong economic growth, both counties would face tough decisions about funding other valuable county services in the future. Whether this concerned citizen's precise dollar projections were accurate, any quibbling with the figures would be over the size of meth's impact and the taxpayers' ability to absorb that cost, not over whether such an impact existed.

Every Person Knows Someone with a Meth Problem

Taken together, interviews with an array of community members suggested widespread concern about the presence of methamphetamine in these two Illinois counties. Criminal justice agencies were most directly affected by the problem, but its impact was wide ranging. One question was whether anyone in these two counties remained untouched by the problem. Most of those interviewed were asked if it were true that just about everyone in their county knew someone who was in trouble because of methamphetamine. The responses varied considerably, from those who doubted the problem was pervasive to those who were relatively confident that most people in their county knew at least one person with a meth problem. Perhaps a more accurate assessment of the situation was provided by a reporter for the *Paris Beacon-News,* a local daily newspaper. He had lived in the area all his life and had reported on meth issues in the paper:

> *Interviewer:* Would it be fair to say that most people in Edgar County know someone who has been affected by meth? Or is that an exaggeration?
>
> *Reporter:* I think that's probably an exaggeration. While I know some people who have been affected by it, that's only because of my work here. My brothers and sisters who live in Chrisman [a town in Illinois] work in other occupations, and they don't have any reason to encounter anyone. Now, it's possible that some people are hiding it and they may know them. But I think if you just walk down the street and ask, "Do you know anybody who used meth?" you'd find several people. But I don't think it would be where everyone in the county has some connection to it, yet.
>
> *Interviewer:* Well, flip it around the other way. When people read the stories in the paper about who has been arrested and booked, is it likely that even if they don't know them personally, the name is familiar to them, the family name is one they would know?

Reporter: That's quite possible, yes. Especially if you are talking family names. We have had some members of the [names omitted] families. Both very old Edgar County names. So people would at least recognize the name, but they may not know that person or their immediate family, but they would certainly recognize the family name.

Respondents were also asked whether they believed the methamphetamine problem was getting better, getting worse, or had leveled off. Most respondents thought the problem was either stable at a high level or had not yet reached its peak. None of the respondents were optimistic about solving the problem completely.

Community Response

The community response to methamphetamine in Edgar and Clark counties was quite remarkable and occurred on several fronts.

Coalition Against Methamphetamine Abuse (CAMA)

The most visible response, and one mentioned by nearly everyone who was interviewed, was the formation of the Coalition Against Methamphetamine Abuse (CAMA). A local reporter said this about the organization:

CAMA is a very unique organization. People who are at the core of CAMA have said this [methamphetamine] is a problem. We've got to deal with it. We can't just turn away. They keep after it. If it wasn't for them, there wouldn't be any community response to speak of. The city government and the county government, especially, are strapped for money. So you are not going to see any official government response to it other than arrest those guys and prosecute them. Put them on probation. Send them through counseling, whatever you need to do. CAMA is a great response. I'm very proud of the people in CAMA for stepping up to the plate and saying "Let's see what we can do," realizing it is a difficult battle to fight. They are not giving up.

CAMA's Mission and Organization

CAMA began in October 2001 when three concerned citizens—the local director of the Department of Human Services for Edgar and Clark counties, a sexual abuse and assault counselor, and a prevention specialist—met to discuss what might be done about the meth problem. After that initial meeting, the organization experienced steady, planned growth and included participants from both Edgar and Clark counties. At the time of this study, CAMA had been in existence for two and one-half years, and attendance at its monthly meetings averaged thirty to forty people—a sizeable number considering the relatively low population of the two counties, and considering that meetings were held on weekday mornings. CAMA had also developed a more formal structure, with by-laws, officers, a board, and committees, each with a particular focus. CAMA had also developed a formal mission statement to guide its activities:[10]

> The Coalition Against Methamphetamine Abuse (CAMA) will work toward community mobilization in Edgar and Clark counties through:
> - Increasing community awareness and collaboration,
> - Supporting education and positive family values, and
> - Reducing accessibility and availability of meth.

The committees, or teams, included the Presentation Team, Laws and Policies Team, CAMA Teens/Kids, Fund Development Team and Resource Scan Team. In 2002–2003 the Presentation Team gave eighty-one presentations in the two counties and around the state. During just the first half of 2004, the team had given fifty-two presentations to approximately 3,500 people. The Laws and Policies Team worked not only to develop policies for the organization but also to have two state laws passed regarding methamphetamine. A local teen who had been a meth user started CAMA Teens/Kids. This group sponsored community activities for kids, marched in local parades, and engaged in activities to increase meth awareness among local youth. Finally, the Fund Development Team successfully marshaled local resources to help the organization—for example, it obtained donations of computer equipment and funds for educational brochures. To this point CAMA had relied primarily on local funding and in-kind contributions, but in 2004 it submitted a proposal for federal funds. That proposal was funded, allowing the organization to expand its already active outreach program.

CAMA's Success

From an organizational standpoint, CAMA avoided the pitfalls that doom many community coalitions. Its continued vitality may be attributed to several factors.

First, CAMA drew in a wide range of people—including professional people from social services, criminal justice, business, education, medicine, and emergency services. The coalition also included adolescents, interested citizens, family members of meth users, and meth users themselves. There was a concerted effort to draw in people with a variety of skills and experiences. The organization utilized experts, but it was not dominated by them, a point emphasized in guides for community organizing.[11] Everyone had a chance for input and participation, and everyone was encouraged to be active. It was no accident that the organization avoided using the word *members* to describe those who attended its meetings, but preferred the word *participants.* Those researchers who study community coalitions stress that inclusiveness and having a meaningful role for participants are key elements of a successful coalition.[12]

Second, local organizing, action, and resources came first, and outside money was sought later, much later. This was important for several reasons. As one community organizing guide has noted:

> . . . all the historical evidence indicates that significant community development takes place only when local community people are committed to investing themselves and their resources in the effort. This observation explains why communities are never built from the top down, or from the outside in . . . [and] it is increasingly futile to wait for significant help to arrive from outside the community. The hard truth is that development must start from within the community.[13]

However, it is not simply that external resources are scarce, but by focusing on the problem and local resources first, a community coalition "keeps its eye on the ball" and is less distracted by outside concerns, who often want a say in how their resources are used. It also makes the coalition dependent on local people, which, in turn, is an incentive to be committed to the work of the coalition. As one guide for building community coalitions observes, "it isn't until the capacities of people are recognized, honored, respected and lifted up that outside resources make much difference."[14] Finally, putting the money second increases the likelihood that people join the organization because of its stated goals and not simply because they sense the possibility of receiving funding. As Kaye and Wolff observe:

> When coalitions are gathered together around the lure of external funding sources, one can never be sure that the partners at the table are not there just for the dollars. This leads to great ambiguity in the startup of these coalitions. The best one can hope for is an open discussion of what brings people to the coalition table.[15]

Third, CAMA set goals for itself that were both clear and achievable. The organization never had the eradication of methamphetamine as a goal, recognizing that such a goal was unattainable. Instead, it had the more modest (and more realistic) objective of "increasing public awareness about the dangers of meth and the rapid increase in its manufacture and use."[16] Within this general objective it also articulated more specific goals, including to increase treatment availability, increase education, sponsor or encourage drug-free activities, train other communities, engage employers, investigate the idea of a drug court, and apply for grants.

Fourth, the leadership of CAMA has been forward looking, anticipating needs and issues before they arose. For example, although the organization appears to have experienced relatively little internal friction, policies and procedures were developed for managing conflict. Similarly, CAMA responded to reports of meth treatment clients using locally purchased kits to defeat drug tests. The Laws and Policies Team helped to pass a state law banning the sale of these kits. In this case the organization responded to a perceived need, even though lobbying for legislation was not part of its original mission.

There is no question that CAMA was successful on several fronts. It raised awareness of the methamphetamine issue in Edgar and Clark counties. It promoted a legislative agenda regarding methamphetamine. CAMA also facilitated cooperation among social services, criminal justice, and the business community. Whether CAMA played a role in reducing or containing the problem of methamphetamine, however, is much harder to prove, at least with existing data.

Media Coverage

While CAMA may have been the most visible sign of community response to the problem of methamphetamine, it was not the only response. There were no television stations located in the two-county area, but there was one daily newspaper, the *Paris Beacon-News*. As the number of methamphetamine labs discovered by the police grew, a local reporter, quoted earlier, decided to cover the issue. His articles included a series about methamphetamine and stories about the work of CAMA. He began reporting on court proceedings involving methamphetamine. As he put it:

> *Reporter:* The Edgar County circuit court has a criminal and traffic call on Monday afternoons and Thursday mornings. And one Friday a month, I think it's the third, they devote to what they call the felony pretrials. Anybody who is charged with a felony and has action pending, they haul them into court to see what progress they can make in the case that day.

> *Interviewer:* I was curious to see the amount of attention your paper focuses on methamphetamine. I grew up in a small community in southern Indiana, and I know it is common in small communities for papers to report on problems in adjoining counties and less so on their own. Was there any agonizing over whether this was something you should do?

> *Reporter:* No. The great thing about working here is that I have a lot of autonomy. I don't have to clear stuff. What happened is that, like other communities, all of a sudden, boom. We had a meth lab, and then the next week another meth lab is raided, and then another meth lab gets raided.

Because it was a new event, something out of the ordinary, they kept saying, "Why don't you go to court, because we know these guys are going to be there, and see what's happening?" It's different. It's news. And after I got going I found that the only way I could track what was going on with these guys was to attend court on a regular basis. And I try to get there.

Interviewer: Up to that point you had not been going to court on a regular basis?

Reporter: No. Not on the court news unless it was something really extraordinary and really out of the usual.

Newspaper coverage undoubtedly did a lot to raise public awareness about methamphetamine and probably contributed to public interest in such groups as CAMA. Both the newspaper and CAMA helped shape an attitude that publicly talking about methamphetamine was acceptable. Small towns are often known for keeping bad news quiet,[17] but in Edgar and Clark counties there was a concerted effort to take the issue public, both within the community and to other communities in the area. When asked about his decision to make the methamphetamine issue a highly visible one through his newspaper stories, the reporter replied:

As far as any kind of concern about community reaction, there wasn't one. I was born in Chrisman, which is just north of here [Paris, Illinois], raised there, and at one point I wrote a story that really wasn't favorable to Chrisman and something that was going on. One of the long-time residents ran into me and said, "You know that sort of thing really shouldn't be written about. It's better if some things just aren't said." And I told him, "Nope. If you don't bring these issues out in public and force people to talk about them, they don't go away. They just sit there and fester." We saw that a couple of years ago when we ran a series during the summer about Edgar County's high teenage birth rate. That's been an ongoing problem for years and years. The paper has addressed it before and at one time there was an organization that tried to deal with it. But it was one of those issues that people just wanted to sweep away. We don't want to talk about it. It was frustrating to write that series and then nothing happens with it.

Nobody wants to address the problem. So I figure the easiest way to address the meth problem is to keep hammering on it. "Hey, these guys are in court today. Oops, they got sentenced. Oops, here are some more guys coming in." And just keep constantly putting it in front of the public—we have people making meth. We have people using meth in the county. It's not going to go away if we don't address it. Writing about it doesn't make it go away, but it makes the public aware. And so I feel I am doing my job.

The president of CAMA pointed out that going public with the issue also made it possible to bring people together to share their knowledge and to work cooperatively on solutions:

People have come together who have never come together before. That's the hopeful side. That's why I think the coalition is the way, that if there is any success it's to be gained that way. Because people are talking with each other and learning each other's vocabulary and learning about how they have to handle things and how they are limited. So there are some bridges we are finding we need to build. So that's really amazing. I think there will be a little bit more understanding. I know that in some communities we are probably bursting their bubble because they moved there or lived there because they think it's the flavor of rural areas and they wanted that serenity, and I know that if there's aggravation at us or anything, it's because we are bursting that.

This quote also highlights one of the unintended benefits of the methamphetamine problem in Edgar and Clark counties. Everyone interviewed agreed that the problem of methamphetamine had brought together people and agencies who might otherwise never have worked together. While this had happened in response to meth, once lines of communication were more open it would likely facilitate cooperative efforts as other problems were identified.

Other Responses

Finally, although CAMA and newspaper coverage were the most visible community responses, there were other indicators. For example, local stores put ephedrine-based cold medicines and lithium batteries behind a counter and limited sales, and this was before state and federal law required such precautions. Store employees also remained alert to suspicious purchases of precursors and notified the police, often providing a vehicle description and license number. Also, a support group was formed in both counties for parents or other family members of methamphetamine users.

One thing noticeably missing from community reaction was hostility toward or hatred of methamphetamine users. Perhaps this is because in smaller communities it is more difficult to vilify someone you know personally. For example, the sheriff's deputy from Edgar County referred to methamphetamine users and cooks sympathetically, even though he was well known for his aggressive pursuit of them:

> *Interviewer:* Are there parts of town that are a particular problem? In some rural communities they talk about the trailer court.
>
> *Deputy:* Well, there is not one certain part. It has nothing to do with how educated you are, how much money you make.
>
> *Interviewer:* It's not a poverty issue, then.
>
> *Deputy:* No, it's an addiction thing. You might think an educated person wouldn't do a thing like that, but they do. They get by with it. They get involved in it. One of them was very educated. What I considered a very intelligent person. I loved talking to him because he was so intelligent. He used to work on our police radios all the time. He got hooked up with methamphetamine and started stealing batteries and started missing work and I got him three times before they ever sent him off to prison. He was a great guy. Good people, bad drugs. That's what I always say, good people bad drugs. They make really bad decisions. Drugs get a hold of them and they can't get away from it. You know I'm not your normal police officer.
>
> *Interviewer:* I haven't heard you use the word *scumbag* yet.
>
> *Deputy:* They are not. They are not. They are people's friends. They are people's family members. It's just a terrible thing.

The deputy had sent members of his own family to prison for meth and had threatened to send another member, not because of animosity toward them but out of frustration at their inability to control the addiction.

Similarly, the sexual abuse counselor did not talk about users with bitterness or hostility, but with compassion. She had a lifelong friend who was addicted to methamphetamine, and her own son was caught up in methamphetamine use. Even people with no close personal ties to methamphetamine users, some of whom would have preferred more prison time for those arrested, expressed little or no hostility to meth users. Perhaps the theme of the community response could be summarized as "tough love"—a belief in treatment but also a recognition that for some meth users prison, even multiple imprisonments, was necessary to push them into taking treatment seriously.

What Did They Think Might Help?

One part of the interview asked respondents what resources or activities might be brought to bear on the methamphetamine problem. There was a range of responses to the question, but no one was optimistic that the problem was going to go away or even substantially diminish in the near future, no matter what was done. The best that most respondents hoped for was to contain the problem.

With this limitation in mind, there were several suggestions of what might be done. One common response was to emphasize prevention to keep new users from starting, particularly to keep young people from becoming involved. Related to this was a belief that more treatment for current users was important, particularly treatment tailored to the methamphetamine user—treatment with frequent drug testing and monitoring of the user. Calls for treatment and prevention were often accompanied by a belief that CAMA's work was important and needed to be continued and expanded.

Another frequent request was for more training for people likely to encounter meth users or meth labs—such as probation officers, business owners, and emergency responders. Along with the need for more training was recognition that more personnel, particularly for treatment and criminal justice, would be helpful. Others suggested additional protective equipment for emergency responders. The fire chief suggested a regional temporary storage facility for the hazardous waste from meth labs so that trucks from across the state would not have to make a trip for the waste from a single lab, but could collect the waste from a number of labs in one trip. He also recommended a regional summit bringing together people from every area affected by the methamphetamine problem, including judges, doctors, and treatment, police, fire, ambulance, and social services. Such a summit, he believed, would facilitate communication among agencies and experts much as had been done locally through CAMA. Still another respondent believed there was a need for a program to encourage businesses to hire former meth users, with economic incentives designed to offset liability and worker's compensation concerns.

Most recommendations required more resources, though the suggestions tended not to be extravagant. It was also recognized that financial resources must be paired with human resources. One respondent, who had worked to secure donations and in-kind contributions to CAMA, summed it up:

> We need more counselors; we need more health specialists helping rehab people; we need people to lead support groups. HRC is just strapped. It is just beat to death. We have so many issues in this town, including meth. We have a prison out here that is empty that could be a halfway house, or a place for counselors and educators. I'm very conservative. The governor closed it. We could turn it into something like that. We need help for that.

> We need to make people more aware of what we are doing. The more you do the more you need. The more you need the more it costs. We've got projectors, PowerPoint stuff to do presentations. We need more people. We need more officers of the law who are trained in this.

> There are three areas: We need more for education and awareness, we need more for rehabilitation, and we need laws that are passed and enforcement to go out and get them. Presence is so important as a deterrent. If they just see you, it's a deterrent. We need more people out there in that deterrent role. It doesn't mean it is going to cure the problem.

We also need job training and human resource services. And that's tough. They are whacking budgets. I'm the guy who goes out in the community and says we need $3,000 for this and $4,000 for that and there are people who when they see me walking in they do two things—they grab their heart and their billfold because they know I am after both. If I get one, I got the other. But you can only get so much blood out of a turnip, and so that's why we need government support. They've written a grant that will help us. We want a coalition with other people. Those are things that we need. We need health care specialists to help rehabilitate these people. You can't lock them up.

Several respondents expressed frustration with the reality that problems from methamphetamine came to the community about the same time that budget shortfalls constrained support from the state. Law enforcement, for example, was frustrated that overcrowding at state prisons was causing early release of convicted meth offenders and thus made imprisonment a less effective threat. Social service providers were similarly concerned about the impact of state budget cuts on vital social services, particularly in those rural areas with limited tax bases. One respondent used this allegory to summarize these concerns:

Respondent: It is almost as if scattered throughout the state of Illinois there are a lot of watering holes for people to go to and survive. Just like in Africa you have watering holes. It seems like the administration isn't too worried about the downstate watering holes and they are drying up. And they are drying up relatively quickly, and the meth problem has either caused some watering holes to dry up quicker or has contaminated what water is left. It looks to me as though at some point we'll have few watering holes left. And what happens to those populations? What happens to the rural areas, the rural communities, when their resources have dried up? Essentially they do not have enough resources to support their communities in a viable manner.

Interviewer: So meth is soaking up resources at the very time that resources are becoming more scarce.

Respondent: Yes, I think at some point, what happens in nature is that the animals move to another watering hole. They try to find one that can support them. But there is a lot of death and carnage in between. I hate to see that happen to people who, if you just look at their lifestyles and their histories, are not migratory by nature. For an animal it is instinctive. For human beings I'm afraid there is going to be a lot more hardship and a lot more people will perish because of it if something really significant doesn't happen.

Overall, in the opinion of these respondents, more resources are needed to deal with the problem of methamphetamine. Their demands are not large, and there is a general understanding that financial resources are particularly difficult to marshal in the current economic climate. The agencies and groups working in these two counties have done a remarkable amount of work with relatively few resources, but their efforts would be substantially bolstered by even a relatively modest infusion of financial support.

A Follow-Up

By any measure Edgar and Clark counties were hit hard by methamphetamine when the interviews were first conducted. Over time, however, some remarkable changes took place. The chief judge in Clark County provided some thought-provoking data that rather dramatically illustrated these changes. His clerk examined all felony cases from January 1, 2000, through October 22, 2007, to identify cases specifically involving methamphetamine charges. These cases did not include other charges, such as burglary, in which methamphetamine use may have been suspected or known, but for which no felony charges were brought specific to methamphetamine. Figure 6.1 illustrates how the percentage of charges for methamphetamine possession or production rose rather dramatically from 2000 to 2003, and then just as precipitously declined through 2007.

The reasons for the startling shift were unclear. The Coalition Against Methamphetamine Abuse discussed the issue, though there was no widely agreed on explanation. Since illicit drug use is an activity that users have a strong incentive to hide, it is difficult to know the true extent of changes

Figure 6.1

Meth Cases as a Percent of All Felony Cases in Clark County, 2000–2007

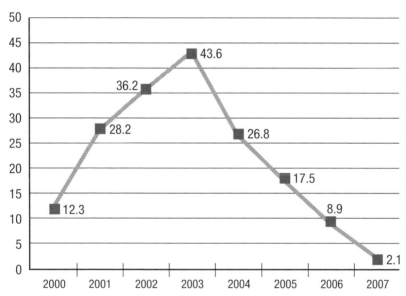

or the precise factors accounting for those changes. Although nothing can be said with certainty, there are a number of possible factors that either individually or in combination may have accounted for the sharp decline.

First, it was about this time that the state and then the federal government began imposing restrictions on access to over-the-counter cold medicines containing ephedrine or pseudoephedrine. Such restrictions may have led to a reduction in the number of methamphetamine labs. As noted in the previous chapter, labs present a highly visible sign of the presence of methamphetamine. Identifying a methamphetamine lab is often the way in which users are ultimately discovered. It is possible that locally produced methamphetamine may have been replaced by imported methamphetamine. A system based on importation rather than on local production is less visible to the public and to law enforcement, making arrests for methamphetamine less likely, and thus creating the illusion that the drug had gone away. It is also possible that a sharp reduction in

local labs produced a genuine shortage of the drug that, in turn, produced a sharp drop in the number of users.

Second, the aggressive activities of community groups, such as the
Coalition Against Methamphetamine Abuse, may have discouraged people
from becoming new users and may have encouraged existing users to quit.
The educational outreach activities of CAMA also may have made the
nonusing public more sensitive to early signs of use. Armed with this
knowledge, friends and family members may have intervened early to
direct new users to treatment or to otherwise pressure them to quit before
their use spun out of control.

Third, not everyone who lived in the community had an interest in
using methamphetamine. Consequently, the pool of people who would
abuse the drug may have been limited. That pool may have shrunk as
aggressive law enforcement, criminal punishment, and treatment took
potential users out of the mix. Further, as social and legal consequences
accumulated for longtime abusers, many of them may have abandoned the
drug.

Fourth, as illustrated in chapter 2, methamphetamine's popularity has
ebbed and flowed over time, a characteristic the drug shares with other
powerful mind-altering substances. It is possible that the precipitous
decline reflects a natural process as users and potential users become aware
of the drug's long-term harmful effects. Further, just as there are difficult-to-
explain collective shifts in styles of clothing or music, drug users may have
shifted their preferences to another drug. As early as 1969 Smith observed
that in San Francisco methamphetamine addicts began switching to heroin
and/or barbiturates, moving from a class of drug that excited and agitated
to one that sedated and calmed.[18] There is anecdotal evidence from both
law enforcement and treatment providers of a switch from methamphetamine to heroin or OxyContin in rural areas of southern Illinois, but only
time will tell if these isolated cases portend a broader pattern.

Perhaps the lesson to be learned from these two rural midwestern counties is that the drug problem is fluid and may quickly morph from one
form to another. Communities must be continuously on the alert for
changes and possess the flexibility to respond.

CONCLUSION

In less than a decade methamphetamine swept through the rural Midwest, rising from obscurity to become one of the most troublesome drugs of abuse. Methamphetamine in much of the Midwest is "homegrown"—a locally produced drug. In addition to problems arising from addiction, the production process leaves a trail of toxic materials that contaminate the air, ground, and water. Meth cooks, their family members, police, emergency responders, and others risk exposure to the toxic meth trash left behind. The study described in this chapter examined the impact of methamphetamine on two rural Illinois counties where the drug had become a major concern. It also looked at how these communities responded to the problem and at what additional resources might further efforts to minimize the problem.

Since illicit drug use is by definition a clandestine activity, it is not possible to know just how many methamphetamine users there are in Edgar and Clark counties, how many methamphetamine labs operate there, or how much ancillary crime results from methamphetamine. What is clear, however, is that at the time of the study methamphetamine affected virtually every citizen in these two counties. For some, the effects were direct—users, their families, and the police all saw the impact of methamphetamine up close. However, methamphetamine had an impact on even those most removed from its direct effect. Homeowners who had no involvement in methamphetamine still found a portion of their taxes used to respond to the problem—arresting, jailing, and treating methamphetamine users, training emergency responders, cleaning up toxic sites, putting out fires from lab explosions, conducting prevention programs in the schools, and the list goes on. If those homeowners lived in the countryside, they might have also found meth trash dumped on their property.

Across the United States, methamphetamine has proven to be a pernicious problem for which there are no easy or obvious solutions. Residents of Edgar and Clark counties mobilized local resources to provide education, treatment, and a variety of other services to address the problem. There is little question that at the time of the study methamphetamine was the source of widespread concern in these communities

and such indicators as arrests and admissions to treatment provided jus-
tification for that concern. By 2007 it appeared that the problem of
methamphetamine was retreating in these counties. Community-level
drug problems often arise as the result of a complex set of circumstances,
and the factors that lead to a diminution of the problem are likely to be
equally complex. Some observers might claim the shift is the result of
federal restrictions on precursors, others might point to the work of
CAMA, others might look to intensive treatment programs, and still others
might credit aggressive police work and punishments. Perhaps it is all of
these things in combination.

It has been argued that states can be laboratories for studying effective
drug policies, as illustrated by the various state laws regulating precursors,
laws that eventually became models for federal legislation. In a similar way
counties such as Edgar and Clark can provide a microcosm for studying
the spread of methamphetamine through the Midwest, as well as insights
into strategies for organizing communities to respond to the problem.

The treatment of methamphetamine dependence is the focus of chapter 7.

CHAPTER 7

Treatment and Recovery Support Resources for Methamphetamine Dependence

Methamphetamine use exists on a continuum, and one's view of the drug and those who consume it can vary markedly depending on whether one encounters experimental use, regular use, regular heavy use, problematic use, mild to moderate dependency, or severe dependency. Media exposés on methamphetamine most often feature severe dependency, with riveting images of human emaciation. Severe dependency has a number of distinguishing features, including tolerance (escalating dosages of the drug are required to achieve the same effect), physical dependence (reflected in acute and postacute withdrawal when drug use is stopped), craving (cellular hunger for the drug), and compulsive drug seeking and drug taking in spite of adverse consequences and resolutions to stop. The essence of methamphetamine dependence is the loss of volitional control over drug intake—the user is no longer free to "just say no." Once use starts, the shutoff valve no longer consistently works. The images of skeletal methamphetamine addicts show the product of a brain disease—a disease of the human will. Those with the most severe methamphetamine problems may require specialized addiction treatment and potentially multiple episodes of such treatment to achieve sustained recovery.

However, severe dependency is just the extreme end of the continuum. Many persons who are involved in casual methamphetamine use and who experience transient, less severe methamphetamine problems will decelerate or stop methamphetamine use through their own personal/family resources or through brief professional intervention involving helpers not trained as addiction specialists. Such helping resources may include family physicians, clergy, pastoral counselors, school counselors, employee assistance counselors and probation officers, as well as counselors and therapists working in a broad spectrum of helping agencies.

Several factors distinguish those who mature out of alcohol and other drug exposure from those who progress to severe alcohol and drug dependence. The latter often exhibit one or more of the following: a family history of alcohol and other drug problems, early onset of alcohol and other drug use, multiple drug use, greater problem severity, co-occurring psychiatric illness, a history of severe physical/sexual victimization in childhood, and low recovery capital (internal and external assets that can be used to initiate and sustain recovery).

This chapter explores the specialized treatment and recovery support resources that are available for persons suffering from methamphetamine dependence. We begin with an overview of addiction treatment in the United States and then talk specifically about treatment of and recovery from methamphetamine dependence.

An Overview of Addiction Treatment

Addiction treatment is the delivery of specialized, professionally directed services to alcohol- and drug-dependent individuals and their families. The goals of such services have been traditionally defined as the achievement of sustained abstinence from primary and secondary drugs (to avoid the propensity to shift from one drug dependency to another) and overall improvement in physical, emotional, and relational health and social functioning.

A 2003 survey of specialized addiction treatment facilities in the United States identified 13,626 facilities with a current enrollment of 1,092,546 clients. More than 60 percent of the facilities surveyed were operated by private nonprofit entities, one-quarter were operated by private for-profit organizations, and the remainder were operated by federal, state, local, or tribal governments.[1] Addiction treatment is financially supported through designated federal and state agencies, private insurance, and fees charged to individual service consumers.

Specialized treatment is provided in three different settings: abstinence-based outpatient programs (78 percent of all programs), inpatient/residential programs (12 percent of programs), and outpatient methadone maintenance programs (10 percent of programs).[2] Inpatient/residential services are indicated for those individuals with more severe and prolonged substance use disorders, acute medical/psychological problems that require intense monitoring and care, a family/social environment that inhibits the initiation of sobriety, or a prior history of failure in outpatient addiction treatment modalities. Abstinence-based outpatient programs address a broad spectrum of drug choices and levels of severity, where methadone maintenance programs are designed specifically for the treatment of addiction to heroin and other opiates. Recent decades also have witnessed intervention programs in the criminal justice system (e.g., drug courts, prison-based therapeutic communities, recovery-focused community reentry programs), as well as multiagency intervention models emanating from the child welfare system that incorporate specialized addiction treatment. These programs are now being refined for the special problems and needs of those dependent on methamphetamine.

The length of involvement in addiction treatment varies by modality and by individual, with the longest lengths of stay usually reserved for those with very severe, complex problems and few recovery supports in their natural environment. A 2000 national study of addiction treatment institutions revealed the following average lengths of stay by modality: detoxification, 5 days; outpatient treatment, 91 days; intensive outpatient treatment, 44 days; short-term residential rehabilitation, 27 days; long-term residential rehabilitation, 75 days; and hospital-based residential treatment, 12 days.[3]

Seen as a whole, the overall effects of addiction treatment are positive. Treatment-related remissions (people no longer meeting DSM-IV criteria for a substance use disorder following treatment) average about 33 percent; substance use decreases by an average of 87 percent following treatment;

and substance-related problems decrease by an average of 60 percent follow-ing treatment.[4] Posttreatment follow-up studies reveal that individuals have highly variable responses to addiction treatment, including those who

- remain continually abstinent following treatment
- immediately return to pretreatment levels of substance use following treatment
- decrease their use to nonproblematic levels or experience less severe problems than before treatment
- abstain initially but return to pretreatment levels of substance use
- relapse following addiction treatment but later migrate to a pat-tern of stable recovery
- recycle between periods of recovery and periods of relapse
- accelerate substance use following treatment

These varied responses to treatment are often viewed as a function of client characteristics, but it is important to note that treatment outcomes vary across programs and even from counselor to counselor.[5] Program characteristics associated with higher recovery outcomes include

- a multidisciplinary staff
- supervising staff trained at the M.A. to Ph.D. level
- a comprehensive assessment process
- a full continuum of care (diversity of treatment modalities)
- family involvement in treatment
- a broad range of ancillary social, medical, and psychiatric services
- assertive linkage to recovery mutual aid groups
- specialized services for women, adolescents, and persons with co-occurring psychiatric illness
- an active program of continuing care following primary treat-ment[6]

The measurable benefits of addiction treatment should not obscure the limitations of such treatment. Limitations include critical areas such as

- attraction (only 10 percent of those who need treatment receive it in any given year and only 25 percent in their lifetime)[7]
- access (waiting lists can generate high pretreatment dropout rates)[8]
- retention (less than half of those admitted to addiction treatment successfully complete treatment)[9]
- length of treatment (many of those who successfully complete treatment do not receive a dose of services associated with long-term recovery outcomes)[10]
- continuing care (only a small minority of clients discharged from addiction treatment participate in posttreatment continuing care activities)[11]
- posttreatment lapse/relapse (over half of those discharged from addiction treatment will resume some alcohol and drug use in the next year),[12] and
- readmission (64 percent of clients admitted to addiction treatment already have one or more past episodes of addiction treatment)[13]

The above data on the outcomes of addiction treatment suggest that severe alcohol and drug dependencies resemble other chronic health disorders (e.g., type 2 diabetes mellitus, hypertension, and asthma) in their etiological complexity, variable pattern of onset, prolonged course, treatment (management rather than cure), and long-term clinical outcomes.[14]

The Treatment of Methamphetamine Dependence

Methamphetamine (with smoking as the most common route of administration) was noted as a primary drug or part of a constellation of multiple drug use among 12 percent of those admitted to addiction treatment in the United States in 2004.[15] The casualties of the surge in methamphetamine use in the United States are evident in the 420 percent increase in methamphetamine-related treatment admissions between 1993 and 2004.[16]

Profile of Those Treated

Compared to others entering addiction treatment in the United States, those seeking help for methamphetamine dependence are more likely to be young, white (although racial diversity is now increasing), unmarried, unemployed, uninsured, men (although female admissions are increasing), educated at less than a high school level, and residents of a rural or small metropolitan community.[17] They often present with a long history of problems from alcohol and drugs other than methamphetamine and most often enter treatment under the supervision of the criminal justice system.[18] This summary blurs the fact that those admitted to treatment for methamphetamine dependency represent multiple subpopulations with very different motivations for use, different patterns of use, and variable treatment needs. We will explore such differences shortly.

Levels of Care

Persons seeking treatment for methamphetamine dependence can be treated in varying levels of care, from acute detoxification to inpatient/residential treatment to outpatient treatment. The most frequently recommended level of care for methamphetamine dependence is intensive outpatient treatment. In this level of care, individuals participate in treatment activities several hours per day, three to five days per week for more than three months, followed by a gradual reduction of treatment appointments and involvement in months of continuing care sessions.[19] The goals of continuing care sessions are to sustain and enhance the gains made during primary treatment.

Pharmacological Treatments

There are a growing number of pharmacological adjuncts in the treatment of addiction.[20] These medications include drugs that can reverse a life-threatening overdose, aids in detoxification, metabolic stabilization agents such as methadone used in the treatment of opiate addiction, aversive agents that provide a chemical shield against impulses to use, neutralizing agents (antagonists) that diminish or eliminate the ability of a drug to induce its desired euphoric effects, anticraving agents that reduce cravings and the euphoric effects of a drug, and medications used to treat co-occurring psychiatric disorders such as depression, bipolar disorder, anxiety disorder, and psychosis. While these medications have been a boon to the treatment of opiate addiction and alcoholism and hold great promise in the treatment of other drug dependencies, medication research has yet to produce comparable medications that can aid the treatment of stimulant dependence.[21] There are no FDA-approved, scientifically validated medicinal specifics for the treatment of methamphetamine-related intoxication, psychosis, dependence, or withdrawal.[22] The National Institute on Drug Abuse is currently investing considerable resources toward the development of such medications.[23]

Behavioral Treatments

At the present time, cognitive behavioral therapy (CBT) and contingency management (CM) techniques are the most research-supported treatments for methamphetamine dependence.[24] Proponents of CBT view addiction as a learned maladaptive behavior pattern that can be corrected by substituting new patterns of thinking and behaving. Key approaches include an analysis of circumstances surrounding drug use, motivational interviewing, social skill training, relapse prevention training, and self-monitoring and correction of thought processes.[25]

CM is the systematic reward of pro-recovery behaviors. An example of CM would be rewarding participation in treatment and recovery support activities with points that can earn vouchers redeemable for desired items (e.g., gifts, bus tokens, movie tickets, dinners, food items). Studies of the use of CM in the treatment of stimulant dependence suggest that CM can increase treatment completion rates and lengthen periods of continuous sobriety.[26] Studies of the use of contingency management techniques have found that such techniques, added to CBT, produce a greater number of drug-free urine samples and longer period of abstinence.[27] While scientific studies suggest great promise for CBT and CM in the treatment of methamphetamine dependence, critics note that these approaches have not generally been effective with very disadvantaged populations.[28]

The Matrix Model

The best-known cognitive behavioral treatment for methamphetamine dependency is the Matrix Model—a sixteen-week intensive outpatient program designed by Dr. Richard Rawson specifically for the treatment of stimulant dependence.[29] This approach has been rigorously evaluated and widely replicated for more than fifteen years. The basic service elements of the Matrix Model include individual and group counseling, relapse prevention training, family education, participation in Twelve Step recovery support groups, random drug and alcohol testing, and a thirty-six-week continuing care program.[30] A 1999 evaluation of the Matrix Model at eight treatment sites compared clients treated in the Matrix Model to clients assigned to "treatment as usual." Those in the Matrix Model had higher retention and completion rates and more negative urine screens during treatment, but posttreatment follow-up outcomes were similar for the two groups.[31]

Methamphetamine Treatment Effectiveness

Popular media have painted a bleak picture of the course of methamphetamine dependence. A 2003 *Rolling Stone Magazine* article claimed that only "6 percent of meth freaks" are able to get and stay drug free. When another stimulant drug, cocaine, first became a national concern in the 1980s, there were similar reports that treatment didn't work with these users. Pessimistic assessments about treatment also accompanied the early spread of crack cocaine. In both cases such reports have since proven inaccurate. Scientific studies of treatment outcomes of those treated for methamphetamine dependence challenge the myth that few if any achieve sustained recovery from methamphetamine addiction. Here is a sampling of such studies.

An early 1992 outcome study by Frawley and Smith of individuals treated for cocaine or methamphetamine dependence found that 53 percent of those treated were abstinent one year following treatment.[32] Brecht and colleagues followed 98 individuals treated for methamphetamine dependence and found 49 percent of them abstinent at the follow-up interview.[33] Rawson and colleagues conducted a follow-up study in 2002 of 114 individuals who had completed outpatient treatment for methamphetamine dependence. They concluded that "two to five years after treatment, there are substantial numbers of former methamphetamine users who are abstinent, employed, and not under the supervision of the criminal justice system."[34] In a confirmation of these findings, follow-up results on 978 individuals treated for methamphetamine dependence as part of the Center for Substance Abuse Treatment's Methamphetamine Treatment Project showed significant reductions in methamphetamine use and related problems at follow-up.[35] Luchansky and colleagues conducted a one-year follow-up to compare treatment outcomes for persons admitted for methamphetamine dependence with those dependent on primary heroin, cocaine, marijuana, and alcohol. Treatment outcomes for 2,782 individuals who were methamphetamine-dependent were similar to those dependent on heroin and cocaine but less positive than those treated for alcohol or marijuana dependence.[36]

In spite of pessimism regarding recovery from methamphetamine dependence expressed in the popular media and by many working on the front lines of this problem, research studies confirm that methamphetamine recovery rates are comparable to those for cocaine and heroin dependence. A 2003 review of methamphetamine treatment outcome studies reported: "We must conclude that clients who report methamphetamine abuse respond favorably to existing treatments."[37]

The Benefits of Ancillary Services

Addiction treatment programs vary widely on the range of available ancillary services they can deliver. Clients with more severe methamphetamine dependence, a greater number and severity of collateral problems, and socioeconomic disadvantages may require a spectrum of ancillary services to initiate and sustain recovery.[38] Such ancillary services include transportation, child care, primary medical care, psychiatric services, case management, and transitional housing or recovery homes.

The Drug Court Model

There are currently more than 1,600 drug courts operating in the United States.[39] What distinguishes drug courts is the unique combination of judicial monitoring (regular status hearings), addiction treatment and case management services, random drug testing, probation supervision, a non-adversarial collaboration between prosecution and defense counsel, and multiagency case conferences for service planning and progress review. At present, more than half of those entering treatment for methamphetamine dependence do so under pressure from criminal justice or child protection authorities.[40] Drug courts challenge the popular idea that it does no good to force addicts into treatment because recovery is possible only for those who really want it. The fact is that those coerced into addiction treatment have long-term recovery rates similar or superior to those who entered treatment without such coercion.[41] Methamphetamine-dependent clients under legal supervision spend a longer time in treatment and have better completion rates than methamphetamine clients without legal supervision.[42] Studies to date have shown the drug court model of managing methamphetamine treatment and recovery to be superior to treatment without this added supervision as measured by higher rates of retention, treatment completion, and days of abstinence during and following treatment.[43] These enhanced outcomes are likely due to a well-defined service continuum, assertive linkage to recovery support groups, and sustained rigorous monitoring and drug testing, as well as the ongoing encouragement of the judge and other members of the drug court team.

Importance of Posttreatment Monitoring and Support

The fact that methamphetamine dependence often has a longer trajectory of physical/psychological recovery than other drug dependencies[44] warrants a longer and potentially more intense course of posttreatment follow-up and support. The more extended duration of craving among those recovering from methamphetamine dependence (compared to those recovering from other drug dependencies) suggests the potential value of a longer period of professional- and peer-based recovery support.

A growing body of scientific evidence suggests that posttreatment monitoring (recovery checkups) and support (recovery coaching) can elevate recovery outcomes for adults[45] and adolescents.[46] Such services can be delivered in face-to-face, telephone-based, and Internet-based formats.

Recovery Mutual Aid Societies

There is a long history of recovery mutual aid groups in the United States and a recent history of the development of such groups specifically for those dependent on stimulants, for example, Cocaine Anonymous (CA) and Crystal Meth Anonymous (CMA). CMA now has meetings in more than thirty states. There is very little scientific information on the use of Twelve Step recovery support groups or alternative recovery support groups as a framework for long-term recovery from methamphetamine dependence. Studies of these groups (mostly studies of Alcoholics Anonymous) suggest that participation in recovery mutual aid groups can enhance long-term recovery outcomes, that this effect is a function of both intensity and duration of participation, and that participation in both professional treatment and recovery mutual aid groups generates recovery rates higher than either activity alone.[47]

Donovan and Wells recently reviewed what is known about the role of recovery support groups in long-term recovery from stimulant dependence (cocaine and methamphetamine). Their major findings include the following:

- Regular Twelve Step meeting attendance is associated with increased abstinence from stimulants, other drugs, and alcohol.
- Dropping out of Twelve Step meeting participation is associated with declines in abstinence rates.
- Stimulant-dependent persons referred to Twelve Step programs exhibit low affiliation rates (ongoing meeting participation), with less than 30 percent affiliation rates in those referred from outpatient treatment and only 40 percent affiliation rates for those referred from inpatient settings.
- There are high rates of attrition in Twelve Step participation following treatment for stimulant dependence.
- The most frequently attended Twelve Step program by those dependent on stimulants is Alcoholics Anonymous, followed by Narcotics Anonymous, Cocaine Anonymous, and Crystal Meth Anonymous.[48]

Procedures to refer each client to a recovery mutual aid society are most effective when they go beyond verbal encouragement and actually link each client to a particular person and/or a particular meeting to which he or she is most likely to respond.[49]

Special Populations

The term *special populations* has been used to describe particular groups of individuals who face unique obstacles to achieving long-term recovery and who may require special support services. In this section, we will briefly acknowledge three such special populations of persons entering treatment for methamphetamine dependence.

Individuals in Rural Communities

Individuals dependent on methamphetamine who live in rural communities constitute a special population for several reasons. First, as this book has made clear, methamphetamine use is very prevalent in some rural communities. Initiating and sustaining recovery within such a social context can be particularly challenging. Second, these same communities may have fewer geographically accessible treatment resources and recovery support groups. Third, the "everyone-knows-everyone" climate and the stigmatized image the user can develop through the experience of drug addiction in such a community can make a new start difficult. Some individuals trying to break out of such an image have described it as "recovering in a fishbowl." These obstacles can be overcome through local educational campaigns and local recovery resource development. The growing phenomenon of online recovery support groups has also offered a needed sanctuary for persons seeking recovery within communities that have few if any local recovery support resources.

Women

Nearly half of treatment admissions for methamphetamine dependence are women—a rate considerably higher than female admissions to treatment for other drug choices. Methamphetamine use tends to have special functions for female users: appetite suppression and weight loss, self-medication of depression, energy enhancement to complete multiple role responsibilities, and social intimacy.[50] Methamphetamine-dependent women have higher dropout rates than men in residential treatment, but higher retention rates and better completion rates in outpatient treatment.[51] The dropout rate in residential treatment may reflect the demands placed on women (e.g., caretaking of children and others) that can make it difficult to remain in residential treatment for any length of time. In at least one study, methamphetamine-dependent women were found to have more severe collateral problems (e.g., severe psychiatric illness) compared to methamphetamine-dependent men entering treatment.[52] These findings are consistent with modern research suggesting that nearly everything related to addiction and recovery is different for women than for men. These findings have spurred the growth of gender-specific treatment and women's only recovery support meetings.

Gay and Bisexual Men

Methamphetamine has become an integral part of urban gay and bisexual male subculture in many cities in the United States. It is used to extend and enhance sexual pleasure and performance and has been linked to the onset of riskier sexual practices and risk for HIV, hepatitis C, and other infections (see chapter 3).[53] While promotional forces for methamphetamine use do exist in the gay community, a growing number and diversity of recovery support meetings and other recovery support institutions can serve to offset such forces.

Treatment Issues

Rawson, Anglin, and Ling recently summarized the special challenges faced in the treatment of methamphetamine dependence:

> Poor treatment engagement rates, high dropout rates, severe paranoia, high relapse rates, ongoing episodes of psychosis, severe craving and protracted dysphoria and anhedonia are clinical challenges that are frequently far more problematic than is seen with standard treatment populations.[54]

We next review special issues that distinguish the treatment of methamphetamine dependence from the treatment of other drug dependencies.

The Question of Motivation

People enter treatment for methamphetamine addiction under quite different circumstances and varying levels of motivation for long-term recovery. The very essence of addiction is the rabid appetite for drug intoxication and the lost capacity to exert volitional control over drug-use decisions. That appetite and that impaired decision-making ability do not dissipate with admission to treatment. Ambivalence about both drug use and abstinence should be considered normal. Recognizing that motivation for treatment and recovery will ebb and flow, treatment providers must carry out frequent status checks and strategies of regular remotivation. What is most important during this earliest stage of engagement is a relationship free of contempt and a stance of regular encouragement. Many people will have entered treatment under crisis with little expectation of long-term recovery. The key here is an environment of acceptance and hope that makes recovery contagious. A key ingredient in creating such an environment is the presence of "real" people with whom clients can identify and who can offer living proof of the transformative power of recovery. Pain can push people into crisis-induced experiments of recovery initiation, but only hope can pull people into the process of long-term recovery.

Biopsychosocial Stabilization

The first goal of treatment is to bring enough order into the life of each client so that treatment can move beyond palliative care. Creating such stability is a task in itself. Physical stabilization must address the symptoms of acute and postacute withdrawal, the treatment of acute medical/dental problems, the assessment of health conditions that may not be initially apparent (e.g., heart damage, HIV, hepatitis C), and the reestablishment of regular patterns of sleep, food intake, and personal hygiene. Hepatitis C is emerging as a special concern in the treatment of methamphetamine addiction. Studies of persons entering treatment for methamphetamine dependence reveal rates of hepatitis C infection above 20 percent and at 70 percent for those injecting methamphetamine.[55]

Psychosocial stabilization can also be a challenge given the cognitive impairments, vacillating mental status, and turbulent family and social relationships that often characterize methamphetamine addiction. Much of early treatment feels like an endless process of putting out fires, but skilled therapeutic support and assertive case management can create the foundation of stability that makes recovery possible. However, achievement of this early honeymoon of stability should not be mistaken for sustainable recovery.

Sexuality

Issues related to sexual functioning in the absence of methamphetamine is a concern for men of all sexual orientations that is often raised early in treatment. During active dependence, methamphetamine becomes so entwined with sexual performance that any posttreatment sexual activity can serve as a trigger for relapse. Learning to have sex without methamphetamine in one's system is an early and ongoing recovery task. Mastery of this task can be aided by communications with addiction treatment professionals and peers in long-term recovery from methamphetamine dependence.

Treatment Retention

Addiction treatment is like antibiotic treatment: clients must get an adequate dose to get its full effects. In both cases, a little bit of treatment can relieve symptoms briefly; but, without a full course of treatment, the disorder returns and often does so in a more virulent form. If the first key to addiction treatment is therapeutic engagement, the second key is ensuring an adequate dose of treatment. Men and women who remain in treatment for methamphetamine dependence longer and participate in the most weekly treatment activities are most likely to be abstinent at follow-up.[56]

Achieving an adequate or optimal dose of treatment services requires mustering the full support of the client's family and kinship network, friends, and co-workers to support the recovery process as well as the full resources of the treatment team. It also means assertively responding to all obstacles to continued treatment involvement, whether those are attitudinal or environmental distractions.

Anhedonia and Craving

From the earliest days of detoxification, the methamphetamine-dependent client is going to mourn the loss of the physical pleasure, confidence, sociability, feelings of power and control, and, for some, enhanced sexual functioning that methamphetamine brought into his or her life.[57] These feelings of loss are often exacerbated by two companion conditions—the lessening or loss of the ability to experience normal physical pleasure (anhedonia) and cellular hunger or craving for methamphetamine and other drugs. This early state manifests itself in what appears to be depression and in flights of fantasy or regular dreams of getting high. It is important to manage such experiences with messages that these feelings and thoughts (1) are normal, (2) lessen in frequency and intensity over time, (3) become less troublesome when verbalized to others in recovery, and (4) are often tied to internal and external cues that can be recognized and avoided. Many clients find diet, aerobic activity, centering rituals (prayer, meditation), and peer or professional recovery support helpful in getting through periods of intense craving and intrusive thoughts of getting high.[58]

Polydrug Use

It is rare for those dependent on methamphetamine not to also have excessive relationships with alcohol and other drugs. Use of other substances frequently predated methamphetamine use and increased (at least periodically) to medicate the unpleasant side effects of methamphetamine.[59] For example, alcohol or opiates may be used to help the meth user come down from a long meth run with a "soft landing." The client entering treatment may be so focused on problems related to methamphetamine that he or she misses this larger pattern of alcohol and drug dependence (e.g., cannabis, sedatives, benzodiazepines, or opiates). There are two lessons to be conveyed to the client: (1) he or she is at increased vulnerability for methamphetamine relapse while under the influence of alcohol and other drugs, and (2) he or she is at increased risk of developing other drug dependencies following methamphetamine dependence. The phenomenon of drug substitution is a common one. Many of the IV methamphetamine injectors of the late 1960s and early 1970s were later admitted for treatment of alcoholism or narcotic addiction.

Co-occurring Psychiatric Disorders

There is high co-occurrence of methamphetamine dependence and psychiatric illness. More than half of those entering treatment with a primary drug choice of methamphetamine present with significant psychiatric symptoms.[60] The relationship between methamphetamine use and psychiatric illness can follow four separate tracks. First, as we noted in chapter 3, acute and chronic methamphetamine intoxication can trigger a toxic organic psychosis that can be mistakenly diagnosed as paranoid schizophrenia. Second, excessive methamphetamine use can be a manifestation of a preexisting psychiatric illness. The onset of methamphetamine use can, for example, be one of a larger cluster of excessive and risk-taking behaviors that are a symptom of bipolar disorder or antisocial personality disorder. Third, methamphetamine use can reflect attempts to self-medicate the symptoms of primary psychiatric illness. An example of such use would be to counter the anhedonia and loss of energy experienced during major depression. A final pattern is the strategic use of methamphetamine to mask or hide the existence (real or feigned) of what the person perceives as a more stigmatized primary psychiatric illness. In this latter pattern, the person often exaggerates the extent of his or her drug use in order to explain symptoms of the psychiatric illness.

The assessment and treatment of the relationship between methamphetamine dependence and other psychiatric illness is difficult and is ideally managed by an integrated team of addiction treatment and psychiatric professionals. Individuals with methamphetamine dependence and a co-occurring psychiatric illness may also benefit from specialized recovery support groups such as Dual Diagnosis Anonymous or Double Trouble in Recovery.

Identity and Lifestyle Reconstruction

Recovery is far more than the removal of drugs from an otherwise unchanged life. Consider the student whose methamphetamine use fuels his or her compulsion to excel, the roguish biker whose methamphetamine use is tied to his or her "outlaw" image, the woman whose methamphetamine use is inseparable from her preoccupation with weight and body image, and the gay man whose methamphetamine use is deeply entangled in his sexual identity and sexual rituals. In recovery, each must disentangle methamphetamine from who he or she is as a person. Such disentanglement requires a fundamental reconstruction of personal identity and daily lifestyle. These are basic questions that must be answered in treatment:

1. Why and how did this happen? (Why me?)

2. What does it mean to have this problem? (How has this problem changed me and my most important relationships and activities?)

3. How did I come to escape this problem? (Why have I survived when others have not? Where does my recovery story begin?)

4. What actions do I need to take today to sustain my recovery?

5. How does this problem affect the future direction of my life? (What is my personal destiny as a person in recovery?)[61]

Spirituality

There are religious, spiritual, and secular pathways to long-term recovery. Being spiritual means that the addicted individual draws on untapped resources within and beyond the self (framed in Twelve Step recovery as a "Higher Power") to initiate and sustain recovery. When persons recovering from methamphetamine dependence talk about the importance of spirituality in recovery, they reference a broad range of experiences. Some talk of a spiritual breakthrough that sparked their recovery—a conversion-like experience that was unplanned, powerful, positive, and permanent.[62] Some talk about a slow process of spiritual growth that altered their relationships with family, community, and God. Still others talk about spirituality in terms of a reconstruction of personal character or personal values or in terms of life meaning and purpose. A growing number of people are using religious experience and affiliation with a community of faith to support their recovery from methamphetamine dependence.

Cultures of Addiction and Cultures of Recovery

Long-term methamphetamine use is often enmeshed in an elaborate culture of significant relationships, places, language, values, symbols, and rituals. It is possible to become as addicted to this culture as to methamphetamine, and the pull of the culture is a major source of relapse. Interestingly, there are equally elaborate cultures of recovery, with their own special relationships and cultural trappings. The challenge is to disengage from the people, places, and things of one culture and replace them with those of another culture that can support long-term recovery. Recovery support groups such as Alcoholics Anonymous, Narcotics Anonymous, Cocaine Anonymous, and Crystal Meth Anonymous constitute such replacement cultures. Those whose lives have been deeply enmeshed in a methamphetamine subculture also may find involvement in recovery homes, recovery schools, recovery industries, and recovery places of worship important to their successful transition into stable recovery. A key role of professional helpers is to facilitate disengagement from the culture of addiction and engagement in a culture of recovery. To achieve this requires knowledge of both cultures and skills in assertively linking clients in treatment to these alternative social worlds.[63]

Lapse and Relapse Management

In the context of efforts to abstain from methamphetamine and other drugs, a "lapse" is an episode of use and a "relapse" is the resumption of compulsive drug use—the latter involving greater quantities of use over greater lengths of time with much greater consequences. A basic primer on the treatment and recovery process would include several key points about the role of lapse and relapse in recovery:

1. Lapses and relapses as a prelude to sustained recovery are common but not inevitable.

2. Relapse is more likely in those with the most severe dependency on methamphetamine and other drugs.

3. A drug-using lapse is usually preceded by lapses in thinking (e.g., "My problem wasn't *that* bad," "I could use a little without

anyone knowing," "Now that my wife and I are back together, I don't need to go to meetings anymore.").

④ Lapse/relapse triggers can be consciously identified and actively avoided.

⑤ Lapses can be aborted early before becoming full-blown relapses.

Perhaps the most important lesson about lapse/relapse is that its risk progressively diminishes over the first five years of recovery, but that some vulnerability for relapse and need for active recovery maintenance remain throughout the person's life.

Helping professionals can take a number of steps to lower relapse rates of the individuals they serve. Five such steps include the following:

① Educate clients and families about relapse prevalence and processes.

② Provide or refer clients for formal relapse prevention training.

③ Assist clients in the development of a relapse prevention plan.

④ Assertively link clients to local communities of recovery, online recovery support groups, and, where needed, recovery community institutions (recovery support centers, recovery homes, recovery schools, recovery ministries).

⑤ Provide posttreatment recovery checkups, stage-appropriate recovery education and, when needed, early reintervention. Ongoing monitoring and support during the first ninety days following discharge from primary inpatient, residential, or outpatient treatment are particularly important.

Ten Steps to Prevent Relapse
from Methamphetamine Dependence

1. Make sobriety a priority: Don't use, no matter what! Find a pathway of recovery that works for you to support this commitment.

2. Sobriety means abstinence from all intoxicants. Avoid the pitfall of drug substitution (and quit smoking!).

3. Attend and participate in treatment continuing care groups and/or peer-based recovery support meetings. And keep going to new meetings until you find a fit.

4. Develop a recovery plan that includes a recovery activities schedule and your steps to avoid relapse. Recovery doesn't happen by accident. You must own and direct it. Set daily goals and take an end-of-day inventory of how you did. Include in your recovery plan how and when you will involve your family members in your recovery process. Be patient; it will take time to re-earn their trust and affection.

5. Cut ties with the people, places, and things associated with your drug use.

6. Develop new sobriety-based friendships and social activities. Find people who have the qualities you would like to recapture or develop.

7. Take care of your body: work on bodily repair, diet, and exercise. And keep working on it!

8. Nurture your spirit. Find things that give your life meaning and purpose.

9. When you fall, get up. Recovery isn't a hundred-yard dash; it is a lifetime marathon.

10. Find opportunities to celebrate your recovery and give back to your family, friends, and community, and to others still wounded.

From Recovery Initiation/Stabilization to Sustained Recovery Maintenance

Recovery involves two quite different processes. The first is initiating and stabilizing recovery—a process that often spans a period of years. The second involves developing rituals of daily life that sustain recovery over time. Professional helpers are usually only involved in the early weeks of the first process, but a movement is growing to provide sustained "recovery check-ups" to people who have been admitted to addiction treatment.[64] Such checkups may have particular utility in supporting long-term recovery from methamphetamine dependence given that this condition may be marked by a long trajectory of neurological, psychological, and social recovery.

Degrees of Recovery

Not all recoveries from methamphetamine dependence look the same. Some individuals will achieve only partial recovery—meaning that permanent abstinence from all drugs is never achieved, but the frequency and intensity of drug use and its related problems have been significantly reduced. Others will achieve full recovery—meaning all methamphetamine use has ceased without other patterns of drug substitution, and the individual exhibits improvements in physical, emotional, and relational health and in social productivity. A third pattern of recovery from methamphetamine dependence involves people who achieve full recovery but then go on to achieve an exceptional level of personal functioning and service to others—not in spite of their recovery but because of the lessons and the strength drawn from their addiction and recovery experiences. The good news about recovery from addiction is not just that recovery is possible and prevalent. It is that many recovering people get better then well.

CONCLUSION

Methamphetamine dependence springs from multiple causes, unfolds in varied patterns and subpopulations of users, and is resolved through varied styles of long-term recovery. Natural recovery from methamphetamine-related problems is possible, but those with severe methamphetamine dependence often require one or more episodes of professional treatment before achieving sustainable recovery. Specialized addiction treatment in the United States enhances long-term recovery outcomes, but is plagued by low attraction, problems of access and retention, low rates of continuing care participation, and high posttreatment relapse and re-admission rates.

Professional treatment of methamphetamine dependence relies predominantly on the use of cognitive behavioral therapies, motivational incentives, and linkage to recovery mutual aid societies. The latter, which include new groups established specifically to support recovery from stimulant dependence, enhance long-term recovery outcomes, particularly when combined with professional treatment. There are special populations of persons treated for methamphetamine dependence who face special obstacles to recovery and who bring special needs to the treatment setting. The treatment of methamphetamine dependence involves addressing special issues unique to this pattern of drug dependency, as well as issues faced by all people seeking to initiate and sustain addiction recovery.

Professional treatment is a crucial but by itself insufficient societal response to the health and social problems produced by methamphetamine dependence.

NOTES

Preface

1. H. C. Covey, "What Is Methamphetamine and How and Why Is It Used?" in *The Methamphetamine Crisis*, ed. H. C. Covey (Westport, CT: Praeger, 2007), 3–22.

Chapter 1

1. C. Luna, "Woman Loved Meth More Than Her Son, Prosecution Says at Trial," *Los Angeles Time* (October 20, 2004), http://www.latimes.com.

2. "Schoolgirls Questioned in Sex-for-Drugs Case," *Los Angeles Times* (May 12, 2005), http://www.latimes.com.

3. K. Zernike, "A Drug Scourge Creates Its Own Form of Orphan," *New York Times* (July 11, 2005), http://www.nytimes.com.

4. S. Gold, "Breast Milk Cited in Meth Fatality," *Los Angeles Times* (January 20, 2003), http://www.latimes.com.

5. "Man Who Killed Five Is Sentenced to Death," *Los Angeles Times* (October 12, 2005), http://www.latimes.com.

6. A. Campo-Flores, "Meth Fallout: 'I Felt My Face Just Melting,'" *Newsweek* (August 8, 2005), http://www.msnbc.msn.com.

7. A discussion of these various waves of panic can be found in J. A. Inciardi, *The War on Drugs IV: The Continuing Saga of the Mysteries and Miseries of Intoxication, Addiction, Crime, and Public Policy* (Boston: Pearson Education, Inc., 2008).

8. R. S. King, *The Next Big Thing? Methamphetamine in the United States* (Washington, DC: The Sentencing Project, 2006).

9. F. Owen, *No Speed Limit: The Highs and Lows of Meth* (New York: St. Martin's Press, 2007).

10. D. Musto, *The American Disease: Origins of Narcotic Control,* expanded ed. (New York: Oxford University Press, 1987); J. Gusfield, *Symbolic Crusade: Status Politics and the American Temperance Movement* (Urbana, IL: University of Illinois Press, 1963).

11. SAMHSA, OAS, *Results from the 2006 National Survey on Drug Use and Health: National Findings,* NSDUH Series H–32, HHS Pub. SMA 07–4293 (2007).

12. SAMHSA, OAS, *Treatment Episode Data Set (TEDS), 1995–2005: National Admissions to Substance Abuse Treatment Services,* DASIS Series S–37, HHS Pub. SMA 07–4234 (2007).

13. Ibid.

14. Ibid.

15. L. D. Johnston, P. M. O'Malley, J. G. Bachman, and J. E. Schulenberg, "Overall, Illicit Drug Use by American Teens Continues Gradual Decline in 2007," University of Michigan News and Information Services, Ann Arbor, MI, (December 11, 2007), http://www.monitoringthefuture.org.

16. L. D. Johnston, P. M. O'Malley, J. G. Bachman, and J. E. Schulenberg, "Teen Drug Use Continues Down in 2006, Particularly Among Older Teens; but Use of Prescription-Type Drugs Remains High," University of Michigan News and Information Services, Ann Arbor, MI, (December 21, 2006), http://www.monitoringthefuture.org.

17. "Methamphetamine Use," *The NSDUH Report* (January 26, 2007), http://oas.samhsa.gov/2k7/meth/meth.pdf.

18. SAMHSA, OAS, *Treatment Episode Data Set (TEDS), 1995–2005.*

19. Z. Zhang, *Drug and Alcohol Use and Related Matters Among Arrestees, 2003,* report for the Arrestee Drug Abuse Monitoring (ADAM) Program, http://www.ncjrs.gov/nij/ADAM2003.pdf.

20. Ibid.

21. Ibid.

22. SAMHSA, OAS, *Treatment Episode Data Set (TEDS), 1995–2005.*

23. M. D. Anglin, C. Burke, B. Perrochet, E. Stamper, and S. Dawud-Noursi, "History of the Methamphetamine Problem," *Journal of Psychoactive Drugs* 32, no. 2 (2000): 139.

24. NIDA, *Methamphetamine Abuse and Addiction,* NIDA Research Report Series, NIH Pub. 02–4210 (2002).

25. P. Jenkins, "'The Ice Age': The Social Construction of a Drug Panic," *Justice Quarterly* 11, no. 1 (1994): 7–31.

26. T. E. Freese, J. Obert, A. Dickow, J. Cohen, and R. H. Lord, "Methamphetamine Abuse: Issues for Special Populations," *Journal of Psychoactive Drugs* 32, no. 2 (2000): 177–82.

27. K. A. Joe-Laidler and P. Morgan, "Kinship and Community: The 'Ice' Crisis in Hawaii," in *Amphetamine Misuse: International Perspectives on Current Trends,* ed. H. Klee (Amsterdam: Harwood Academic Publishers, 1997), 163–79.

28. Cited in "Methamphetamine Use," *The NSDUH Report.*

29. National Center on Addiction and Substance Abuse (CASA) at Columbia University, *No Place to Hide: Substance Abuse in Mid-Size Cities and Rural America* (January 2000), http://www.casacolumbia.org/absolutenm/articlefiles/380No%20Place%20to%20Hide.pdf.

30. R. W. Bauer, "Methamphetamine in Illinois: An Examination of an Emerging Drug," *Illinois Criminal Justice Information Authority Research Bulletin* 1, no. 2 (2003): 1–12.

31. B. Warner and C. G. Leukefeld, "Rural-Urban Differences in Substance Use and Treatment Utilization Among Prisoners," *American Journal of Drug and Alcohol Abuse* 27 (2001): 265–80.

32. K. M. Grant, S. S. Kelley, S. Agrawal, J. L. Meza, J. R. Meyer, and D. J. Romberger, "Methamphetamine Use in Rural Midwesterners," *American Journal on Addictions* 16, no. 2 (March 2007): 79–84.

33. "Demographic and Geographic Variations in Injection Drug Use," *The NSDUH Report* (July 19, 2007), http://www.oas.samhsa.gov/2k7/idu/idu.htm.

34. M. Evans, *National Methamphetamine Initiative Survey: The Status of the Methamphetamine Threat and Impact on Indian Lands,* report prepared for the Bureau of Indian Affairs Law Enforcement Services by the New Mexico Investigative Support Center (April 12, 2006).

35.   P. Kraman, *Drug Abuse in America—Rural Meth* (Lexington, KY: The Council of State Governments, 2004); Methamphetamine Interagency Task Force, *Final Report* (January 2000), http://www.ncjrs.org/pdffiles1/nij/180155.pdf; R. A. Weisheit, D. N. Falcone, and L. E. Wells, *Crime and Policing in Rural and Small-Town America,* 3rd ed. (Long Grove, IL: Waveland Press, 2006).

36.   B. M. Lester, A. M. Arria, C. Derauf, P. Grant, L. Lagasse, E. Newman, R. Z. Shah, S. Stewart, and T. Wouldes, "Methamphetamine Exposure: A Rural Early Intervention Challenge," *Zero to Three* 26, no. 4 (March 2006): 30–36.

37.   P. J. Draus, H. A. Siegal, R. G. Carlson, R. S. Falck, and J. Wang, "Cracking the Cornfields: Recruiting Illicit Stimulant Drug Users in Rural Ohio," *The Sociological Quarterly* 46, no. 1 (Winter 2005): 165–89.

38.   SAMHSA, OAS, *2006 National Survey on Drug Use and Health: Detailed Tables,* http://oas.samhsa.gov/NSDUH/2k6NSDUH/tabs/Sect8peTabs1to46.htm#Tab843B.

39.   Johnston et al., "Overall, Illicit Drug Use by American Teens Continues Gradual Decline in 2007."

40.   SAMHSA, OAS, *Treatment Episode Data Set (TEDS), 1995–2005.*

41.   Ibid., Table 3.1b.

42.   Inciardi, *The War on Drugs IV.*

43.   SAMHSA, OAS, *Results from the 2006 National Survey on Drug Use and Health.*

44.   L. D. Johnston, P. M. O'Malley, J. G. Bachman, and J. E. Schulenberg, *Demographic Subgroup Trends for Various Licit and Illicit Drugs, 1975–2006,* Monitoring the Future Occasional Paper, Number 67 (Ann Arbor, MI: Institute for Social Research, 2007), http://www.monitoringthefuture.org.

45.   SAMHSA, OAS, *Treatment Episode Data Set (TEDS), 1995–2005.*

46.   Ibid.

Chapter 2

1.   I (White) have collaborated with my colleague Randall Webber for more than thirty years on understanding the principles that underlie cyclical drug trends. I wish to acknowledge his contributions to the insights presented in this chapter. Some of the principles discussed in this chapter have been referenced in two earlier works: W. White and R. Webber, "Substance Use Trends: History and Principles," *Counselor* 4, no. 3 (2003): 18–20; W. White, "OxyContin Addiction: A New Drug, but an Old Problem," in *When Painkillers Become Dangerous: What Everyone Needs to Know About OxyContin and Other Prescription Drugs* (Center City, MN: Hazelden, 2004), 99–138.

2.   R. A. Weisheit and J. Fuller, "Methamphetamines in the Heartland: A Review and Initial Exploration, *Journal of Crime and Justice* 27, no. 1 (2004): 131–51; T. Zábranský, "Methamphetamine in the Czech Republic," *Journal of Drug Issues* 37, no. 1 (2007): 155–80.

3.   S. Fukui, K. Wada, and M. Iyo, "Epidemiology of Amphetamine Abuse in Japan and Its Social Implications," in *Amphetamine and Its Analogs: Psychopharmacology, Toxicology, and Abuse,* ed. A. K. Cho and D. S. Segal (San Diego, CA: Academic Press, 1994), 459–78; H. Brill and T. Hirose, "The Rise and Fall of a Methamphetamine Epidemic: Japan 1945–55," *Seminars in Psychiatry* 1 (1969): 179–94.

4. C. O. Jackson, "The Amphetamine Inhaler: A Case Study of Medical Abuse," in *Amphetamine Use, Misuse, and Abuse: Proceedings of the National Amphetamine Conference, 1978*, ed. D. E. Smith, D. R. Wesson, M. E. Buxton, R. B. Seymour, J. T. Ungerleider, J. P. Morgan, A. J. Mandell, and G. Jara (Boston: G.K. Hall & Co., 1979), 35–45.

5. J. C. Kramer, V. S. Fischman, and D. C. Littlefield, "Amphetamine Abuse: Pattern and Effects of High Dose Taken Intravenously," *Journal of the American Medical Association* 201 (1967): 305–309.

6. R. C. Smith, "The World of the Haight-Ashbury Speed Freak," *Journal of Psychedelic Drugs* 2 (1969): 172–88; W. Burroughs, *Speed* (New York: Olympia Press, 1970).

7. K. Beebe and E. Walley, "Smokable Methamphetamine 'Ice': An Old Drug in a Different Form," *American Family Physician* 51, no. 2 (1995): 449–53; R. F. Calkins, G. B. Aktan, and K. L. Hussain, "Methcathinone: The Next Illicit Stimulant Epidemic," *Journal of Psychoactive Drugs* 27, no. 3 (1995): 277–85; A. K. Cho, "Ice: A New Dosage Form of an Old Drug," *Science* 249 (1990): 631–34; K. A. Joe-Laidler and P. Morgan, "Kinship and Community: The 'Ice' Crisis in Hawaii," in *Amphetamine Misuse: International Perspectives on Current Trends*, ed. H. Klee (Amsterdam: Harwood Academic Publishers, 1997), 163–79.

8. Cho, "Ice: A New Dosage Form of an Old Drug"; M. A. Miller, "Trends and Patterns of Methamphetamine Smoking in Hawaii," in *Methamphetamine Abuse: Epidemiologic Issues and Implications*, ed. M. Miller and N. J. Kozel, NIDA Research Monograph Series 115 (1991), 113–33; Beebe and Walley, "Smokable Methamphetamine 'Ice.'"

9. J. H. Tanne, "Methamphetamine Epidemic Hits Middle America," *British Medical Journal* 332, no. 7538 (2006): 982.

10. M. D. Anglin, C. Burke, B. Perrochet, E. Stamper, and D. Dawud-Noursi, "History of the Methamphetamine Problem," *Journal of Psychoactive Drugs* 32, no. 2 (2000): 137–41; Miller, "Trends and Patterns of Methamphetamine Smoking in Hawaii."

11. J. C. Kramer, "Introduction to Amphetamine Abuse," *Journal of Psychedelic Drugs* 2, no. 2 (1969): 1–16; Weisheit and Fuller, "Methamphetamines in the Heartland."

12. W. R. Bett, "Benzedrine Sulphate in Clinical Medicine: A Survey of the Literature," *Postgraduate Medical Journal* (August 1946): 205–18; L. Grinspoon and P. Hedblom, *The Speed Culture: Amphetamine Use and Abuse in America* (Cambridge, MA: Harvard University Press, 1975).

13. N. Rasmussen, *On Speed: The Many Lives of Amphetamine* (New York: New York University Press, 2008).

14. Quoted in Bett, "Benzedrine Sulphate in Clinical Medicine," 217.

15. Ibid.

16. Rasumussen, *On Speed.*

17. Anglin et al., "History of the Methamphetamine Problem"; H. Suwaki, S. Fukui, and K. Konuma, "Methamphetamine Abuse in Japan: Its 45 Year History and the Current Situation," in *Amphetamine Misuses: International Perspectives on Current Trends*, ed. H. Klee (Amsterdam: Harwood Academic Publishers, 1997), 199–214.

18. Joe-Laidler and Morgan, "Kinship and Community."

19. Brill and Hirose, "The Rise and Fall of a Methamphetamine Epidemic."

20. Rasmussen, *On Speed.*

21. Fukui, Wada, and Iyo, "Epidemiology of Amphetamine Abuse in Japan and Its Social Implications"; Suwaki, Fukui, and Konuma, "Methamphetamine Abuse in Japan."

22. B. Angrist and S. Gershon, "Amphetamine Abuse in New York City, 1966–1968," *Seminars in Psychiatry* 1 (1969): 195–207.

23. C. O. Jackson, "The Amphetamine Democracy: Medicinal Abuse in the Popular Culture," *The South Atlantic Quarterly* 74, no. 3 (1975): 308–23.

24. Bett, "Benzedrine Sulphate in Clinical Medicine," 205.

25. Jackson, "The Amphetamine Inhaler," 36.

26. Jackson, "The Amphetamine Democracy."

27. M. A. Miller and A. L. Hughes, "Epidemiology of Amphetamine Use in the United States," in *Amphetamine and Its Analogs: Psychopharmacology, Toxicology, and Abuse,* ed. A. K. Cho and D. S. Segal (San Diego, CA: Academic Press, 1994), 439–57.

28. Brill and Hirose, "The Rise and Fall of a Methamphetamine Epidemic."

29. Fukui, Wada, and Iyo, "Epidemiology of Amphetamine Abuse in Japan and Its Social Implications."

30. SAMHSA, OAS, *Treatment Episode Data Set (TEDS): 1993–1998: National Admissions to Substance Abuse Treatment Services,* DASIS Series S–11, http://wwwdasis.samhsa.gov/teds98/1998_teds_rpt.pdf.

31. Brill and Hirose, "The Rise and Fall of a Methamphetamine Epidemic."

32. D. Brown, "Globalization, Iowa Pork, and Hometown Tweakers," *Journal of Popular Culture* 34, no. 4 (2001): 35–48.

33. Weisheit and Fuller, "Methamphetamines in the Heartland."

34. T. E. Freese, J. Obert, A. Dickow, J. Cohen, and R. H. Lord, "Methamphetamine Abuse: Issues for Special Populations," *Journal of Psychoactive Drugs* 32, no. 2 (2000): 177–82.

35. White and Webber, "Substance Use Trends."

36. Miller and Hughes, "Epidemiology of Amphetamine Use in the United States."

37. K. Morimoto, "The Problem of the Abuse of Amphetamines in Japan," *Bulletin on Narcotics* 9 (1957): 8–12; Fukui, Wada, and Iyo, "Epidemiology of Amphetamine Abuse in Japan and Its Social Implications."

38. Jackson, "The Amphetamine Democracy."

39. J. P. Morgan, "Amphetamine," in *Substance Abuse: Clinical Problems and Perspectives,* ed. J. H. Lowinson and P. Ruiz (Baltimore: Williams & Wilkins, 1981), 167–84.

40. P. Jenkins, "'The Ice Age': The Social Construction of a Drug Panic," *Justice Quarterly* 11, no. 1 (1994): 7–31.

41. Suwaki, Fukui, and Konuma, "Methamphetamine Abuse in Japan."

42. W. White, "Themes in Chemical Prohibition," in *Drugs in Perspective* (Rockville, MD: National Drug Abuse Center/National Institute on Drug Abuse, 1979), 117–82; Jenkins, "'The Ice Age.'"

43. Jenkins, "'The Ice Age.'"

44. H. Klee, "Patterns of Amphetamine Misuse in Seven Nations: Factors Affecting Growth and Decline," in *Amphetamine Misuse: International Perspectives on Current Trends,* ed. H. Klee (Amsterdam: Harwood Academic Publishers, 1997), 291–319.

45. Jackson, "The Amphetamine Inhaler."

46. Morgan, "Amphetamine," 181.

47. Weisheit and Fuller, "Methamphetamines in the Heartland."

48. H. Suwaki, "Methamphetamine Abuse in Japan," *Substance Use and Misuse* 32, no. 12/13 (1997): 1817–22; Suwaki, Fukui, and Konuma, "Methamphetamine Abuse in Japan"; Brill and Hirose, "The Rise and Fall of a Methamphetamine Epidemic."

49. White, "OxyContin Addiction."

50. Brill and Hirose, "The Rise and Fall of a Methamphetamine Epidemic."

51. Suwaki, "Methamphetamine Abuse in Japan."

52. Klee, "Patterns of Amphetamine Misuse in Seven Nations."

53. Suwaki, "Methamphetamine Abuse in Japan."

54. Fukui, Wada, and Iyo, "Epidemiology of Amphetamine Abuse in Japan and Its Social Implications."

55. D. Coyhis and W. White, *Alcohol Problems in Native America: The Untold Story of Resistance and Recovery—The Truth About the Lie* (Colorado Springs, CO: White Bison, Inc., 2006).

56. Fukui, Wada, and Iyo, "Epidemiology of Amphetamine Abuse in Japan and Its Social Implications."

57. R. A. Weisheit, *The Impact of Methamphetamine on Illinois Communities: An Ethnography* (Chicago, IL: Illinois Criminal Justice Information Authority, 2004).

Chapter 3

1. R. L. Balster and C. R. Schuster, "A Comparison of D-Amphetamine, L-Amphetamine, and Methamphetamine Self-Administration in Rhesus Monkeys," *Pharmacology, Biochemistry and Behavior* 1 (1973): 67–71.

2. D. E. Espelin and A. K. Done, "Amphetamine Poisoning: Effectiveness of Chlorpromazine," *New England Journal of Medicine* 278, no. 25 (1968): 1361–65.

3. Q. Yu, D. F. Larson, and R. R. Watson, "Heart Disease, Methamphetamine and AIDS," *Life Sciences* 73 (2003): 129–40.

4. E. M. Brecher, *Licit and Illicit Drugs: The Consumers Union Report on Narcotics, Stimulants, Depressants, and Inhalants—Including Caffeine, Nicotine, and Alcohol* (Boston: Little Brown, 1972).

5. Ibid.

6. T. E. Albertson, R. W. Derlet, and B. E. Van Hoozen, "Methamphetamine and the Expanding Complications of Amphetamines," *Western Journal of Medicine* 170 (1999): 214–19.

7. F. G. Castro, E. H. Barrington, M. A. Walton, and R. A. Rawson, "Cocaine and Methamphetamine: Differential Addiction Rates," *Psychology of Addictive Behaviors* 14, no. 4 (2000): 390–96.

8. L. Grinspoon and P. Hedblom, *The Speed Culture: Amphetamine Use and Abuse in America* (Cambridge, MA: Harvard University Press, 1975), 62.

9. H. Becker, *Outsiders: Studies in the Sociology of Deviance* (New York: The Free Press, 1963); N. E. Zinberg, *Drug, Set, and Setting: The Basis for Controlled Intoxicant Use* (New Haven, CT: Yale University Press, 1984).

10. F. Owen, *No Speed Limit: The Highs and Lows of Meth* (New York: St. Martin's Press, 2007), 2–3.

11. T. Nordahl, R. Salo, and M. Leamon, "Neuropsychological Effects of Chronic Methamphetamine Use on Neurotransmitters and Cognition: A Review," *Journal of Neuropsychiatry and Clinical Neurosciences* 15, no. 3 (August 2003): 317–25.

12. A. H. Beckett and M. Roland, "Urinary Excretion Kinetics of Amphetamine in Man," *Journal of Pharmacy and Pharmacology* 17 (May 1965): 628–39.

13. Beckett and Roland, "Urinary Excretion Kinetics of Amphetamine in Man"; J. P. Morgan, "Amphetamine," in *Substance Abuse: Clinical Problems and Perspectives,* ed. J. H. Lowinson and P. Ruiz (Baltimore: Williams & Wilkins, 1981), 167–84.

14. B. M. Angrist and S. Gershon, "Psychiatric Sequelae of Amphetamine Abuse," in *Psychiatric Complications of Medical Drugs,* ed. R. I. Shader (New York: Raven Press Publishers, 1972), 175–99; N. E. Gary and P. Saidi, "Methamphetamine Intoxication: A Speedy New Treatment," *American Journal of Medicine* 64, no. 3 (1978): 537–40; Morgan, "Amphetamine."

15. Albertson, Derlet, and Van Hoozen, "Methamphetamine and the Expanding Complications of Amphetamines"; K. Beebe and E. Walley, "Smokable Methamphetamine 'Ice': An Old Drug in a Different Form," *American Family Physician* 51, no. 2 (1995): 449–53; C. W. Callaway and R. F. Clark, "Hyperthermia in Psychostimulant Overdose," *Annals of Emergency Medicine* 24 (1994): 68–76; G. A. Smets, K. A. Bronselaer, K. B. De Munnynck, K. C. De Feyter, W. Van de Voorde, and M. A. Sabbe, "Amphetamine Toxicity in the Emergency Department," *European Journal of Emergency Medicine* 12, no. 4 (2005): 193–97.

16. K. Sullivan, "Man Sentenced in Meth-from-Urine Mishap," *San Francisco Chronicle* (December 3, 2005), http://www.sfgate.com.

17. D. Wu, S. V. Otton, T. Inaba, W. Kalow, and E. M. Sellers, "Interactions of Amphetamine Analogs with Human Liver CYP2D6," *Biochemical Pharmacology* 53 (1997): 1605–12; A. K. Cho and W. P. Melega, "Patterns of Methamphetamine Abuse and Their Consequences," *Journal of Addictive Diseases* 21 (2002): 21–34; Smets et al., "Amphetamine Toxicity in the Emergency Department."

18. R. B. Rothman, M. H. Baumann, C. M. Dersch, D. V. Romero, K. C. Rice, F. I. Carroll, and J. S. Partilla, "Amphetamine-Type Central Nervous System Stimulants Release Norepinephrine More Potently Than They Release Dopamine and Serotonin," *Synapse* 39 (2001): 32–41.

19. E. H. Ellinwood, "The Epidemiology of Stimulant Abuse," in *Drug Use: Epidemiological and Sociological Approaches,* ed. E. Josephson and E. E. Carroll (Washington, DC: Hemisphere Publishing Corporation, 1974), 303–29; T. Newton, A. D. Kalechstein, S. Duran, N. Vansluis, and W. Ling, "Methamphetamine Abstinence Syndrome: Preliminary Findings," *American Journal of the Addictions* 13, no. 3 (2004): 248–55; R. A. Rawson, M. D. Anglin, and W. Ling, "Will the Methamphetamine Problem Go Away?" *Journal of Addictive Diseases* 21, no. 1 (2002): 5–19.

20. A. Moszczynska, P. Fitzmaurice, L. Ang, K. S. Kalasinsky, G. A. Schmunk, F. J. Peretti, S. S. Aiken, D. J. Wickham, and S. J. Kish, "Why Is Parkinsonism Not a Feature of Human Methamphetamine Users?" *Brain* 127, no. 2 (2004): 363–70.

21. C. W. Meredith, C. Jaffe, K. Ang-Lee, and A. J. Saxon, "Implications of Chronic Methamphetamine Use: A Literature Review," *Harvard Review of Psychiatry* 13, no. 3 (2005): 141–54.

22. Albertson, Derlet, and Van Hoozen, "Methamphetamine and the Expanding Complications of Amphetamines"; E. A. De Letter, M. H. A. Piette, W. E. Lambert, and J. A. C. M. Cordonnier, "Amphetamines as Potential Inducers of Fatalities: A Review in the District of Ghent from 1976–2004," *Medicine, Science & the Law* 46, no. 1 (January 2006): 37–65; J. C. Kramer, "Introduction to Amphetamine Abuse," *Journal of Psychedelic Drugs* 2, no. 2 (1969): 1–16; J. C. Kramer, "Amphetamine Abuse," in *North American Symposium on Drugs and Drug Abuse,* ed. W. White and R. F. Albando (Philadelphia, PA: North American Publishing Company, 1974), 42–48; E. G. Zalis and L. F. Parmiley, "Fatal Amphetamine Poisoning," *Archives of Internal Medicine* 112 (1963): 822–26.

23. B. K. Logan, C. L. Fligner, and T. Haddix, "Cause and Manner of Death in Fatalities Involving Methamphetamine," *Journal of Forensic Science* 43, no. 1 (1998): 28–34.

24. Beebe and Walley, "Smokable Methamphetamine 'Ice'"; R. W. Derlet, P. Rice, B. Z. Horowitz, and R. V. Lord, "Amphetamine Toxicity: Experience with 127 Cases," *Journal of Emergency Medicine* 7 (1989): 157–61.

25. De Letter et al., "Amphetamines as Potential Inducers of Fatalities"; Callaway and Clark, "Hyperthermia in Psychostimulant Overdose"; H. Kalant and O. J. Kalant, "Death in Amphetamine Users: Causes and Rates," *Canadian Medical Association Journal* 112 (1975): 299–304; T. Kojima, I. Une, J. Noda, K. Sakai, and K. Yamamoto, "A Fatal Methamphetamine Poisoning Associated with Hyperpyrexia," *Forensic Science International* 24 (1984): 87–93.

26. Logan, Fligner, and Haddix, "Cause and Manner of Death in Fatalities Involving Methamphetamine."

27. Kalant and Kalant, "Death in Amphetamine Users."

28. Kramer, "Introduction to Amphetamine Abuse," 4.

29. L. Grinspoon and J. B. Bakalar, "The Amphetamines: Medical Uses and Health Hazards," in *Amphetamine Use, Misuse, and Abuse: Proceedings of the National Amphetamine Conference, 1978,* ed. D. E. Smith, D. R. Wesson, M. E. Buxton, R. B. Seymour, J. T. Ungerleider, J. P. Morgan, A. J. Mandell, and G. Jara (Boston, MA: G.K. Hall & Co, 1979), 18–34.

30. J. C. Kramer, V. S. Fischman, and D. C. Littlefield, "Amphetamine Abuse: Pattern and Effects of High Dose Taken Intravenously," *Journal of the American Medical Association* 201 (1967): 305–309.

31. Ibid.

32. K. M. Grant, S. S. Kelley, S. Agrawal, J. L. Meza, J. R. Meyer, and D. J. Romberger, "Methamphetamine Use in Rural Midwesterners," *American Journal on Addictions* 16, no. 2 (March 2007): 79–84.

33. Cited in Angrist and Gershon, "Psychiatric Sequelae of Amphetamine Abuse."

34. A. N. G. Clark and G. D. Mankikar, "D-Amphetamine in Elderly Patients' Refractory to Rehabilitation Procedures," *Journal of the American Geriatrics Society* 27, no. 4 (1979): 174–77.

35. M. D. Anglin, C. Burke, B. Perrochet, E. Stamper, and S. Dawud-Noursi, "History of the Methamphetamine Problem," *Journal of Psychoactive Drugs* 32, no. 2 (2000): 137–41; A. Baker and N. K. Lee, "A Review of Psychosocial Interventions for Amphetamine Use," *Drug and Alcohol Review* 22 (2003): 323–35; F. J. Couper, M. Pemberton, A. Jarvis, M. Hughes,

and B. K. Logan, "Prevalence of Drug Use in Commercial Tractor-Trailer Drivers," *Journal of Forensic Sciences* 47 (2002): 562–67; C. O. Jackson, "The Amphetamine Democracy: Medicinal Abuse in the Popular Culture," *The South Atlantic Quarterly* 74, no. 3 (1975): 308–23; C. O. Jackson, "The Amphetamine Inhaler: A Case Study of Medical Abuse," in *Amphetamine Use, Misuse, and Abuse: Proceedings of the National Amphetamine Conference, 1978,* ed. D. E. Smith, D. R. Wesson, M. E. Buxton, R. B. Seymour, J. T. Ungerleider, J. P. Morgan, A. J. Mandell, and G. Jara (Boston: G.K. Hall & Co., 1979), 35–45; J. W. Rawlin, "Street Level Abusage of Amphetamines," in *Amphetamine Abuse,* ed. J. R. Russo (Springfield, IL: Charles C. Thomas, 1968), 51–65.

36. Kramer, "Introduction to Amphetamine Abuse"; Kramer, "Amphetamine Abuse."

37. M. Brecht, A. O'Brien, C. von Mayrhauser, and M. D. Anglin, "Methamphetamine Use Behaviors and Gender Differences," *Addictive Behaviors* 29 (2004): 89–106; S. D. Comer, C. L. Hart, A. S. Ward, M. Haney, R. W. Foltin, and M. W. Fishman, "Effects of Repeated Oral Methamphetamine Administration in Humans," *Psychopharmacology* 155 (2001): 397–404.

38. E. H. Ellinwood, "Assault and Homicide Associated with Amphetamine Abuse," *American Journal of Psychiatry* 127 (1971): 1170–75; E. M. Gorman, C. W. Clark, K. R. Nelson, T. Applegate, E. Amato, and A. Scrol, "A Community Social Work Study of Methamphetamine Use Among Women: Implications for Social Work Practice, Education and Research," *Journal of Social Work Practice in the Addictions* 3, no. 3 (2003): 41–62; Kramer, "Amphetamine Abuse"; J. B. Murray, "Psychophysiological Aspects of Amphetamine-Methamphetamine Abuse," *The Journal of Psychology* 132, no. 2 (1998): 227–37; S. Snyder, "A 'Model Schizophrenia' Mediated by Catecholamines," in *Amphetamine Use, Misuse, and Abuse: Proceedings of the National Amphetamine Conference, 1978,* ed. D. E. Smith, D. R. Wesson, M. E. Buxton, R. B. Seymour, J. T. Ungerleider, J. P. Morgan, A. J. Mandell, and G. Jara (Boston: G.K. Hall & Co, 1979), 189–204.

39. M. R. Gossop, B. P. Bradley, and R. K. Brewis, "Amphetamine Withdrawal and Sleep Disturbance," *Drug and Alcohol Dependence* 10 (1982): 177–83.

40. C. Bradley, "The Behavior of Children Receiving Benzedrine," *American Journal of Psychiatry* 94 (1937): 577–85.

41. C. Johanson, K. A. Frey, L. H. Lundahl, P. Keenan, N. Lockhart, J. Roll, G. P. Galloway, R. A. Koeppe, M. R. Kilbourn, T. Robbins, and C. R. Schuster, "Cognitive Function and Nigrostriatal Markers in Abstinent Methamphetamine Abusers," *Psychopharmacology* 185, no. 3 (April 2006): 327–38; R. W. Foltin and S. M. Evans, "Performance Effects of Drugs of Abuse: A Methodological Survey," *Human Psychopharmacology* 8 (1993): 9–19.

42. R. M. Ridley and H. F. Baker, "Stereotypy in Monkeys and Humans," *Psychological Medicine* 12 (1982): 61–72.

43. J. V. Baranski and R. A. Pigeau, "Self-Monitoring Cognitive Performance During Sleep Deprivation: Effects of Modafinil, D-Amphetamine and Placebo," *Journal of Sleep Research* 6 (1997): 84–91.

44. P. M. Thompson, K. M. Hayashi, S. L. Simon, J. A. Geaga, M. S. Hong, Y. Sui, J. Y. Lee, A. W. Toga, W. Ling, and E. D. London, "Structural Abnormalities in the Brains of Human Subjects Who Use Methamphetamine," *The Journal of Neuroscience* 24, no. 26 (2004): 6028–36.

45. B. Weiss, "Enhancement of Performance by Amphetamine-Like Drugs," in *Abuse of Central Stimulants: Symposium Arranged by the Swedish Committee on International Health Relations Stockholm, November 25–27, 1968,* ed. F. Sjöqvist and M. Tottie (Stockholm: Almqvist & Wiksell, 1968), 31–60; S. L. Simon, C. Domier, J. Carnell, P. Brethen, R. Rawson, and W. Ling, "Cognitive Impairment in Individuals Currently Using Methamphetamine," *The American Journal on Addictions* 9, no. 3 (2000): 222–31.

46. S. L. Simon, J. Dacey, S. Glynn, R. Rawson, and W. Ling, "The Effect of Relapse on Cognition in Abstinent Methamphetamine Users," *Journal of Substance Abuse Treatment* 27 (2004): 59–66.

47. J. R. Monterosso, A. R. Aron, X. Cordova, J. Xu, and E. D. London, "Deficits in Response Inhibition Associated with Chronic Methamphetamine Abuse," *Drug and Alcohol Dependence* 79 (2005): 273–77.

48. Meredith et al., "Implications of Chronic Methamphetamine Use."

49. Foltin and Evans, "Performance Effects of Drugs of Abuse."

50. B. Weiss and V. G. Laties, "Enhancement of Human Performance by Caffeine and the Amphetamines," *Pharmacology Review* 14 (March 1962): 1–36.

51. Johanson et al., "Cognitive Function and Nigrostriatal Markers in Abstinent Methamphetamine Abusers."

52. Jackson, "The Amphetamine Democracy."

53. K. G. Low and A. E. Gendaszek, "Illicit Use of Psychostimulants Among College Students: A Preliminary Study," *Psychology, Health & Medicine* 7, no. 3 (2002): 283–87.

54. J. Leo, "Attention Deficit Disorder: Good Science or Good Marketing?" *Skeptic* 8, no. 1 (2000): 63–69.

55. Low and Gendaszek, "Illicit Use of Psychostimulants Among College Students."

56. B. K. Logan, "Methamphetamine and Driving Impairment," *Journal of Forensic Science* 41 (1996): 457–64; Weiss and Laties, "Enhancement of Human Performance by Caffeine and the Amphetamines."

57. P. M. Hurst, "Amphetamines and Driving," *Alcohol, Drugs & Driving* 3, no. 1 (January–March 1987): 13–17.

58. Owen, *No Speed Limit,* 88.

59. Logan, "Methamphetamine and Driving Impairment."

60. Ibid.

61. I. Gustavsen, J. Mørland, and J. G. Bramness, "Impairment Related to Blood Amphetamine and/or Methamphetamine Concentrations in Suspected Drugged Drivers," *Accident Analysis & Prevention* 38, no. 3 (May 2006): 490–95.

62. A. J. Ryan, "Use of Amphetamines in Athletics," *Journal of the American Medical Association* 170, no. 5 (May 30, 1959): 562.

63. P. V. Karpovich, "Effect of Amphetamine Sulfate on Athletic Performance," *Journal of the American Medical Association* 170, no. 5 (May 30, 1959): 558–61.

64. G. M. Smith and H. K. Beecher, "Amphetamine Sulfate and Athletic Performance," *Journal of the American Medical Association* 170, no. 5 (May 30, 1959): 542–57.

65. Ibid., 557.

66. Ryan, "Use of Amphetamines in Athletics."

67. P. Shekelle, M. Hardy, S. C. Morton, M. Maglione, M. Suttorp, E. Roth, L. Jungvig, W. Mojica, J. Gagne, S. Rhodes, and E. McKinnon, *Ephedra and Ephedrine for Weight Loss and Athletic Performance Enhancement: Clinical Efficacy and Side Effects,* Evidence Report/Technology Assessment No. 76, AHRQ Pub. 03–E022 (February 2003).

68. Jackson, "The Amphetamine Democracy"; Grinspoon and Hedblom, *The Speed Culture.*

69. Brecher, *Licit and Illicit Drugs.*

70. S. F. Asnis and R. C. Smith, "Amphetamine Abuse and Violence," *Journal of Psychedelic Drugs* 10, no. 4 (1978): 371–77; R. Cornum, J. Caldwell, and K. Cornum, "Stimulant Use in Extended Flight Operations," *Airpower Journal* 11 (Spring 1997): 53–58.

71. Cornum et al., "Stimulant Use in Extended Flight Operations."

72. J. A. Caldwell, J. L. Caldwell, J. S. Crowley, and H. D. Jones, "Sustaining Helicopter Pilot Performance with Dexedrine During Periods of Sleep Deprivation," *Aviation, Space, and Environmental Medicine* 66 (1995): 930–37; J. A. Caldwell and J. L. Caldwell, "An In-Flight Investigation of the Efficacy of Dextroamphetamine for Sustaining Helicopter Pilot Performance," *Aviation Space and Environmental Medicine* 68, no. 12 (1997): 1073–1080; J. A. Caldwell, J. L. Caldwell, and J. S. Crowley, "Sustaining Female Helicopter Pilot Performance with Dexedrine During Sleep Deprivation," *International Journal of Aviation Psychology* 7, no. 1 (1997): 15–36; J. A. Caldwell, N. K. Smythe, P. A. Leduc, and J. L. Caldwell, "Efficacy of Dexedrine for Maintaining Aviator Performance During 64 Hours of Sustained Wakefulness: A Simulator Study," *Aviation, Space, and Environmental Medicine* 71 (2000): 7–18; D. L. Emonson and R. D. Vanderbeek, "The Use of Amphetamines in U.S. Air Force Tactical Operations During Desert Shield and Storm," *Aviation, Space, and Environmental Medicine* 66, no. 3 (1995): 260–63; Naval Strike and Air Warfare Center, *Performance Maintenance During Continuous Flight Operations: A Guide for Flight Surgeons,* Report Number NAVMED P–6410 (January 1, 2000).

73. S. A. Shappell, D. F. Neri, and C. A. Dejohn, "Simulated Sustained Flight Operations and Performance, Part 2: Effects of Dextro-Methamphetamine," *Military Psychology* 4 (1992): 267–87.

74. Cornum et al., "Stimulant Use in Extended Flight Operations," 55.

75. Ibid., 55.

76. Caldwell and Caldwell, "An In-Flight Investigation of the Efficacy of Dextroamphetamine for Sustaining Helicopter Pilot Performance," 1079.

77. C. L. Hart, A. S. Ward, M. Haney, J. Nasser, and R. W. Foltin, "Methamphetamine Attenuates Disruptions in Performance and Mood During Simulated Night-Shift Work," *Psychopharmacology* 169 (2003): 42–51; C. L. Hart, M. Haney, J. Nasser, and R. W. Foltin, "Combined Effects of Methamphetamine and Zolpidem on Performance and Mood During Simulated Night Shift Work," *Pharmacology Biochemistry and Behavior* 81 (2005): 559–68.

78. T. R. Guilarte, "Is Methamphetamine Abuse a Risk Factor in Parkinsonism?" *Neurotoxicology* 22, no. 6 (2001): 725–31.

79. J. W. Langston and P. Ballard, "Chronic Parkinsonism in Humans Due to a Product of Meperidine-Analog Synthesis," *Science* 219, no. 4587 (1983): 979–80; P. A. Ballard, J. W. Tetrud, and J. W. Langston, "Permanent Human Parkinsonism Due to 1-Methyl-4-Phenyl-1,2,3,6-Tetrahydropyridine (MPTP)," *Neurology* 35 (1985): 949–56.

80. C. M. Tanner, R. Ottman, S. M. Goldman, J. Ellenberg, P. Chan, R. Mayeux, and J. W. Langston, "Parkinson's Disease in Twins: An Etiologic Study," *Journal of the American Medical Association* 281, no. 4 (January 27, 1999): 341–46.

81. M. A. Miller and A. L. Hughes, "Epidemiology of Amphetamine Use in the United States," in *Amphetamine and Its Analogs: Psychopharmacology, Toxicology, and Abuse,* ed. A. K. Cho and D. S. Segal (San Diego, CA: Academic Press, 1994), 439–57.

82. F. K. Goodwin, "Behavioral Effects of L-DOPA in Man," in *Psychiatric Complications of Medical Drugs,* ed. R. I. Shader (New York: Raven Press Publishers, 1972), 149–74; B. M. Angrist and S. Gershon, "Clinical Effects of Amphetamine and L-DOPA on Sexuality and Aggression," *Comprehensive Psychiatry* 17, no. 6 (1976): 715–22.

83. Meredith et al., "Implications of Chronic Methamphetamine Use."

84. S. Mintzer, S. Hickenbottom, and S. Gilman, "Parkinsonism after Taking Ecstasy," *New England Journal of Medicine* 340, no. 18 (1999): 1443.

85. K. Ahmad, "Asia Grapples with Spreading Amphetamine Abuse," *The Lancet* 361 (May 31, 2003): 1878–79; M. Farrell, J. Marsden, R. Ali, and W. Ling, "Methamphetamine: Drug Use and Psychoses Become a Major Public Health Issue in the Asia Pacific Region," *Addiction* 97, no. 7 (2002): 771–72.

86. Snyder, "A 'Model Schizophrenia' Mediated by Catecholamines"; Murray, "Psychophysiological Aspects of Amphetamine-Methamphetamine Abuse."

87. J. van Os, M. Hanssen, R. V. Bijl, and A. Ravelli, "Strauss (1969) Revisited: A Psychosis Continuum in the General Population?" *Schizophrenia Research* 45 (2000): 11–20.

88. M. Srisurapanont, R. Ali, J. Marsden, A. Sunga, K. Wada, and M. Monteiro, "Psychotic Symptoms in Methamphetamine Psychotic In-Patients," *International Journal of Neuropsychopharmacology* 6, no. 4 (2003): 347–52.

89. Ellinwood, "Assault and Homicide Associated with Amphetamine Abuse."

90. P. H. Connell, *Amphetamine Psychosis* (London: Oxford University Press, 1958).

91. D. Young and W. B. Scoville, "Paranoid Psychosis in Narcolepsy and the Possible Danger of Benzedrine Treatment," *Medical Clinics of North America* 22 (1938): 637–46.

92. M. Herman and S. H. Nagler, "Psychoses Due to Amphetamine," *Journal of Nervous and Mental Disease* 120 (1954): 268–72.

93. B. Angrist and S. Gershon, "Amphetamine Abuse in New York City, 1966–1968," *Seminars in Psychiatry* 1 (1969): 195–207.

94. Angrist and Gershon, "Psychiatric Sequelae of Amphetamine Abuse"; J. D. Griffith, J. H. Cavanaugh, and J. A. Oates, "Psychosis Induced by the Administration of D-Amphetamine to Human Volunteers," in *Psychotomimetic Drugs,* ed. D. H. Efron (New York: Raven Press, 1970), 287–94; Connell, *Amphetamine Psychosis.*

95. R. McKetin, J. McLaren, D. I. Lubman, and L. Hides, "The Prevalence of Psychotic Symptoms Among Methamphetamine Users," *Addiction* 101, no. 10 (October 2006): 1473–78.

96. S. Antelman, A. J. Eichler, C. A. Black, and D. Kocan, "Interchangeability of Stress and Amphetamine Sensitization," *Science* 207, no. 18 (1980): 329–31; B. Angrist, "Amphetamine Psychosis: Clinical Variations of the Syndrome," in *Amphetamine and Its Analogs: Psychopharmacology, Toxicology, and Abuse,* ed. A. K. Cho and D. S. Segal (New York: Academic Press, 1994), 387–414.

97. Meredith et al., "Implications of Chronic Methamphetamine Use."

98. C. Chen, S. Lin, P. C. Sham, D. Ball, E. Loh, C. C. Hsiao, Y. L. Chiang, S. C. Ree, C. H. Lee, and R. M. Murray, "Premorbid Characteristics and Comorbidity of Methamphetamine Users with and without Psychosis," *Psychological Medicine* 33 (2003): 1407–14; C. Chen, S. Lin, P. C. Sham, D. Ball, E. Loh, and R. Murray, "Morbid Risk for Psychiatric Disorder Among the Relatives of Methamphetamine Users with and without Psychosis," *American Journal of Medical Genetics, Part B* 136B (2005): 87–91; McKetin et al., "The Prevalence of Psychotic Symptoms Among Methamphetamine Users."

99. P. Beamish and L. G. Kiloh, "Psychosis Due to Amphetamine Consumption," *Journal of Mental Science* 106 (1960): 337–44; Chen et al., "Premorbid Characteristics and Comorbidity of Methamphetamine Users with and without Psychosis"; Chen et al., "Morbid Risk for Psychiatric Disorder Among the Relatives of Methamphetamine Users with and without Psychosis."

100. C. von Mayrhauser, M. Brecht, and M. D. Anglin, "Use Ecology and Drug Use Motivation of Methamphetamine Users Admitted to Substance Abuse Treatment Facilities in Los Angeles: An Emerging Profile," *Journal of Addictive Diseases* 21, no. 1 (2002): 53.

101. E. H. Ellinwood and M. M. Kilbey, "Amphetamine Stereotypy: The Influence of Environmental Factors and Prepotent Behavioural Patterns on Its Topography and Development," *Biological Psychiatry* 10 (1975): 3–16; Ridley and Baker, "Stereotypy in Monkeys and Humans."

102. G. Rylander, "Clinical and Medico-Criminological Aspects of Addiction to Central Nervous System Stimulants," in *Abuse of Central Stimulants: Symposium Arranged by the Swedish Committee on International Health Relations Stockholm, November 25–27, 1968,* ed. F. Sjöqvist and M. Tottie (Stockholm: Almqvist & Wiksell, 1968), 251–74; G. Rylander, "Psychoses and the Punding and Choreiform Syndromes in Addiction to Central Stimulant Drugs," *Folia Psychiatrica, Neurologica Et Neurochirurgica* 75 (1972): 203–12.

103. P. Morgan and J. E. Beck, "The Legacy and the Paradox: Hidden Contexts of Methamphetamine Use in the United States," in *Amphetamine Misuse: International Perspectives on Current Trends,* ed. H. Klee (Amsterdam: Harwood Academic Publishers, 1997), 135–62.

104. A. Randrup and I. Munkvad, "Stereotyped Activities Produced by Amphetamine in Several Animal Species and Man," *Psychopharmacologia* 1 (1967): 300–310.

105. E. H. Ellinwood, A. Sudilovsky, and L. M. Nelson, "Evolving Behavior in the Clinical and Experimental Amphetamine (Model) Psychosis," *American Journal of Psychiatry* 130 (1973): 1088–93.

106. G. V. Rebec and T. R. Bashore, "Some Critical Issues in Assessing the Behavioral Effects of Amphetamine," *Neuroscience and Biobehavioral Reviews* 8 (1984): 153–59.

107. K. Lan, Y. Yin, F. Yu, C. Lin, and P. Chu, "Clinical Manifestations and Prognostic Features of Acute Methamphetamine Intoxication," *Journal of Formosa Medical Association* 97 (1998): 528–33.

108. P. L. Brown, R. A. Wise, and E. A. Kiyatkin, "Brain Hyperthermia Is Induced by Methamphetamine and Exacerbated by Social Interaction," *The Journal of Neuroscience* 23, no. 9 (2003): 3924–29.

109. T. Xie, U. D. McCann, S. Kim, J. Yuan, and G. A. Ricaurte, "Effect of Temperature on Dopamine Transporter Function and Intracellular Accumulation of Methamphetamine: Implications for Methamphetamine-Induced Dopaminergic Neurotoxicity," *The Journal of Neuroscience* 20, no. 20 (October 15, 2000): 7838–45.

110. Brown et al., "Brain Hyperthermia Is Induced by Methamphetamine and Exacerbated by Social Interaction."

111. L. Matuszewich and B. K. Yamamoto, "Chronic Stress Augments the Long-Term and Acute Effects of Methamphetamine," *Neuroscience* 124 (2004): 637–46.

112. M. Duenwald, "Baseball: An Herb Under Scrutiny," *New York Times* (February 19, 2003), http://www.nytimes.com.

113. E. A. Kiyatkin, "Brain Hyperthermia During Physiological and Pathological Conditions: Causes, Mechanisms, and Functional Implications," *Current Neurovascular Research* 1, no. 1 (2004): 77–90.

114. Callaway and Clark, "Hyperthermia in Psychostimulant Overdose."

115. Angrist and Gershon, "Psychiatric Sequelae of Amphetamine Abuse"; Callaway and Clark, "Hyperthermia in Psychostimulant Overdose"; De Letter et al., "Amphetamines as Potential Inducers of Fatalities"; Kalant and Kalant, "Death in Amphetamine Users"; Smets et al., "Amphetamine Toxicity in the Emergency Department"; Lan et al., "Clinical Manifestations and Prognostic Features of Acute Methamphetamine Intoxication."

116. Smets et al., "Amphetamine Toxicity in the Emergency Department."

117. Callaway and Clark, "Hyperthermia in Psychostimulant Overdose"; A. Meeks and R. Stevens, "The Latest Rage: Methamphetamine Abuse," *Resident Staff Physician* 50 (2004): 26–30; M. D. Ginsberg, M. Hertzman, and W. W. Schmidt-Nowara, "Amphetamine Intoxication with Coagulopathy, Hyperthermia, and Reversible Renal Failure," *Annals of Internal Medicine* 73 (1970): 81–85; Lan et al., "Clinical Manifestations and Prognostic Features of Acute Methamphetamine Intoxication."

118. Espelin and Done, "Amphetamine Poisoning"; Meeks and Stevens, "The Latest Rage: Methamphetamine Abuse."

119. Brecht et al., "Methamphetamine Use Behaviors and Gender Differences"; Von Mayrhauser et al., "Use Ecology and Drug Use Motivation of Methamphetamine Users Admitted to Substance Abuse Treatment Facilities in Los Angeles."

120. F. Di Cugno, C. J. Perec, and A. A. Tocci, "Salivary Secretion and Dental Caries Experience in Drug Addicts," *Archives of Oral Biology* 26 (1981): 363–67.

121. Ibid.

122. P. J. Redfearn, N. Agrawal, and L. H. Mair, "An Association Between the Regular Use of 3,4 Methylenedioxy-Methamphetamine (Ecstasy) and Excessive Wear of the Teeth," *Addiction* 93, no. 5 (1998): 745–48; A. J. Duxbury, "Ecstasy—Dental Implications," *British Dental Journal* 175 (1993): 38.

123. Beckett and Roland, "Urinary Excretion Kinetics of Amphetamine in Man"; J. W. Shaner, "Caries Associated with Methamphetamine Abuse," *Journal of the Michigan Dental Association* 84 (September 2002): 42–47; J. W. Shaner, N. Kimmes, T. Saini, and P. Edwards, "'Meth Mouth': Rampant Caries in Methamphetamine Abusers," *AIDS Patient Care & Standards* 20, no. 3 (March 2006): 146–50.

124. J. R. Richards and B. T. Brofeldt, "Patterns of Tooth Wear Associated with Methamphetamine Use," *Journal of Periodontology* 71, no. 8 (August 2000): 1371–74; Di Cugno et al., "Salivary Secretion and Dental Caries Experience in Drug Addicts."

125. Di Cugno et al., "Salivary Secretion and Dental Caries Experience in Drug Addicts."

126. Shaner, "Caries Associated with Methamphetamine Abuse."

127. T. S. Saini, P. C. Edwards, N. S. Kimmes, L. R. Carroll, J. W. Shaner, and F. J. Dowd, "Etiology of Xerostomia and Dental Caries Among Methamphetamine Abusers," *Oral Health and Preventive Dentistry* 3 (2005): 189–95.

128. A. M. Howe, "Methamphetamine and Childhood and Adolescent Caries," *Australian Dental Journal* 40, no. 5 (1995): 340.

129. Richards and Brofeldt, "Patterns of Tooth Wear Associated with Methamphetamine Use."

130. Duxbury, "Ecstasy—Dental Implications."

131. C. McGrath and B. Chan, "Oral Health Sensations Associated with Illicit Drug Abuse," *British Dental Journal* 198, no. 3 (February 12, 2005): 159–62.

132. Redfearn et al., "An Association Between the Regular Use of 3,4 Methylenedioxy-Methamphetamine (Ecstasy) and Excessive Wear of the Teeth."

133. H. Kalant, "The Pharmacology and Toxicology of 'Ecstasy' (MDMA) and Related Drugs," *Canadian Medical Association Journal* 167, no. 7 (2001): 917–28; Redfearn et al., "An Association Between the Regular Use of 3,4 Methylenedioxy-Methamphetamine (Ecstasy) and Excessive Wear of the Teeth"; Shaner et al., "'Meth Mouth.'"

134. Howe, "Methamphetamine and Childhood and Adolescent Caries."

135. T. J. Pallasch and C. E. Joseph, "Oral Manifestations of Drug Abuse," *Journal of Psychoactive Drugs* 19 (1987): 375–77.

136. See, for example, L. A. Assael, "Methamphetamine: An Epidemic of Oral Health Neglect, Loss of Access to Care, Abuse, and Violence," *Journal of Oral and Maxillofacial Surgery* 63, no. 9 (September 2005): 1253–54.

137. J. Schafer, "The Meth-Mouth Myth: Our Latest Moral Panic," *Slate* (August 9, 2005), http://slate.msn.com/id/2124160.

138. Howe, "Methamphetamine and Childhood and Adolescent Caries."

139. S. Kaye, R. McKetin, J. Duflou, and S. Darke, "Methamphetamine and Cardiovascular Pathology: A Review of the Evidence," *Addiction* 102, no. 8 (2007): 1204–11.

140. Kaye et al., "Methamphetamine and Cardiovascular Pathology: A Review of the Evidence"; M. Wijetunga, R. Bahn, J. Lindsay, and S. Karch, "Acute Coronary Syndrome and Crystal Methamphetamine Use: A Case Series," *Hawaii Medical Journal* 63 (2004): 8–13; S. D. Turnipseed, J. R. Richards, J. D. Kirk, D. B. Diercks, and E. A. Amsterdam, "Frequency of Acute Coronary Syndrome in Patients Presenting to the Emergency Department with Chest Pain after Methamphetamine Abuse," *Journal of Emergency Medicine* 24 (2003): 369–73.

141. C. I. Swalwell and G. G. Davis, "Methamphetamine as a Risk Factor for Acute Aortic Dissection," *Journal of Forensic Sciences* 44, no. 1 (January 1999): 23–26; G. G. Davis and C. I. Swalwell, "Acute Aortic Dissections and Ruptured Berry Aneurysm Associated with Methamphetamine Abuse," *Journal of Forensic Sciences* 39 (1994): 1481–85.

142. J. Mendelson, R. T. Jones, R. Upton, and P. Jacob, "Methamphetamine and Ethanol Interactions in Humans," *Clinical Pharmacology and Therapeutics* 57, no. 5 (1995): 559–68; Albertson, Derlet, and Van Hoozen, "Methamphetamine and the Expanding Complications of Amphetamines."

143. Wijetunga et al., "Acute Coronary Syndrome and Crystal Methamphetamine Use."

144. Kaye et al., "Methamphetamine and Cardiovascular Pathology."

145. K. J. Varner, B. A. Ogden, J. Delcarpio, and S. Meleg-Smith, "Cardiovascular Responses Elicited by the 'Binge' Administration of Methamphetamine," *The Journal of Pharmacology and Experimental Therapeutics* 301 (2002): 152–59; K. Yoshida, A. Morimoto, T. Makisumi, and N. Murakami, "Cardiovascular, Thermal and Behavioral Sensitization to Methamphetamine in Freely Moving Rats," *Journal of Pharmacology and Experimental Therapy* 267 (1993): 1538–43.

146. Kaye et al., "Methamphetamine and Cardiovascular Pathology."

147. E. J. Poulsen, M. J. Mannis, and S. D. Chang, "Keratitis in Methamphetamine Abusers," *Cornea* 15, no. 5 (1996): 477–82; R. S. Chuck, J. M. Williams, and M. A. Goldberg, "Recurrent Corneal Ulcerations Associated with Smokable Methamphetamine Abuse," *American Journal of Ophthalmology* 121, no. 5 (1996): 571–72.

148. R. Sachs, B. M. Zagelbaum, and P. S. Hersh, "Corneal Complications Associated with the Use of Crack Cocaine," *Ophthalmology* 100 (1993): 187–91; M. B. Strominger, R. Sachs, and P. S. Hersch, "Microbial Keratitis with Crack Cocaine," *Archives of Ophthalmology* 108 (1990): 1672.

149. Poulsen et al., "Keratitis in Methamphetamine Abusers."

150. C. Derauf, L. L. Lagasse, L. M. Smith, P. Grant, R. Shah, A. Arria, M. Huestis, W. Haning, A. Strauss, S. D. Grotta, J. Liu, and B. M. Lester, "Demographic and Psychosocial Characteristics of Mothers Using Methamphetamine During Pregnancy: Preliminary Results of the Infant Development, Environment, and Lifestyle Study (IDEAL)," *American Journal of Drug & Alcohol Abuse* 33, no. 2 (April 2007): 281–89; L. Billing, M. Eriksson, G. Steneroth, and R. Zetterstrom, "Predictive Indicators for Adjustment in 4-Year-Old Children Whose Mothers Used Amphetamine During Pregnancy," *Child Abuse & Neglect* 12 (1988): 503–507; L. Billing, M. Erikkson, B. Jonsson, B. Steneroth, and R. Zetterstrom, "The Influence of Environmental Factors on Behavioural Problems in 8-Year-Old Children Exposed to Amphetamine During Fetal Life," *Child Abuse & Neglect* 18 (1994): 3–9; L. Cernerud, M. Eriksson, B. Jonsson, G. Steneroth, and R. Zetterstrom, "Amphetamine Addiction During Pregnancy: 14-Year Follow-Up of Growth and School Performance," *Acta Paediratrica* 85 (1996): 204–208; B. M. Lester, A. M. Arria, C. Derauf, P. Grant, L. Lagasse, E. Newman, R. Z. Shah, S. Stewart, and T. Wouldes, "Methamphetamine Exposure: A Rural Early Intervention Challenge," *Zero to Three* 26, no. 4 (March 2006): 30–36; L. Smith, M. L. Yonekura, T. Wallace, N. Berman, J. Kuo, and C. Berkowitz, "Effects of Prenatal Methamphetamine Exposure on Fetal Growth and Drug Withdrawal Symptoms in Infants Born at Term," *Journal of Developmental and Behavioral Pediatrics* 24, no. 1 (2003): 17–23.

151. Mendelson et al., "Methamphetamine and Ethanol Interactions in Humans."

152. M. J. Ellenhorn, S. Schonwald, G. Ordog, and J. Wasserberger, "Amphetamines and Designer Drugs" in *Ellenhorn's Medical Toxicology: Diagnosis and Treatment of Human Poisoning* (Baltimore, MD: Williams & Wilkins, 1997), 340–55.

153. A. S. Oro and S. D. Dixon, "Perinatal Cocaine and Methamphetamine Exposure: Maternal and Neonatal Correlates," *The Journal of Pediatrics* 111, no. 4 (1987): 571–78.

154. Smith et al., "Effects of Prenatal Methamphetamine Exposure on Fetal Growth and Drug Withdrawal Symptoms in Infants Born at Term."

155. Lester et al., "Methamphetamine Exposure."

156.   L. Keith, W. Donald, M. Rosner, M. Mitchell, and J. Bianchi, "Obstetric Aspects of Perinatal Addiction," in *Drug Use in Pregnancy: Mother and Child,* ed. I. J. Chasnoff (Boston: MTP Press Limited, 1986), 23–41.

157.   S. Schnoll, "Pharmacological Basis of Perinatal Addiction," in *Drug Use in Pregnancy: Mother and Child,* ed. I. J. Chasnoff (Boston: MTP Press Limited, 1986), 7–16.

158.   Ibid., 8.

159.   R. A. Weisheit and J. Fuller, "Methamphetamines in the Heartland: A Review and Initial Exploration, *Journal of Crime and Justice* 27, no. 1 (2004): 131–51.

160.   A. K. Cho, "Ice: A New Dosage Form of an Old Drug," *Science* 249 (1990): 631–34.

161.   S. D. Dixon, "Effects of Transplacental Exposure to Cocaine and Methamphetamine in the Neonate," *Western Journal of Medicine* 150 (1989): 436–42.

162.   Schnoll, "Pharmacological Basis of Perinatal Addiction."

163.   Lester et al., "Methamphetamine Exposure," 32.

164.   Billing et al., "Predictive Indicators for Adjustment in 4-Year-Old Children Whose Mothers Used Amphetamine During Pregnancy"; Billing et al., "The Influence of Environmental Factors on Behavioural Problems in 8-Year-Old Children Exposed to Amphetamine During Fetal Life"; Cernerud et al., "Amphetamine Addiction During Pregnancy."

165.   Lester et al., "Methamphetamine Exposure," 35.

166.   M. Brecht and C. von Mayrhauser, "Differences Between Ecstasy-Using and Nonusing Methamphetamine Users," *Journal of Psychoactive Drugs* 34, no. 2 (2002): 215–23.

167.   L. Greenwell and M. Brecht, "Self-Reported Health Status Among Treated Methamphetamine Users," *American Journal of Drug and Alcohol Abuse* 29, no. 1 (2003): 75–104.

168.   Brecht et al., "Methamphetamine Use Behaviors and Gender Differences"; J. Hando and W. Hall, "HIV Risk-Taking Behaviour Among Amphetamine Users in Sydney, Australia," *Addiction* 89, no. 1 (1994): 79–85; Y. Hser, D. Huang, C. Chou, C. Teruya, and M. D. Anglin, "Longitudinal Patterns of Treatment Utilization and Outcomes Among Methamphetamine Abusers: A Growth Curve Modeling Approach," *The Journal of Drug Issues* 33, no. 4 (2003): 921–37; S. M. Strauss and G. P. Falkin, "Women Offenders Who Use and Deal Methamphetamine: Implications for Mandated Drug Treatment," *Women and Criminal Justice* 12, no. 4 (2001): 77–97.

169.   S. Semple, T. L. Patterson, and I. Grant, "The Context of Sexual Risk Behavior Among Heterosexual Methamphetamine Users," *Addictive Behaviors* 29 (2004): 807–10; Thompson et al., "Structural Abnormalities in the Brains of Human Subjects Who Use Methamphetamine."

170.   "Methamphetamine Use, Abuse, and Dependence: 2002, 2003, and 2004," *NSDUH Report* (September 16, 2005).

171.   L. Wu, D. J. Pilowsky, W. M. Wechsberg, and W. E. Schlenger, "Injection Drug Use Among Stimulant Users in a National Sample," *The American Journal of Drug and Alcohol Abuse* 30, no. 1 (2004): 61–83.

172.   W. A. Zule and D. P. Desmond, "An Ethnographic Comparison of HIV Risk Behaviors Among Heroin and Methamphetamine Injectors," *American Journal of Drug and Alcohol Abuse* 25 (1999): 1–23.

173. A. Brinker, A. Mosholder, S. D. Schech, M. Burgess, and M. Avigan, "Indication and Use of Drug Products Used to Treat Attention-Deficit/Hyperactivity Disorder: A Cross-Sectional Study with Inference on the Likelihood of Treatment in Adulthood," *Journal of Child and Adolescent Psychopharmacology* 17, no. 3 (2007): 328–33.

174. Callaway and Clark, "Hyperthermia in Psychostimulant Overdose."

175. Ellenhorn et al., "Amphetamines and Designer Drugs."

176. *Pulse Check: National Trends in Drug Abuse, Summer 1998* (Washington, DC: Office of National Drug Control Policy, 1998).

177. S. H. Kollins, E. K. MacDonald, and C. R. Rush, "Assessing the Abuse Potential of Methylphenidate in Nonhuman and Human Subjects: A Review," *Pharmacology Biochemistry and Behavior* 68, no. 3 (2001): 611–27; C. R. Rush, W. D. Essman, C. A. Simpson, and R. W. Baker, "Reinforcing and Subject-Rated Effects of Methylphenidate and D-Amphetamine in Non-Drug-Abusing Humans," *Journal of Clinical Psychopharmacology* 21, no. 3 (2001): 273–86.

178. Bradley, "The Behavior of Children Receiving Benzedrine."

179. Ibid., 579.

180. Cited in W. R. Bett, "Benzedrine Sulphate in Clinical Medicine: A Survey of the Literature," *Postgraduate Medical Journal* (August 1946): 217.

181. J. O. Cole, "The Amphetamines in Child Psychiatry: A Review," *Seminars in Psychiatry* 1, no. 2 (1969): 175.

182. R. P. Allen, D. Safer, and L. Covi, "Effects of Psychostimulants on Aggression," *The Journal of Nervous and Mental Diseases* 160, no. 2 (1975): 138–45.

183. P. R. Breggin, "Psychostimulants in the Treatment of Children Diagnosed with ADHD: Part 1—Acute Risks and Psychological Effects," *Ethical Human Sciences and Services* 1, no. 1 (1999): 13–34; Leo, "Attention Deficit Disorder."

184. Breggin, "Psychostimulants in the Treatment of Children Diagnosed with ADHD."

185. T. E. Wilens, S. V. Faraone, J. Biederman, and S. Gunawardene, "Does Stimulant Therapy of Attention-Deficit/Hyperactivity Disorder Beget Later Substance Abuse? A Meta-Analytic Review of the Literature," *Pediatrics* 111, no. 1 (January 2003): 179–85.

186. Leo, "Attention Deficit Disorder."

187. J. R. Parr, A. Ward, and S. Inman, "Current Practice in the Management of Attention Deficit Disorder with Hyperactivity (ADHD)," *Child: Care, Health & Development* 29, no. 3 (2003): 215–18.

188. L. M. Robison, D. A. Sclar, T. L. Skaer, and R. S. Galin, "National Trends in the Prevalence of Attention-Deficit/Hyperactivity Disorder and the Prescribing of Methylphenidate Among School-Age Children: 1990–1995," *Clinical Pediatrics* 38, no. 4 (1999): 209–17.

189. International Narcotics Control Board, "Measures to Counter Illicit Manufacture of, Trafficking in and Abuse of Stimulants," summary of a Special Session of the United Nations General Assembly (1998), http://www.incb.org/pdf/e/ga/incb-sti.pdf.

190. G. Harris, "Panel Advises Disclosure of Drugs' Psychotic Effects," *New York Times* (March 23, 2006), http://www.nytimes.com.

191. SAMHSA, "Emergency Department Visits Involving ADHD Stimulant Medications," *The New Dawn Report* 29 (2006): 1–4.

192. S. Nano, "Heart Screening Urged for ADHD Kids," *Chicago Tribune* (April 21, 2008), http://www.chicagotribune.com.

193. J. M. Zito, D. J. Safer, S. dos Reis, J. F. Gardner, M. Boles, and F. Lynch, "Trends in the Prescribing of Psychotropic Medications to Preschoolers," *Journal of the American Medical Association* 283, no. 8 (2000): 1025–30; M. D. Rappley, "Actual Psychotropic Medication Use in Preschool Children," *Infants & Young Children* 19, no. 2 (2006): 154–63; S. H. Kollins and L. Greenhill, "Evidence Base for the Use of Stimulant Medication in Preschool Children with ADHD," *Infants & Young Children* 19, no. 2 (2006): 132–41.

194. L. Greenhill, S. Kollins, H. Abikoff, J. McCracken, M. Riddle, J. Swanson, J. McGrough, S. Wigal, T. Wigal, B. Vitiello, A. Skrobala, K. Posner, J. Ghuman, C. Cunningham, M. Davies, S. Chuang, and T. Cooper, "Efficacy and Safety of Immediate-Release Methylphenidate Treatment for Preschoolers with ADHD," *Journal of the American Academy of Child & Adolescent Psychiatry* 45, no. 11 (2006): 1284–93.

195. J. Swanson, L. Greenhill, T. Wigal, S. Kollins, A. Stehli, M. Davies, S. Chuang, B. Vitiello, A. Skrobala, K. Posner, H. Abikoff, M. Oatis, J. McCracken, J. McGough, M. Riddle, J. Ghuman, C. Cunningham, and S. Wigal, "Stimulant-Related Reductions of Growth Rates in the PATS," *Journal of the American Academy of Child & Adolescent Psychiatry* 45, no. 11 (2006): 1304–13.

196. P. Firestone, L. M. Musten, S. Pisterman, J. Mercer, and S. Bennett, "Short-Term Side Effects of Stimulant Medication Are Increased in Preschool Children with Attention-Deficit/Hyperactivity Disorder: A Double-Blind Placebo-Controlled Study," *Journal of Child and Adolescent Psychopharmacology* 8 (1998): 13–25; T. Wigal, L. Greenhill, S. Chuang, J. McGough, B. Vitiello, A. Skrobala, J. Swanson, S. Wigal, H. Abikoff, S. Kollins, J. McCracken, M. Riddle, K. Posner, J. Ghuman, M. Davies, B. Thorp, and A. Stehli, "Safety and Tolerability of Methylphenidate in Preschool Children with ADHD," *Journal of the American Academy of Child & Adolescent Psychiatry* 45, no. 11 (2006): 1294–1303.

197. For example, see S. E. Nissen, "ADHD Drugs and Cardiovascular Risk," *New England Journal of Medicine* 354 (2006): 1445–48; J. Biederman, T. J. Spencer, T. E. Wilens, J. B. Prince, and S. V. Faraone, "Treatment of ADHD with Stimulant Medications: Response to Nissen Perspective in the *New England Journal of Medicine*," *Journal of the American Academy of Child and Adolescent Psychiatry* 45, no. 10 (2006): 1147–50.

198. Brecht and von Mayrhauser, "Differences Between Ecstasy-Using and Nonusing Methamphetamine Users."

199. D. Nichols, "The Chemistry of MDMA," in Ecstasy: *The Complete Guide,* ed. J. Holland (Rochester, VT: Park Street Press, 2001), 39–53.

200. K. L. R. Jansen and L. Theron, "Ecstasy (MDMA), Methamphetamine, and Date Rape (Drug-Facilitated Sexual Assault): A Consideration of the Issues," *Journal of Psychoactive Drugs* 38, no. 1 (March 2006): 1–12.

201. Ellenhorn et al., "Amphetamines and Designer Drugs."

202. Jansen and Theron, "Ecstasy (MDMA), Methamphetamine, and Date Rape (Drug-Facilitated Sexual Assault)," 7.

203. J. Holland, ed., *Ecstasy: The Complete Guide* (Rochester, VT: Park Street Press, 2001).

204. P. Kalix, "Khat: A Plant with Amphetamine Effects," *Journal of Substance Abuse Treatment* 5, no. 3 (1988): 163–69; P. Kalix, "The Pharmacology of Psychoactive Alkaloids from *Ephedra and Catha,*" *Journal of Ethnopharmacology* 32 (1991): 201–208.

205. Kalix, "Khat: A Plant with Amphetamine Effects."

206. J. Zelger, H. Schorno, and E. Carlini, "Behavioural Effects of Cathinone, an Amine Obtained from *Catha Edulis:* Comparisons with Amphetamine, Norpseudoephedrine, Apomorphine, and Nomifensine," *Bulletin on Narcotics* 32 (1980): 67–81; C. Pantelis, C. Hindler, and J. Taylor, "Use and Abuse of Khat: Distribution, Pharmacology, Side Effects, and Description of Psychosis Attributed to Khat Chewing," *Psychological Medicine* 19 (1989): 657–68; Kalix, "The Pharmacology of Psychoactive Alkaloids from *Ephedra and Catha.*"

207. Kalix, "Khat: A Plant with Amphetamine Effects."

208. "44 Arrested in 6 States in Suspected Drug Ring," *New York Times* (July 27, 2006), http://www.nytimes.com.

209. R. A. Glennon, R. Young, B. R. Martin, and T. A. Dalcason, "Methcathinone ('Cat'): An Enantiomeric Potency Comparison," *Pharmacology Biochemistry and Behavior* 50, no. 4 (1995): 601–606.

210. H. Belhadj-Tahar and N. Sadeg, "Methcathinone: A New Postindustrial Drug," *Forensic Science International* 153 (2005): 99–101.

211. Hart et al., "Methamphetamine Attenuates Disruptions in Performance and Mood During Simulated Night-Shift Work"; Hart et al., "Combined Effects of Methamphetamine and Zolpidem on Performance and Mood During Simulated Night Shift Work."

212. Logan, "Methamphetamine and Driving Impairment."

213. M. Perez-Reyes, W. R. White, S. A. McDonald, R. E. Hicks, A. R. Jeffcoat, J. M. Hill, and C. E. Cook, "Clinical Effects of Daily Methamphetamine Administration," *Clinical Neuropharmacology* 14, no. 4 (1991): 352–58.

214. Meredith et al., "Implications of Chronic Methamphetamine Use."

215. G. C. Wagner, G. A. Ricaurte, L. S. Seiden, C. R. Schuster, R. J. Miller, and J. Westley, "Long-Lasting Depletion of Striatal Dopamine and Loss of Dopamine Uptake Sites Following Repeated Administration of Methamphetamine," *Brain Research* 181 (1980): 151–60.

216. Ibid.

217. Thompson et al., "Structural Abnormalities in the Brains of Human Subjects Who Use Methamphetamine."

218. Simon et al., "The Effect of Relapse on Cognition in Abstinent Methamphetamine Users."

219. S. Simon, K. Richardson, J. Dacey, S. Glynn, C. P. Domier, R. A. Rawson, and W. Ling, "A Comparison of Patterns of Methamphetamine and Cocaine Use," *Journal of Addictive Diseases* 21, no. 1 (2002): 35–44; T. Ernst, L. Chang, M. Leonido-Yee, and O. Speck, "Evidence for Long-Term Neurotoxicity Associated with Methamphetamine Abuse," *Neurology* 54 (2000): 1344–49; C. L. Hart, A. S. Ward, M. Haney, R. W. Foltin, and M. W. Fischman, "Methamphetamine Self-Administration by Humans," *Psychopharmacology* 157 (2001): 75–81.

220. J. R. Richards, S. W. Bretz, E. B. Johnson, S. D. Turnipseed, B. T. Brofeldt, and R. W. Derlet, "Methamphetamine Abuse and Emergency Department Utilization," *Western Journal of Medicine* 170 (1999): 198–202; H. Sekine, S. Nagao, H. Kuribara, and Y. Nakahara, "Behavioral Effects of N-Cyanomethylmethamphetamine, a Product Derived from Smoking Methamphetamine with Tobacco, in Mice and Rats," *Pharmacology Biochemistry and Behavior* 57 (1997): 167–72.

221. D. Waldorf, C. Reinarman, and S. Murphy, *Cocaine Changes: The Experiences of Using and Quitting* (Philadelphia: Temple University Press, 1991).

Chapter 4

1. P. Goldstein, "The Drugs/Violence Nexus: A Tripartite Conceptual Framework," *Journal of Drug Issues* 15 (1985): 493–506.

2. W. L. White, "Substance Use and Violence: Understanding the Nuances of the Relationship," *Addiction Professional* 2, no. 1 (2004): 13–19.

3. S. Fukui, K. Wada, and M. Iyo, "Epidemiology of Amphetamine Abuse in Japan and Its Social Implications," in *Amphetamine and Its Analogs: Psychopharmacology, Toxicology, and Abuse,* ed. A. K. Cho and D. S. Segal (San Diego, CA: Academic Press, 1994), 459–78; H. Brill and T. Hirose, "The Rise and Fall of a Methamphetamine Epidemic: Japan 1945-55," *Seminars in Psychiatry* 1 (1969): 179–94.

4. C. O. Jackson, "The Amphetamine Democracy: Medicinal Abuse in the Popular Culture," *The South Atlantic Quarterly* 74, no. 3 (1975): 308–23.

5. J. C. Kramer, V. S. Fischman, and D. C. Littlefield, "Amphetamine Abuse: Pattern and Effects of High Dose Taken Intravenously," *Journal of the American Medical Association* 201 (1967): 305–309; R. C. Smith, "The World of the Haight-Ashbury Speed Freak," *Journal of Psychedelic Drugs* 2 (1969): 172–88.

6. R. H. Blum, "Drugs and Violence," in *Crimes of Violence,* vol. 13, A Staff Report to the National Commission on the Causes and Prevention of Violence (Washington, DC: U.S. Government Printing Office, 1969), 1489.

7. I. Sommers and D. Baskin, *The Social Consequences of Methamphetamine Use* (Lewiston, NY: The Edwin Mellen Press, 2004); A. Baskin-Sommers and I. Sommers, "The Co-occurrence of Substance Use and High-Risk Behaviors," *Journal of Adolescent Health* 38, no. 5 (May 2006): 609–11.

8. J. Cartier, D. Farabee, and M. L. Prendergast, "Methamphetamine Use, Self-Reported Violent Crime, and Recidivism Among Offenders in California Who Abuse Substances," *Journal of Interpersonal Violence* 21, no. 4 (April 2006): 435–45.

9. E. H. Ellinwood, "Assault and Homicide Associated with Amphetamine Abuse," *American Journal of Psychiatry* 127 (1971): 1170–75; E. H. Ellinwood, "The Epidemiology of Stimulant Abuse," in *Drug Use: Epidemiological and Sociological Approaches,* ed. E. Josephson and E. E. Carroll (Washington, DC: Hemisphere Publishing Corporation, 1974), 303–29.

10. D. S. Bell, "The Experimental Reproduction of Amphetamine Psychosis," *Archives of General Psychiatry* 29 (1973): 35–40; D. Bell and W. Trethowan, "Amphetamine Addiction and Disturbed Sexuality," *Archives of General Psychiatry* 4 (1961): 74–78.

11. S. Asnis and R. C. Smith, "Amphetamine Abuse and Violence," in *Amphetamine Use, Misuse, and Abuse: Proceedings of the National Amphetamine Conference, 1978,* ed. D. E. Smith, D. R. Wesson, M. E. Buxton, R. B. Seymour, J. T. Ungerleider, J. P. Morgan, A. J. Mandell, and G. Jara (Boston: G.K. Hall & Co., 1979), 213.

12. Sommers and Baskin, *The Social Consequences of Methamphetamine Use.*

13. Ibid.

14. B. Link and A. Stueve, "Psychotic Symptoms and the Violent/Illegal Behavior of Mental Patients Compared to Community Controls," in *Violence and Mental Disorder*, ed. J. Monahan and H. Steadman (Chicago: University of Chicago Press, 1998), 137–60.

15. E. H. Ellinwood, "Amphetamine Psychosis I: Description of the Individuals and Processes," *Journal of Nervous and Mental Disease* 144 (1967): 277.

16. E. H. Ellinwood, "Amphetamine Psychosis II," *Journal of Neuropsychiatry* 4 (1968): 47.

17. B. Angrist and S. Gershon, "Amphetamine Abuse in New York City, 1966–1968," *Seminars in Psychiatry* 1 (1969): 195–207; Smith, "The World of the Haight-Ashbury Speed Freak."

18. C. Dobkin and N. Nicosia, "The War on Drugs: Methamphetamine, Public Health, and Crime" (June 18, 2008), http://people.ucsc.edu/~cdobkin/Papers/Methamphetamine.pdf.

19. R. A. Weisheit and J. Fuller, "Methamphetamines in the Heartland: A Review and Initial Exploration," *Journal of Crime and Justice* 27, no. 1 (2004): 131–51.

20. C. von Mayrhauser, M. Brecht, and M. D. Anglin, "Use Ecology and Drug Use Motivation of Methamphetamine Users Admitted to Substance Abuse Treatment Facilities in Los Angeles: An Emerging Profile," *Journal of Addictive Diseases* 21, no. 1 (2002): 45–60.

21. G. Rylander, "Clinical and Medico-Criminological Aspects of Addiction to Central Nervous System Stimulants," in *Abuse of Central Stimulants: Symposium Arranged by the Swedish Committee on International Health Relations Stockholm, November 25–27, 1968*, ed. F. Sjöqvist and M. Tottie (Stockholm: Almqvist & Wiksell, 1968), 251–74.

22. Asnis and Smith, "Amphetamine Abuse and Violence" in *Amphetamine Use, Misuse, and Abuse.*

23. B. M. Angrist and S. Gershon, "Psychiatric Sequelae of Amphetamine Abuse," in *Psychiatric Complications of Medical Drugs*, ed. R. I. Shader (New York: Raven Press Publishers, 1972), 175–99.

24. H. Klee, "HIV Risks for Women Drug Injectors: Heroin and Amphetamine Users Compared," *Addiction* 88, no. 8 (1993): 1055–62.

25. J. J. Collins, ed., *Drinking and Crime: Perspectives on the Relationships Between Alcohol Consumption and Criminal Behavior* (New York: The Guilford Press, 1981); R. Parker, "Bringing 'Booze' Back In: The Relationship Between Alcohol and Homicide," *Journal of Research in Crime and Delinquency* 32 (1995): 3–38; R. Parker and K. Auerhahn, "Alcohol, Drugs and Violence," *Annual Review of Sociology* 24 (1998): 291–311; P. N. S. Hoaken and S. H. Stewart, "Drugs of Abuse and the Elicitation of Human Aggressive Behavior," *Addictive Behaviors* 28 (2003): 1533–54; Blum, "Drugs and Violence."

26. S. S. Bull, P. Piper, and C. Rietmeijer, "Men Who Have Sex with Men and Also Inject Drugs—Profiles of Risk Related to the Synergy of Sex and Drug Injection Behaviors," *Journal of Homosexuality* 42, no. 3 (2002): 31–51; M. Cretzmeyer, M. V. Sarrazin, D. L. Huber, R. I. Block, and J. A. Hall, "Treatment of Methamphetamine Abuse: Research Findings and Clinical Directions," *Journal of Substance Abuse Treatment* 24 (2003): 267–77; Klee, "HIV Risks for Women Drug Injectors"; S. J. Semple, I. Grant, and T. L. Patterson, "Female Methamphetamine Users: Social Characteristics and Sexual Risk Behavior," *Women & Health* 40, no. 3 (2004): 35–50; S. Simon, K. Richardson, J. Dacey, S. Glynn, C. P. Domier, R. A. Rawson, and W. Ling, "A Comparison of Patterns of Methamphetamine and Cocaine Use," *Journal of Addictive Diseases* 21, no. 1 (2002): 35–44.

27. Angrist and Gershon, "Psychiatric Sequelae of Amphetamine Abuse," 187.

28. S. Wright and H. Klee, "Violent Crime, Aggression and Amphetamine: What Are the Implications for Treatment Services?" *Drugs: Education, Prevention Policy* 8, no. 1 (2001): 73–90.

29. A. N. G. Clark and G. D. Mankikar, "D-Amphetamine in Elderly Patients' Refractory to Rehabilitation Procedures," *Journal of the American Geriatrics Society* 27, no. 4 (1979): 174–77.

30. Sommers and Baskin, *The Social Consequences of Methamphetamine Use.*

31. W. Hall and J. Hando, "Route of Administration and Adverse Effects of Amphetamine Use Among Young Adults in Sydney, Australia," *Drug and Alcohol Review* 13 (1994): 277–84.

32. Cartier et al., "Methamphetamine Use, Self-Reported Violent Crime, and Recidivism Among Offenders in California Who Abuse Substances."

33. R. W. Derlet, P. Rice, B. Z. Horowitz, and R. V. Lord, "Amphetamine Toxicity: Experience with 127 Cases," *Journal of Emergency Medicine* 7 (1989): 157–61.

34. S. B. Karch, B. G. Stevens, and C. Ho, "Methamphetamine-Related Deaths in San Francisco: Demographic, Pathologic and Toxicologic Profiles," *Journal of Forensic Sciences* 44, no. 2 (March 1999): 359–68; H. Kalant and O. J. Kalant, "Death in Amphetamine Users: Causes and Rates," *Canadian Medical Association Journal* 112 (1975): 299–304.

35. D. N. Bailey and R. G. Shaw, "Cocaine- and Methamphetamine-Related Deaths in San Diego County (1987): Homicides and Accidental Overdoses," *Journal of Forensic Sciences* 34, no. 2 (1989): 407–22.

36. B. K. Logan, C. L. Fligner, and T. Haddix, "Cause and Manner of Death in Fatalities Involving Methamphetamine," *Journal of Forensic Science* 43, no. 1 (1998): 28–34.

37. P. W. Vik and T. Ross, "Methamphetamine Use Among Incarcerated Women," *Journal of Substance Use* 8, no. 2 (2003): 69–77.

38. J. B. Cohen, A. Dickow, K. Horner, J. E. Zweben, J. Balabis, D. Vandersloot, and C. Reiber, "Abuse and Violence History of Men and Women in Treatment for Methamphetamine Dependence," *The American Journal on Addictions* 12 (2003): 377–85.

39. K. L. R. Jansen and L. Theron, "Ecstasy (MDMA), Methamphetamine, and Date Rape (Drug-Facilitated Sexual Assault): A Consideration of the Issues," *Journal of Psychoactive Drugs* 38, no. 1 (March 2006): 9

40. R. P. Allen, D. Safer, and L. Covi, "Effects of Psychostimulants on Aggression," *The Journal of Nervous and Mental Diseases* 160, no. 2 (1975): 138–45.

41. K. Miczek and J. W. Tidey, "Amphetamines: Aggressive and Social Behavior," in *Pharmacology and Toxicology of Amphetamine and Related Designer Drugs,* ed. K. Asghar and E. De Souza, NIDA Research Monograph Series 94 (1989), 68–100.

42. A. Randrup and I. Munkvad, "Stereotyped Activities Produced by Amphetamine in Several Animal Species and Man," *Psychopharmacologia* 1 (1967): 300–310.

43. R. M. Ridley and H. F. Baker, "Stereotypy in Monkeys and Humans," *Psychological Medicine* 12 (1982): 61–72.

44. Baskin-Sommers and Sommers, "The Co-occurrence of Substance Use and High-Risk Behaviors"; A. Baskin-Sommers and I. Sommers, "Methamphetamine Use and Violence Among Young Adults," *Journal of Criminal Justice* 34 (2006): 661–74; A. H. Brown, C. P. Domier, and R. A. Rawson, "Stimulants, Sex, and Gender," *Sexual Addiction & Compulsivity* 12, no. 2–3 (2005): 169–80; J. A. Brown and M. Hohman, "The Impact of Methamphetamine on Parenting," *Journal of Social Work Practice in the Addictions* 6, no. 1–2 (2006): 63–88; Cohen et al., "Abuse and Violence History of Men and Women in Treatment for Methamphetamine Dependence"; K. Joe, "Ice Is Strong Enough for a Man, but Made for a Woman: A Social Cultural Analysis of Crystal Methamphetamine Use Among Asian Pacific Americans," *Crime, Law and Social Change* 22, no. 3 (1995): 269–89; S. Magura and A. B. Laudet, "Parental Substance Abuse and Child Maltreatment: Review and Implications for Intervention," *Children and Youth Services Review* 3 (1996): 193–220; I. Sommers and D. Baskin, "Methamphetamine Use and Violence," *Journal of Drug Issues* 36, no. 1 (Winter 2006): 77–96; L. Wermuth, "Methamphetamine Use: Hazards and Social Influences," *Journal of Drug Education* 30, no. 4 (2000): 423–33.

45. K. A. Joe, "The Lives and Times of Asian-Pacific American Women Drug Users: An Ethnographic Study of Their Methamphetamine Use," *Journal of Drug Issues* 26, no. 1 (1996): 199–218; Brown and Hohman, "The Impact of Methamphetamine on Parenting"; T. E. Freese, J. Obert, A. Dickow, J. Cohen, and R. H. Lord, "Methamphetamine Abuse: Issues for Special Populations," *Journal of Psychoactive Drugs* 32, no. 2 (2000): 177–82.

46. P. Morgan and J. E. Beck, "The Legacy and the Paradox: Hidden Contexts of Methamphetamine Use in the United States," in *Amphetamine Misuse: International Perspectives on Current Trends,* ed. H. Klee (Amsterdam: Harwood Academic Publishers, 1997), 135–62.

47. Joe, "Ice Is Strong Enough for a Man, but Made for a Woman"; W. Haight, T. Jacobsen, J. Black, L. Kingery, K. Sheridan, and C. Mulder, "'In These Bleak Days': Parent Methamphetamine Abuse and Child Welfare in the Rural Midwest," *Children and Youth Services Review* 27 (2005): 949–71; W. Haight, T. Ostler, J. Black, K. Sheridan, and L. Kingery, "A Child's-Eye View of Parent Methamphetamine Abuse: Implications for Helping Foster Families to Succeed," *Children and Youth Services Review* 29, no. 1 (2007): 1–15; M. Brecht, A. O'Brien, C. von Mayrhauser, and M. D. Anglin, "Methamphetamine Use Behaviors and Gender Differences," *Addictive Behaviors* 29 (2004): 89–106.

48. C. E. Grella, Y. Hser, and Y. Huang, "Mothers in Substance Abuse Treatment: Differences in Characteristics Based on Involvement with Child Welfare Services," *Child Abuse & Neglect* 30, no. 1 (2006): 55–73.

49. Magura and Laudet, "Parental Substance Abuse and Child Maltreatment"; Parker and Auerhahn, "Alcohol, Drugs and Violence."

50. Freese et al., "Methamphetamine Abuse."

51. Baskin-Sommers and Sommers, "Methamphetamine Use and Violence Among Young Adults," 669.

52. Wermuth, "Methamphetamine Use"; E. M. Gorman, C. W. Clark, K. R. Nelson, T. Applegate, E. Amato, and A. Scrol, "A Community Social Work Study of Methamphetamine Use Among Women: Implications for Social Work Practice, Education and Research," *Journal of Social Work Practice in the Addictions* 3, no. 3 (2003): 41–62.

53. J. T. Carey and J. Mandel, "A San Francisco Bay Area 'Speed' Scene," *Journal of Health and Social Behavior* 9, no. 2 (1968): 170.

54. Brown and Hohman, "The Impact of Methamphetamine on Parenting."

55. L. Billing, M. Erikkson, B. Jonsson, B. Steneroth, and R. Zetterstrom, "The Influence of Environmental Factors on Behavioural Problems in 8-Year-Old Children Exposed to Amphetamine During Fetal Life," *Child Abuse & Neglect* 18 (1994): 3–9.

56. L. Smith, M. L. Yonekura, T. Wallace, N. Berman, J. Kuo, and C. Berkowitz, "Effects of Prenatal Methamphetamine Exposure on Fetal Growth and Drug Withdrawal Symptoms in Infants Born at Term," *Journal of Developmental and Behavioral Pediatrics* 24, no. 1 (2003): 17–23.

57. Haight et al., "A Child's-Eye View of Parent Methamphetamine Abuse."

58. Ibid., 6.

59. Ibid., 8.

60. Weisheit and Fuller, "Methamphetamines in the Heartland."

61. R. A. Weisheit, D. N. Falcone, and L. E. Wells, *Crime and Policing in Rural and Small-Town America,* 3rd ed. (Long Grove, IL: Waveland Press, 2006).

62. N. Websdale, *Rural Woman Battering and the Justice System* (Thousand Oaks, CA: Sage, 1998).

63. National Association of Counties, "The Criminal Effect of Meth on Communities" and "The Impact of Meth on Children," *The Meth Epidemic in America, Two Surveys of U.S. Counties* (July 5, 2005), 1–12.

64. Ibid.

65. Dobkin and Nicosia, "The War on Drugs."

66. J. C. Ball, L. Rosen, J. A. Flueck, and D. N. Nurco, "The Criminality of Heroin Addicts: When Addicted and When Off Opiates," in *The Drugs-Crime Connection,* ed. J. A. Inciardi (Beverly Hills, CA: Sage, 1981), 39–65; M. D. Anglin and F. Speckart, "Narcotics Use and Crime: A Multi Sample, Multi Method Analysis," *Criminology* 26 (1988): 197–233.

67. F. H. Gawin, "Drugs and Eros: Reflections on Aphrodisiacs," *Journal of Psychedelic Drugs* 10, no. 3 (1978): 227–36.

68. Rylander, "Clinical and Medico-Criminological Aspects of Addiction to Central Nervous System Stimulants."

69. R. A. Rawson, A. Washton, C. P. Domier, and C. Reiber, "Drugs and Sexual Effects: Role of Drug Type and Gender," *Journal of Substance Abuse Treatment* 22 (2002): 103–108; Gorman et al., "A Community Social Work Study of Methamphetamine Use Among Women"; Klee, "HIV Risks for Women Drug Injectors"; H. Klee, "Sexual Risk Among Amphetamine Misusers: Prospects for Change," in *AIDS: Rights, Risk and Reason,* ed. P. Aggleton, P. Davies, and G. Hart (London: The Falmer Press, 1992), 77–84.

70. Klee, "Sexual Risk Among Amphetamine Misusers"; Bell and Trethowan, "Amphetamine Addiction and Disturbed Sexuality."

71. Gawin, "Drugs and Eros."

72. G. R. Gay and D. W. Sheppard, "Sex in the 'Drug Culture,'" *Medical Aspects of Human Sexuality* 6, no. 10 (1972): 28–47; A. J. Schilder, T. M. Lampinen, M. L. Miller, and R. S. Hogg, "Crystal Methamphetamine and Ecstasy Differ in Their Relation to Unsafe Sex Among Young Gay Men," *Canadian Journal of Public Health* 96, no. 5 (September-October 2005): 340–43.

73. Gawin, "Drugs and Eros"; Gay and Sheppard, "Sex in the 'Drug Culture.'"

74. Cited in T. Lyons, G. Chandra, and J. Goldstein, "Stimulant Use and HIV Risk Behavior: The Influence of Peer Support Group Participation," *AIDS Education and Prevention* 18, no. 5 (2006): 468.

75. S. P. Kurtz, "Post-Circuit Blues: Motivations and Consequences of Crystal Meth Use Among Gay Men in Miami," *AIDS and Behavior* 9, no. 1 (2005): 63–72.

76. K. C. Brouwer, P. Case, R. Ramos, C. Magis-Rodriguez, J. Bucardo, T. L. Patterson, and S. A. Strathdee, "Trends in Production, Trafficking, and Consumption of Methamphetamine and Cocaine in Mexico," *Substance Use and Misuse* 41, no. 5 (May 2006): 707–27; M. C. Clatts, L. A. Goldsamt, and H. Yi, "Club Drug Use Among Young Men Who Have Sex with Men in NYC: A Preliminary Epidemiological Profile," *Substance Use & Misuse* 40 (2005): 1317–30; Angrist and Gershon, "Amphetamine Abuse in New York City, 1966–1968"; Brecht et al., "Methamphetamine Use Behaviors and Gender Differences"; P. N. Halkitis, M. T. Shrem, and F. W. Martin, "Sexual Behavior Patterns of Methamphetamine-Using Gay and Bisexual Men," *Substance Use & Misuse* 40, no. 5 (2005): 703–19; C. J. Reback and C. E. Grella, "HIV Risk Behaviors of Gay and Bisexual Male Methamphetamine Users Contacted Through Street Outreach," *Journal of Drug Issues* 29, no. 1 (1999): 155–66.

77. Haight et al., "A Child's-Eye View of Parent Methamphetamine Abuse."

78. M. Brecht and C. von Mayrhauser, "Differences Between Ecstasy-Using and Nonusing Methamphetamine Users," *Journal of Psychoactive Drugs* 34, no. 2 (2002): 215–23.

79. Cited in E. M. Gorman, B. Barr, A. Hansen, B. Robertson, and C. Green, "Speed, Sex, Gay Men, and HIV: Ecological and Community Perspectives," *Medical Anthropology Quarterly* 11, no. 4 (1997): 505.

80. Angrist and Gershon, "Amphetamine Abuse in New York City, 1966–1968"; J. R. Guss, "Sex Like You Can't Even Imagine: 'Crystal,' Crack and Gay Men," in *Addictions in the Gay and Lesbian Community,* ed. J. R. Guss and J. Drescher (New York: The Haworth Press, 2000), 105–22.

81. Morgan and Beck, "The Legacy and the Paradox"; J. Hando and W. Hall, "HIV Risk-Taking Behaviour Among Amphetamine Users in Sydney, Australia," *Addiction* 89, no. 1 (1994): 79–85.

82. D. Frosch, S. Shoptaw, A. Huber, R. A. Rawson, and W. Ling, "Sexual HIV Risk Among Gay and Bisexual Male Methamphetamine Abusers," *Journal of Substance Abuse Treatment* 13, no. 6 (1996): 483–86; Guss, "Sex Like You Can't Even Imagine."

83. P. N. Halkitis, J. T. Parsons, and L. Wilton, "An Exploratory Study of Contextual and Situational Factors Related to Methamphetamine Use Among Gay and Bisexual Men in New York City," *Journal of Drug Issues* 33 (2003): 413–32; Schilder et al., "Crystal Methamphetamine and Ecstasy Differ in Their Relation to Unsafe Sex Among Young Gay Men."

84. S. J. Semple, J. Zians, I. Grant, and T. L. Patterson, "Sexual Compulsivity in a Sample of HIV-Positive Methamphetamine-Using Gay and Bisexual Men," *AIDS and Behavior* 10, no. 5 (September 2006): 587–98; C. J. Reback, S. Larkins, and S. Shoptaw, "Changes in the Meaning of Sexual Risk Behaviors Among Gay and Bisexual Male Methamphetamine Abusers Before and After Drug Treatment," *AIDS and Behavior* 8, no. 1 (2004): 87–98.

85. Frosch et al., "Sexual HIV Risk Among Gay and Bisexual Male Methamphetamine Abusers"; Gay and Sheppard, "Sex in the 'Drug Culture.'"

86. Brown and Hohman, "The Impact of Methamphetamine on Parenting."

87. Ellinwood, "Amphetamine Psychosis I"; Ellinwood, "Amphetamine Psychosis II"; E. H. Ellinwood, "Amphetamine Psychosis: A Multidimensional Process," *Seminars in Psychiatry* 1, no. 2 (1969): 208–26.

88. Gay and Sheppard, "Sex in the 'Drug Culture'"; D. Farabee, M. Prendergast, and J. Cartier, "Methamphetamine Use and HIV Risk Among Substance-Abusing Offenders in California," *Journal of Psychoactive Drugs* 34, no. 3 (2002): 295–300.

89. R. D. Chessick, "The 'Pharmacogenic Orgasm' in the Drug Addict," *Archives of General Psychiatry* 3 (November 1960): 117–28.

90. Gay and Sheppard, "Sex in the 'Drug Culture.'"

91. Gorman et al., "A Community Social Work Study of Methamphetamine Use Among Women"; M. Gorman, "A Tale of Two Epidemics: HIV and Stimulant Use," *Focus* 13, no. 4 (1998): 1–3.

92. K. Kall and A. Nilsonne, "Preference for Sex on Amphetamines: A Marker for HIV Risk Behaviour Among Male Intravenous Amphetamine Users in Stockholm," *AIDS Care* 7, no. 2 (1995): 171–88.

93. Gawin, "Drugs and Eros"; Angrist and Gershon, "Amphetamine Abuse in New York City, 1966–1968."

94. Brown, Domier, and Rawson, "Stimulants, Sex, and Gender."

95. Gorman et al., "A Community Social Work Study of Methamphetamine Use Among Women"; Joe, "The Lives and Times of Asian-Pacific American Women Drug Users."

96. Brown, Domier, and Rawson, "Stimulants, Sex, and Gender."

97. B. M. Angrist and S. Gershon, "Clinical Effects of Amphetamine and L-DOPA on Sexuality and Aggression," *Comprehensive Psychiatry* 17, no. 6 (1976): 715–22.

98. Gay and Sheppard, "Sex in the 'Drug Culture'"; Baskin-Sommers and Sommers, "The Co-occurrence of Substance Use and High-Risk Behaviors"; Klee, "HIV Risks for Women Drug Injectors."

99. Gay and Sheppard, "Sex in the 'Drug Culture.'"

100. A. L. Copeland and J. L. Sorensen, "Differences Between Methamphetamine Users and Cocaine Users in Treatment," *Drug and Alcohol Dependence* 62 (2001): 91–95; Farabee, Prendergast, and Cartier, "Methamphetamine Use and HIV Risk Among Substance-Abusing Offenders in California"; Gorman, "A Tale of Two Epidemics."

101. C. Breen, L. Degenhardt, S. Kinner, R. Bruno, R. Jenkinson, A. Matthews, and J. Newman, "Alcohol Use and Risk Taking Among Regular Ecstasy Users," *Substance Use & Misuse* 41, no. 8 (2006): 1095–1109.

102. Klee, "HIV Risks for Women Drug Injectors."

103. Bull, Piper, and Rietmeijer, "Men Who Have Sex with Men and Also Inject Drugs"; Clatts, Goldsamt, and Yi, "Club Drug Use Among Young Men Who Have Sex with Men in NYC"; Farabee, Prendergast, and Cartier, "Methamphetamine Use and HIV Risk Among Substance-Abusing Offenders in California"; Freese et al., "Methamphetamine Abuse"; Frosch et al., "Sexual HIV Risk Among Gay and Bisexual Male Methamphetamine Abusers"; E. M. Gorman and R. T. Carroll, "Substance Abuse and HIV: Considerations with Regard to Methamphetamines and Other Recreational Drugs for Nursing Practice and Research," *Journal of the Association of Nurses in AIDS Care* 11, no. 2 (2000): 51–62; Halkitis, Parsons, and Wilton, "An Exploratory Study of Contextual and Situational Factors Related to Methamphetamine Use Among Gay and Bisexual Men in New York City"; P. N. Halkitis, B. N. Fischgrund, and J. T. Parsons, "Explanations for Methamphetamine Use Among Gay and Bisexual Men in New York City," *Substance Use & Misuse* 40 (2005): 1331–45; F. Molitor, S. R. Truax, J. D. Ruiz, and R. K. Sun, "Association of Methamphetamine Use During Sex with Risky Sexual Behaviors and HIV Infection Among Non-Injection Drug Users," *Western Journal of Medicine* 168, no. 2 (1998): 93–97; F. Molitor, J. D. Ruiz, N. Flynn, J. Mikanda, R. K. Sun, and R. Anderson, "Methamphetamine Use and Sexual and Injection Risk Behaviors Among Out-of-Treatment Injection Drug Users," *American Journal of Drug and Alcohol Abuse* 25, no. 3 (1999): 475–93; Reback and Grella, "HIV Risk Behaviors of Gay and Bisexual Male Methamphetamine Users Contacted Through Street Outreach"; S. Semple, T. L. Patterson, and I. Grant, "Motivations Associated with Methamphetamine Use Among HIV+ Men Who Have Sex with Men," *Journal of Substance Abuse Treatment* 22 (2002): 149–56; S. J. Semple, T. L. Patterson, and I. Grant, "Binge Use of Methamphetamine Among HIV-Positive Men Who Have Sex with Men: Pilot Data and HIV Prevention Implications," *AIDS Education and Prevention* 15 (2003): 133–47; S. J. Semple, T. L. Patterson, and I. Grant, "A Comparison of Injection and Non-injection Methamphetamine-Using HIV Positive Men Who Have Sex with Men," *Drug and Alcohol Dependence* 76 (2004): 203–12; R. Stall and D. W. Purcell, "Intertwining Epidemics: A Review of Research on Substance Use Among Men Who Have Sex with Men and Its Connection to the AIDS Epidemic," *AIDS and Behavior* 4 (2000): 181–92; W. A. Zule and D. P. Desmond, "An Ethnographic Comparison of HIV Risk Behaviors Among Heroin and Methamphetamine Injectors," *American Journal of Drug and Alcohol Abuse* 25 (1999): 1–23.

104. P. N. Halkitis, J. T. Parsons, and M. J. Stirratt, "A Double Epidemic: Crystal Methamphetamine Drug Use in Relation to HIV Transmission Among Gay Men," *Journal of Homosexuality* 41, no. 2 (2001): 17–35.

105. Reback and Grella, "HIV Risk Behaviors of Gay and Bisexual Male Methamphetamine Users Contacted Through Street Outreach."

106. Gorman and Carroll, "Substance Abuse and HIV"; Gorman, "A Tale of Two Epidemics"; Gorman et al., "A Community Social Work Study of Methamphetamine Use Among Women."

107. T. M. Vogt, J. F. Perz, C. K. Van Houten, R. Harrington, T. Hansuld, S. Bialek, R. Johnson, R. Bratlie, and I. T. Williams, "An Outbreak of Hepatitis B Virus Infection Among Methamphetamine Injectors: The Role of Sharing Injection Drug Equipment," *Addiction* 101, no. 5 (May 2006): 726–30.

108. E. Stone, P. Heagerty, E. Vittinghoff, J. M. Douglas, B. A. Koblin, K. H. Mayer, C. L. Celum, M. Gross, G. E. Woody, M. Marmor, G. R. Seage, and S. Buchbinder, "Correlates of Condom Failure in a Sexually Active Cohort of Men Who Have Sex with Men," *Journal of Acquired Immune Deficiency Syndrome and Human Retrovirology* 20 (1999): 495–501.

109. G. R. Twitchell, A. Huber, C. J. Reback, and S. Shoptaw, "Comparison of General and Detailed HIV Risk Assessments Among Methamphetamine Abusers," *AIDS and Behavior* 6, no. 2 (June 2002): 153–62.

110. R. Ellis, M. Childers, M. Cherner, D. Lazaretto, S. Letendre, and I. Grant, "Increased Human Immunodeficiency Virus Loads in Active Methamphetamine Users Are Explained by Reduced Effectiveness of Antiretroviral Therapy," *The Journal of Infectious Diseases* 188 (2003): 1820–26.

111. A. Nath, W. F. Maragos, M. J. Avison, F. A. Schmitt, and J. R. Berger, "Acceleration of HIV Dementia with Methamphetamine and Cocaine," *Journal of Neurovirology* 7 (2001): 66–71.

112. C. L. Carey, S. P. Woods, J. D. Rippeth, R. Gonzalez, R. K. Heaton, and I. Grant, "Additive Deleterious Effects of Methamphetamine Dependence and Immunosuppression on Neuropsychological Functioning in HIV Infection," *AIDS & Behavior* 10, no. 2 (March 2006): 185–90; J. D. Rippeth, R. K. Heaton, C. L. Carey, T. D. Marcotte, D. J. Moore, R. Gonzalez, T. Wolfson, I. Grant, and the HNRC Group, "Methamphetamine Dependence Increases Risk of Neuropsychological Impairment in HIV Infected Persons," *Journal of the International Neuropsychological Society* 10 (2004): 1–14.

113. W. Fals-Stewart, "Neurocognitive Defects and Their Impact on Substance Abuse Treatment," *Journal of Addictions and Offender Counseling* 13 (1993): 46–57.

114. D. G. Ostrow, "The Role of Drugs in the Sexual Lives of Men Who Have Sex with Men: Continuing Barriers to Researching This Question," *AIDS and Behavior* 4 (2000): 205–19.

115. G. Mansergh, G. Marks, G. N. Colfax, R. Guzman, M. Rader, and S. Buchbinder, "'Barebacking' in a Diverse Sample of Men Who Have Sex with Men," *AIDS* 16 (2002): 653–59.

116. Ostrow, "The Role of Drugs in the Sexual Lives of Men Who Have Sex with Men."

117. Mansergh et al., "'Barebacking' in a Diverse Sample of Men Who Have Sex with Men."

118. S. Hirschfield, R. H. Remien, M. Humberstone, I. Walavalkar, and M. A. Chiasson, "Substance Use and High-Risk Sex Among Men Who Have Sex with Men: A National Online Study in the USA," *AIDS Care* 16, no. 8 (2004): 1036–47; P. Halkitis and J. T. Parsons, "Intentional Unsafe Sex (Barebacking) Among HIV-Positive Gay Men Who Seek Sexual Partners on the Internet," *AIDS Care* 15, no. 3 (2003): 367–78; Halkitis, Parsons, and Wilton, "An Exploratory Study of Contextual and Situational Factors Related to Methamphetamine Use Among Gay and Bisexual Men in New York City."

119. G. N. Colfax, E. Vittinghoff, M. J. Husnik, D. McKirnan, S. Buchbinder, B. Koblin, C. Celum, M. Chesney, Y. Huang, K. Mayer, S. Bozeman, F. N. Judson, K. J. Bryant, T. J. Coates, and the EXPLORE Study Team, "Substance Use and Sexual Risk: A Participant and Episode-Level Analysis Among a Cohort of Men Who Have Sex with Men," *American Journal of Epidemiology* 159 (2004): 1002–12; Hirschfield et al., "Substance Use and High-Risk Sex Among Men Who Have Sex with Men"; P. N. Halkitis and J. T. Parsons, "Recreational Drug Use and HIV Risk Sexual Behavior Among Men Frequenting Urban Gay Venues," *Journal of Gay & Lesbian Social Services* 14, no. 4 (2002): 19–38.

120. Semple, Patterson, and Grant, "Motivations Associated with Methamphetamine Use Among HIV+ Men Who Have Sex with Men," 154.

121. T. L. Patterson, S. J. Semple, J. K. Zians, and S. A. Strathdee, "Methamphetamine-Using HIV-Positive Men Who Have Sex with Men: Correlates of Polydrug Use," *Journal of Urban Health* 82, supplement 1 (2005): 1120–26.

122. Hirschfield et al., "Substance Use and High-Risk Sex Among Men Who Have Sex with Men."

123. J. Paul, R. Stall, and F. Davis, "Sexual Risk for HIV Transmission Among Gay/Bisexual Men in Substance Abuse Treatment," *AIDS Education and Prevention* 5, no. 1 (1993): 11–24.

124. Semple et al., "Sexual Compulsivity in a Sample of HIV-Positive Methamphetamine-Using Gay and Bisexual Men."

125. Colfax et al., "Substance Use and Sexual Risk."

126. Gorman et al., "Speed, Sex, Gay Men, and HIV"; M. Gorman, "Speed Use and HIV Transmission," *Focus* 11, no. 7 (1996): 4–6; Frosch et al., "Sexual HIV Risk Among Gay and Bisexual Male Methamphetamine Abusers"; Paul, Stall, and Davis, "Sexual Risk for HIV Transmission Among Gay/Bisexual Men in Substance Abuse Treatment."

127. Cited in Lyons, Chandra, and Goldstein, "Stimulant Use and HIV Risk Behavior," 468.

128. Semple et al., "Sexual Compulsivity in a Sample of HIV-Positive Methamphetamine-Using Gay and Bisexual Men"; Clatts, Goldsamt, and Yi, "Club Drug Use Among Young Men Who Have Sex with Men in NYC"; Semple, Patterson, and Grant, "A Comparison of Injection and Non-injection Methamphetamine-Using HIV Positive Men Who Have Sex with Men."

129. Hirschfield et al., "Substance Use and High-Risk Sex Among Men Who Have Sex with Men."

130. Stall and Purcell, "Intertwining Epidemics."

131. Ostrow, "The Role of Drugs in the Sexual Lives of Men Who Have Sex with Men."

132. Stall and Purcell, "Intertwining Epidemics."

133. Halkitis and Parsons, "Recreational Drug Use and HIV Risk Sexual Behavior Among Men Frequenting Urban Gay Venues."

134. Both cited in Lyons, Chandra, and Goldstein, "Stimulant Use and HIV Risk Behavior," 468.

135. Guss, "Sex Like You Can't Even Imagine."

136. J. W. Rawlin, "Street Level Abusage of Amphetamines," in *Amphetamine Abuse,* ed. J. R. Russo (Springfield, IL: Charles C. Thomas, 1968), 51–65.

137. M. A. ElSohly and S. J. Salamone, "Prevalence of Drugs Used in Cases of Alleged Sexual Assault," *Journal of Analytical Toxicology* 23 (1999): 141–46.

138. Grella, Hser, and Huang, "Mothers in Substance Abuse Treatment."

139. B. M. Lester, A. M. Arria, C. Derauf, P. Grant, L. Lagasse, E. Newman, R. Z. Shah, S. Stewart, and T. Wouldes, "Methamphetamine Exposure: A Rural Early Intervention Challenge," *Zero to Three* 26, no. 4 (March 2006): 30–36.

140. V. M. Skeers, "Illegal Methamphetamine Drug Laboratories: A New Challenge for Environmental Health Professionals," *Journal of Environmental Health* 55, no. 3 (1992): 6–10; Wermuth, "Methamphetamine Use."

141. Morgan and Beck, "The Legacy and the Paradox."

142. Haight et al., "A Child's-Eye View of Parent Methamphetamine Abuse," 5.

143. National Association of Counties, "The Criminal Effect of Meth on Communities" and "The Impact of Meth on Children"; Weisheit and Fuller, "Methamphetamines in the Heartland."

144. C. W. Huddleston, "Drug Courts: An Effective Strategy for Communities Facing Methamphetamine," *Bureau of Justice Assistance Bulletin* (May 2005): 1–16.

145. S. J. Altshuler, "Drug-Endangered Children Need a Collaborative Community Response," *Child Welfare* 54, no. 2 (2005): 171–90; L. A. Assael, "Methamphetamine: An Epidemic of Oral Health Neglect, Loss of Access to Care, Abuse, and Violence," *Journal of Oral and Maxillofacial Surgery* 63, no. 9 (September 2005): 1253–54; R. A. Rawson, R. Gonzales, and P. Brethen, "Treatment of Methamphetamine Use Disorder: An Update," *Journal of Substance Abuse Treatment* 23 (2002): 145–50.

146. Brown and Hohman, "The Impact of Methamphetamine on Parenting"; Haight et al., "'In These Bleak Days'"; Haight et al., "A Child's-Eye View of Parent Methamphetamine Abuse"; M. Hohman, R. Oliver, and W. Wright, "Methamphetamine Abuse and Manufacture: The Child Welfare Response," *Social Work* 49, no. 3 (2004): 373–81; Huddleston, "Drug Courts."

147. Quoted in Haight et al., "'In These Bleak Days,'" 958.

148. Haight et al., "'In These Bleak Days'"; Haight et al., "A Child's-Eye View of Parent Methamphetamine Abuse"; Brown and Hohman, "The Impact of Methamphetamine on Parenting."

149. Brown and Hohman, "The Impact of Methamphetamine on Parenting."

150. T. Ostler, W. Haight, and J. Black, "Case Series: Mental Health Needs and Perspectives of Rural Children Reared by Parents Who Abuse Methamphetamine," *Journal of the American Academy of Child and Adolescent Psychiatry* 46, no. 4 (April 2007): 505.

151. A. Sun, M. P. Freese, and M. Fitzgerald, "An Exploratory Study of Drug-Exposed Infants: Case Substantiation and Subsequent Child Maltreatment," *Child Welfare* 86, no. 3 (May/June 2007): 33–50.

152. Magura and Laudet, "Parental Substance Abuse and Child Maltreatment," 200.

153. S. Davis, "Comprehensive Interventions for Affecting the Parenting Effectiveness of Chemically Dependent Women," *Journal of Obstetric, Gynecologic, and Neonatal Nursing* 26 (September/October 1997): 604–605.

154. Grella, Hser, and Huang, "Mothers in Substance Abuse Treatment."

155. C. S. Brooks, B. Zuckerman, A. Bamforth, J. Cole, and M. Kaplan-Sanoff, "Clinical Issues Related to Substance-Involved Mothers and Their Infants," *Infant Mental Health Journal* 15, no. 2 (1994): 202–17.

156. Davis, "Comprehensive Interventions for Affecting the Parenting Effectiveness of Chemically Dependent Women"; P. Nair, M. M. Black, M. Schuler, V. Keane, L. Snow, and B. A. Rigney, "Risk Factors for Disruption in Primary Caregiving Among Infants of Substance Abusing Women," *Child Abuse & Neglect* 21, no. 11 (1997): 1039–51.

157. Joe, "Ice Is Strong Enough for a Man, but Made for a Woman."

158. Blum, "Drugs and Violence," 1466.

Chapter 5

1. H. Klee, "Patterns of Amphetamine Misuse in Seven Nations: Factors Affecting Growth and Decline," in *Amphetamine Misuse: International Perspectives on Current Trends,* ed. H. Klee (Amsterdam: Harwood Academic Publishers, 1997), 291–319.

2. P. Reuter, "Can the Borders Be Sealed?" in *Drugs, Crime and the Criminal Justice System,* ed. R. A. Weisheit (Cincinnati, OH: Anderson Publishing, 1990), 18.

3. Klee, "Patterns of Amphetamine Misuse in Seven Nations."

4. P. Chouvy and J. Meissonnier, *Yaa Baa: Production, Traffic, and Consumption of Methamphetamine in Mainland Southeast Asia* (Singapore: Singapore University Press, 2004).

5. NIDA, Community Epidemiology Work Group (CEWG), "Advance Report and Highlights/Executive Summary: Abuse of Stimulants and Other Drugs," Epidemiologic Trends in Drug Abuse (January 2005), http://www.drugabuse.gov/PDF/CEWG/AdvReport_Vol1_105.pdf.

6. Constructed from exhibit 4 and exhibit 7 in Drug Enforcement Administration, *Drug Trafficking in the United States,* http://www.usdoj.gov/dea/concern/drug_trafficking.html.

7. Drug Enforcement Administration, *Guidelines for Law Enforcement for the Cleanup of Clandestine Drug Laboratories* (2005), http://www.usdoj.gov/dea/resources/redbook.pdf.

8. National Drug Intelligence Center, *National Drug Threat Assessment 2003,* http://www.usdoj.gov/ndic/pubs3/3330/meth.htm.

9. M. A. Miller, "History and Epidemiology of Amphetamine Abuse in the United States," in *Amphetamine Misuse: International Perspectives on Current Trends,* ed. H. Klee (Amsterdam: Harwood Academic Publishers, 1997), 116.

10. E. M. Brecher, *Licit and Illicit Drugs: The Consumers Union Report on Narcotics, Stimulants, Depressants, and Inhalants—Including Caffeine, Nicotine, and Alcohol* (Boston: Little Brown, 1972); R. Smith, "Traffic in Speed: Illegal Manufacture and Distribution," *Journal of Psychedelic Drugs* 2 (1969): 30–41; Miller, "History and Epidemiology of Amphetamine Abuse in the United States."

11. Smith, "Traffic in Speed."

12. Cited in K. S. Puder, D. V. Kagan, and J. P. Morgan, "Illicit Methamphetamine: Analysis, Synthesis, and Availability," *American Journal of Drug and Alcohol Abuse* 14, no. 4 (1988): 464.

13. Puder, Kagan, and Morgan, "Illicit Methamphetamine."

14. R. L. Sexton, R. G. Carlson, C. G. Leukefeld, and B. M. Booth, "Patterns of Illicit Methamphetamine Production ('Cooking') and Associated Risks in the Rural South: An Ethnographic Exploration," *Journal of Drug Issues* 36, no. 4 (2006): 853–76; R. Sexton, R. G. Carlson, C. G. Leukefeld, and B. M. Booth, "Methamphetamine Use and Adverse Consequences in the Rural Southern United States: An Ethnographic Overview," *Journal of Psychoactive Drugs,* SARC supplement 3 (November 2006): 393–404.

15. F. Owen, *No Speed Limit: The Highs and Lows of Meth* (New York: St. Martin's Press, 2007), 24.

16. R. A. Weisheit, *Domestic Marijuana: A Neglected Industry* (Westport, CT: Greenwood Press, 1992).

17. Owen, *No Speed Limit,* 23.

18. Uncle Fester, *Secrets of Methamphetamine Manufacture,* 7th ed. (Port Townshend, WA: Loompanics Unlimited, 2005).

19. Owen, *No Speed Limit,* 53.

20. V. M. Skeers, "Illegal Methamphetamine Drug Laboratories: A New Challenge for Environmental Health Professionals," *Journal of Environmental Health* 55, no. 3 (1992): 6–10.

21. National Drug Intelligence Center, *National Drug Threat Assessment 2003.*

22. H. F. Skinner, "Methamphetamine Synthesis Via HI/Red Phosphorous Reduction of Ephedrine," *Forensic Science International* 48 (1990): 128–34, http://www.rhodium.ws/chemistry/meth.hi-rp.html.

23. National Drug Intelligence Center, *National Drug Threat Assessment 2007,* http://www.usdoj.gov/ndic/pubs21/21137/21137p.pdf.

24. *Drug Identification Bible* (Grand Junction, CO: Amera-Chem, Inc., 2001).

25. Owen, *No Speed Limit.*

26. Drug Enforcement Administration, "Chemical Diversion," *Methamphetamine Situation in the United States* (March 1996), http://www.fas.org/irp/agency/doj/dea/product/meth/diversion.htm.

27. Drug Enforcement Administration, "Chemical Diversion"; Owen, *No Speed Limit.*

28. "Cooking Up Solutions to a Cooked Up Menace: Responses to Methamphetamine in a Federal System," *Harvard Law Review* 119, no. 8 (June 2006): 2508–29.

29. National Alliance for Model State Drug Laws, *Restrictions on Over-the-Counter Sales/Purchases of Products Containing Pseudoephedrine* (2007), http://www.namsdl.org/resources/Pseudoephedrine%20Products%20Overview%20-%20 November%202006%20Revised%20Version.pdf.

30. National Alliance for Model State Drug Laws, *State Ammonia Provisions* (2004-2006), http://www.namsdl.org/resources/Ammonia%20Chart%208.01.pdf.

31. Sexton et al., "Methamphetamine Use and Adverse Consequences in the Rural Southern United States."

32. J. K. Cunningham and L. Liu, "Impacts of Federal Ephedrine and Pseudoephedrine Regulations on Methamphetamine-Related Hospital Admissions," *Addiction* 98, no. 9 (2003): 1229–37.

33. P. Reuter and J. P. Caulkins, "Does Precursor Regulation Make a Difference?" *Addiction* 98, no. 9 (2003): 1177–79.

34. R. L. Sexton, R. G. Carlson, C. G. Leukefeld, and B. M. Booth, "Methamphetamine Producers and Users' Reactions to Pseudoephedrine Legislation in the Rural South," *Journal of Crime and Justice* (forthcoming).

35. C. Dobkin and N. Nicosia, "The War on Drugs: Methamphetamine, Public Health, and Crime" (June 18, 2008), http://people.ucsc.edu/~cdobkin/Papers/Methamphetamine.pdf.

36. Ibid., 3.

37. Sexton et al., "Patterns of Illicit Methamphetamine Production ('Cooking') and Associated Risks in the Rural South," 870.

38. National Drug Intelligence Center, *National Drug Threat Assessment 2007,* 7–8.

39. P. Jenkins, "'The Ice Age': The Social Construction of a Drug Panic," *Justice Quarterly* 11, no. 1 (1994): 10.

40. K. C. Brouwer, P. Case, R. Ramos, C. Magis-Rodriguez, J. Bucardo, T. L. Patterson, and S. A. Strathdee, "Trends in Production, Trafficking, and Consumption of Methamphetamine and Cocaine in Mexico," *Substance Use and Misuse* 41, no. 5 (May 2006): 712.

41. D. Leinwand, "DEA: Flavored Meth Use on the Rise," *USA Today* (March 25, 2007), http://www.usatoday.com.

42. National Association of Counties, "Meth Ado About Nothing? Flavored Meth Stories Smack of Fearmongering," *Methamphetamine Newsletter* (August 2007): 4–6.

43. National Drug Intelligence Center, *National Methamphetamine Threat Assessment 2008,* 10, http://www.usdoj.gov/ndic/pubs26/26594/26594p.pdf.

44. United Nations Office on Drugs and Crime, *2007 World Drug Report,* http://www.unodc.org/pdf/research/wdr07/WDR_2007.pdf.

45. Ibid., 127.

46. United Nations Office on Drugs and Crime, *2007 World Drug Report.*

47. United Nations, *United Nations Convention Against Illicit Traffic in Narcotic Drugs and Psychotropic Substances, 1988,* http://www.incb.org/pdf/e/conv/convention_1988_en.pdf.

48. U.S. Department of State, Bureau for International Narcotics and Law Enforcement Affairs, "Chemical Controls," *International Narcotics Control Strategy Report* (2006), http://www.state.gov/p/inl/rls/nrcrpt/2006/vol1/html/62105.htm.

49. Owen, *No Speed Limit.*

50. Chouvy and Meissonnier, *Yaa Baa.*

51. Ibid.

52. Ibid.

53. United Nations Office on Drugs and Crime, *2007 World Drug Report.*

54. Ibid.

55. Ibid.

56. M. C. Longo, S. M. Henry-Edwards, R. E. Humeniuk, P. Christie, and R. L. Ali, "Impact of the Heroin 'Drought' on Patterns of Drug Use and Drug-Related Harms," *Drug and Alcohol Review* 23 (June 2004): 143–50.

57. United Nations Office on Drugs and Crime, *2007 World Drug Report.*

58. T. Zábranský, "Methamphetamine in the Czech Republic," *Journal of Drug Issues* 37, no. 1 (2007): 155–80; United Nations Office on Drugs and Crime, *2007 World Drug Report.*

59. United Nations Office on Drugs and Crime, *2007 World Drug Report.*

60. Ibid.

61. G. D. Irvine and L. Chin, "The Environmental Impact and Adverse Health Effects of the Clandestine Manufacture of Methamphetamine," in *Methamphetamine Abuse: Epidemiologic Issues and Implications,* ed. M. Miller and N. J. Kozel, NIDA Research Monograph Series 115 (1991), 33–46.

62. Dakota Gasification Company, "Anhydrous Ammonia Safety Information: Everything You Ever Wanted to Know but Didn't Want to Ask," http://www.dakotagas.com/Products/Safety%20Information/Anhydrous_Ammonia_Sa.html#top.

63. C. V. Schwab, M. Hanna, and L. Miller, "Play It Safe with Anhydrous Ammonia" (2002), National Ag Safety Database, http://www.cdc.gov/nasd/docs/d001001d001100/d001062/d001062.html.

64. J. Nowatzki, "Anhydrous Ammonia: Managing the Risks" (2008), North Dakota State University Agriculture and University Extension, http://www.ag.ndsu.edu/pubs/ageng/safety/ae1149-1.htm.

65. J. W. Martyny, S. L. Arbuckle, C. S. McCammon, and N. Erb, "Chemical Exposures Associated with Clandestine Methamphetamine Laboratories Using the Anhydrous Ammonia Method of Production," report for the National Jewish Medical and Research Center (March 2004), http://www.njc.org/pdf/Ammonia%20Meth.pdf; J. W. Martyny, S. L. Arbuckle, C. S. McCammon, E. J. Esswein, and N. Erb, "Chemical Exposures Associated with Clandestine Methamphetamine Laboratories," report for the National Jewish Medical and Research Center (January 2004), http://www.njc.org/pdf/Chemical_Exposures.pdf; J. W. Martyny, S. L. Arbuckle, C. S. McCammon, and N. Erb, "Methamphetamine Contamination on Environmental Surfaces Caused by Simulated Smoking of Methamphetamine," report for the National Jewish Medical and Research Center (July 2004), http://www.njc.org/pdf/Meth%20smoking%20experiment.pdf; J. W. Martyny, M. VanDyke, C. S. McCammon, N. Erb, and S. L. Arbuckle, "Chemical Exposures Associated with Clandestine Methamphetamine Laboratories Using the Hypophosphorous and Phosphorous Flake Method of Production," report for the National Jewish Medical and Research Center (September 23, 2005), http://www.njc.org/pdf/meth-hypo-cook.pdf; J. W. Martyny, N. Erb, S. L. Arbuckle, and M. VanDyke, "A 24-Hour Study to Investigate Chemical Exposures Associated with Clandestine Methamphetamine Laboratories," report for the National Jewish Medical and Research Center (August 11, 2005), http://www.njc.org/pdf/Meth-24hour-study.pdf.

66. Martyny et al., "Chemical Exposures Associated with Clandestine Methamphetamine Laboratories Using the Anhydrous Ammonia Method of Production."

67. CDC, "Public Health Consequences Among First Responders to Emergency Events Associated with Illicit Methamphetamine Laboratories—Selected States, 1996–1999," *Morbidity and Mortality Weekly Report* 49, no. 45 (2000): 1021–24; P. Charukamnoetkanok and M. D. Wagoner, "Facial and Ocular Injuries Associated with Methamphetamine Production Accidents," *American Journal of Ophthalmology* 138, no. 5 (November 2004): 875–76.

68. M. Mitka, "Meth Lab Fires Put Heat on Burn Centers," *Journal of the American Medical Association* 294, no. 16 (October 26, 2005): 2009.

69. P. Warner, J. P. Connolly, N. S. Gibran, D. M. Heimbach, and L. H. Engrav, "The Methamphetamine Burn Patient," *Journal of Burn Care and Rehabilitation* 24, no. 5 (September-October 2003): 275–78.

70. A. P. Santos, A. K. Wilson, C. A. Hornung, H. C. Polk, J. L. Rodriguez, and G. A. Franklin, "Methamphetamine Laboratory Explosions: A New and Emerging Burn Injury," *Journal of Burn Care and Rehabilitation* 26, no. 3 (2005): 228–32.

71. A. Campo-Flores, "Meth Fallout: 'I Felt My Face Just Melting,'" *Newsweek* (August 8, 2005), http://www.msnbc.msn.com.

72. R. R. Danks, L. A. Wibbenmeyer, L. D. Faucher, K. C. Sihler, G. P. Kealey, P. Chang, M. Amelon, and R. W. Lewis, "Methamphetamine-Associated Burn Injuries: A Retrospective Analysis," *Journal of Burn Care and Rehabilitation* 25, no. 5 (September–October 2004): 425–29.

73. Santos et al., "Methamphetamine Laboratory Explosions."

74. Danks et al., "Methamphetamine-Associated Burn Injuries."

75. Santos et al., "Methamphetamine Laboratory Explosions," 232.

76. J. L. Burgess, "Phosphine Exposure from a Methamphetamine Laboratory Investigation," *Clinical Toxicology* 39, no. 2 (2001): 165–68.

77. L. J. Willers-Russo, "Three Fatalities Involving Phosphine Gas, Produced as a Result of Methamphetamine Manufacturing," *Journal of Forensic Sciences* 44 (1999): 647.

78. Ibid.

79. Burgess, "Phosphine Exposure from a Methamphetamine Laboratory Investigation."

80. R. L. Norton, K. W. Kauffman, D. B. Chandler, B. T. Burton, J. Gordon, and L. R. Foster, "Intravenous Lead Poisoning Associated with Methamphetamine Use," *Veterinarian and Human Toxicology* 31 (1989): 379, cited in B. T. Burton, "Heavy Metal and Organic Contaminants Associated with Illicit Methamphetamine Production," in *Methamphetamine Abuse: Epidemiologic Issues and Implications,* ed. M. Miller and N. J. Kozel, NIDA Research Monograph Series 115 (1991), 47–59.

81. J. V. Allcott, R. A. Barnhart, and L. A. Mooney, "Acute Lead Poisoning in Two Users of Illicit Methamphetamine," *Journal of the American Medical Association* 258 (1987): 510–11; CDC, "Epidemiologic Notes and Reports Lead Poisoning Associated with Intravenous Methamphetamine Use—Oregon, 1988," *Morbidity and Mortality Weekly Report* 38, no. 48 (1989): 830–31.

82. "How Your Thyroid Works" (2005), EndocrineWeb.com, http://www.endocrineweb.com/thyfunction.html.

83. R. Mathur, "Thyroid & Iodine—Part 2" (2006), MedicineNet.com, http://www.medicinenet.com/script/main/art.asp?articlekey=18395.

84. U.S. Department of Justice, National Drug Intelligence Center, "Iodine in Methamphetamine Production," Information Brief 2002–L0490-002 (2002), 1.

85. Martyny et al., "Chemical Exposures Associated with Clandestine Methamphetamine Laboratories."

86. CDC, "Acute Public Health Consequences of Methamphetamine Laboratories—16 States, January 2000–June 2004," *Morbidity and Mortality Weekly Report* 54, no. 14 (2005): 356–59.

87. Skeers, "Illegal Methamphetamine Drug Laboratories."

88. J. L. Burgess, D. F. Kovalchick, E. M. Siegel, T. A. Hysong, and S. A. McCurdy, "Medical Surveillance of Clandestine Drug Laboratory Investigators," *Journal of Occupational and Environmental Medicine* 44, no. 2 (2002): 184–89.

89. Martyny et al., "Chemical Exposures Associated with Clandestine Methamphetamine Laboratories Using the Anhydrous Ammonia Method of Production"; Martyny et al., "Chemical Exposures Associated with Clandestine Methamphetamine Laboratories"; Martyny et al., "Methamphetamine Contamination on Environmental Surfaces Caused by Simulated Smoking of Methamphetamine"; Martyny et al., "Chemical Exposures Associated with Clandestine Methamphetamine Laboratories Using the Hypophosphorous and Phosphorous Flake Method of Production"; Martyny et al., "A 24-Hour Study to Investigate Chemical Exposures Associated with Clandestine Methamphetamine Laboratories."

90. Martyny et al., "Chemical Exposures Associated with Clandestine Methamphetamine Laboratories Using the Anhydrous Ammonia Method of Production," 24.

91. CDC, "Public Health Consequences Among First Responders to Emergency Events Associated with Illicit Methamphetamine Laboratories—Selected States, 1996–1999."

92. J. L. Burgess, S. Barnhart, and H. Checkoway, "Investigating Clandestine Drug Laboratories: Adverse Medical Effects in Law Enforcement Personnel," *American Journal of Industrial Medicine* 30 (1996): 488–94.

93. W. C. Holton, "Unlawful Lab Leftovers," *Environmental Health Perspectives* 109, no. 12 (2001): A576.

94. Irvine and Chin, "The Environmental Impact and Adverse Health Effects of the Clandestine Manufacture of Methamphetamine."

95. E. I. Krause, "Take My Property Please! Who Should Bear the Burden of Cleaning Up Toxic Methamphetamine Lab Waste?" *Catholic University Law Review* 56 (2006): 187–224.

96. Holton, "Unlawful Lab Leftovers."

97. G. D. Irvine and L. Chin, "The Environmental Impact and Adverse Health Effects of the Clandestine Manufacture of Methamphetamine," *Substance Use and Misuse* 32, no. 12/13 (1997): 1811–12.

98. Krause, "Take My Property Please!"

99. Drug Enforcement Administration, National Clandestine Laboratory Register, http://www.dea.gov/seizures/index.html.

100. G. Hargreaves, "Clandestine Drug Labs: Chemical Time Bombs," *FBI Law Enforcement Bulletin* 69 (2000): 1–6; Holton, "Unlawful Lab Leftovers."

101. T. Manning, "Drug Labs and Endangered Children," *FBI Law Enforcement Bulletin* 68 (1999): 10–17.

102. D. Hannan, "Meth Labs: Understanding Exposure Hazards and Associated Problems," *Professional Safety* 48 (June 2005): 28.

103. Z. R. Gates, "Obeying the 'Speed' Limit: Framing the Appropriate Role of EPA Criminal Enforcement Actions Against Clandestine Drug Laboratory Operators," *Penn State Environmental Law Review* 13, no. 2 (2005): 173–215.

104. K. Farst, J. M. Duncan, M. Moss, R. M. Ray, E. Kokoska, and L. P. James, "Methamphetamine Exposure Presenting as Caustic Ingestions in Children," *Annals of Emergency Medicine* 49, no. 3 (March 2007): 341–43.

105. Manning, "Drug Labs and Endangered Children."

106. "Methamphetamine Control," Illinois Public Act 094–0556, http://www.ilga.gov/legislation/publicacts/94/PDF/094-0556.pdf.

107. J. C. O'Connor, J. F. Chriqui, and D. C. McBride, "Developing Lasting Legal Solutions to the Dual Epidemics of Methamphetamine Production and Use," *North Dakota Law Review* 82 (2006): 1165–94.

108. H. E. Hopper, "Exploring the Evolution of Drug Endangered Children's Movement and Drug Courts," *North Dakota Law Review* 82 (2006): 1443–59.

109. Hopper, "Exploring the Evolution of Drug Endangered Children's Movement and Drug Courts"; S. J. Altshuler, "Drug-Endangered Children Need a Collaborative Community Response," *Child Welfare* 54, no. 2 (2005): 171–90.

110. The National Alliance for Drug Endangered Children (NADEC), http://www.nationaldec.org.

111. Michigan Drug Endangered Children (DEC) Response Protocol (2006), http://www.methresources.gov.

112. Michigan Drug Endangered Children (DEC) Medical Protocol (2006), http://www.methresources.gov.

Chapter 6

1. R. W. Bauer, "Methamphetamine in Illinois: An Examination of an Emerging Drug," *Illinois Criminal Justice Information Authority Research Bulletin* 1, no. 2 (2003): 1–12.

2. Ibid.

3. R. A. Weisheit and J. Fuller, "Methamphetamines in the Heartland: A Review and Initial Exploration, *Journal of Crime and Justice* 27, no. 1 (2004): 131–51.

4. Population, employment, and similar characteristics of Edgar and Clark counties are drawn from the Institute of Government and Public Affairs at the University of Illinois, *Illinois Statistical Abstract 2003*, http://www.igpa.uiuc.edu/abstract.

5. See Indiana Senator Connie Sipes's 2004 summer newsletter at http://www.in.gov/legislative/senate_democrats/homepages/s46/Sipes.pdf. See also Indiana State Police, "Methamphetamine Report," prepared for the Government Reform Committee's Subcommittee on Criminal Justice, Drug Policy, and Human Resources (February 6, 2004).

6. See the Illinois State Police Web site that maps meth lab seizures and provides counts by county at http://www.isp.state.il.us/crime/methinillinois.htm.

7. J. M. Klofas, "The Jail and the Community," *Justice Quarterly* 7, no. 1 (1990): 69–102; G. L. Mays and J. A. Thompson, "Mayberry Revisited: The Characteristics and Operation of America's Small Jails," *Justice Quarterly* 5, no. 3 (1988): 421–40.

8. Drawn from the Institute of Government and Public Affairs at the University of Illinois, *Illinois Statistical Abstract 2003*.

9. See W. J. Lefever, *Report Operating Cost Study Proposed Clark County Jail: Additions and Revisions* (July 10, 2004).

10. From the Human Resources Center of Edgar and Clark Counties, Coalition Against Methamphetamine Abuse (CAMA) Web site, http://www.hrcec.org/cama.htm.

11. See G. Kaye and T. Wolff, eds., *From the Ground Up: A Workbook on Coalition Building and Community Development* (Amherst, MA: AHEC/Community Partners, 1997).

12. Ibid.

13. J. P. Kretzman and J. L. McKnight, *Building Communities from the Inside Out: A Path Toward Finding and Mobilizing a Community's Assets* (Evanston, IL: Northwestern University, 1993), 5.

14. Ibid.

15. Kaye and Wolff, *From the Ground Up,* 46.

16. From the Human Resources Center of Edgar and Clark Counties, Coalition Against Methamphetamine Abuse (CAMA) Web site, http://www.hrcec.org/cama.htm.

17. R. Weisheit, D. N. Falcone, and L. E. Wells, *Crime and Policing in Rural and Small-Town America,* 2nd ed. (Prospect Heights, IL: Waveland Press, 1999).

18. R. Smith, "Traffic in Speed: Illegal Manufacture and Distribution," *Journal of Psychedelic Drugs* 2 (1969): 30–41.

Chapter 7

1. SAMHSA, OAS, *The DASIS Report: The National Survey of Substance Abuse Treatment Services (N-SSATS): 2003,* http://oas.samhsa.gov/2k5/nssats/nssats.cfm.

2. A. T. McLellan and K. Meyers, "Contemporary Addiction Treatment: A Review of Systems Problems for Adults and Adolescents," *Biological Psychiatry* 56, no. 10 (2004): 764–70.

3. SAMHSA, OAS, *Treatment Episode Data Set (TEDS), 1992-2000: National Admissions to Substance Abuse Treatment Services,* DASIS Series S-17, HHS Pub. SMA 07–3727 (2002), http://wwwdasis.samhsa.gov/teds00/TEDS_2K_index.htm.

4. W. R. Miller, S. T. Walters, and M. E. Bennett, "How Effective Is Alcoholism Treatment in the United States?" *Journal of Studies on Alcohol* 62, no. 2 (2001): 211–20.

5. A. T. McLellan, G. R. Grissom, P. Brill, J. Durell, D. S. Metsger, and C. P. O'Brien, "Private Substance Abuse Treatments: Are Some Programs More Effective Than Others?" *Journal of Substance Abuse Treatment* 10 (1993): 243–54; A. T. McLellan, G. E. Woody, L. Luborsky, and L. Goehl, "Is the Counselor an 'Active Ingredient' in Substance Abuse Rehabilitation? An Examination of Treatment Success Among Four Counselors," *Journal of Nervous and Mental Disorders* 176, no. 7 (1988): 423–30.

6. H. A. Siegal, R. C. Rapp, L. Li, P. Saha, and K. Kirk, "The Role of Case Management in Retaining Clients in Substance Abuse Treatment: An Exploratory Analysis," *Journal of Drug Issues* 27, no. 4 (1997): 821–31; McLellan et al., "Private Substance Abuse Treatments"; A. T. McLellan, T. A. Hagan, M. Levine, F. Gould, K. Meyers, M. Bencivengo, and J. Durell, "Supplemental Social Services Improve Outcomes in Public Addiction Treatment," *Addiction* 93, no. 10 (1998): 1489–99.

7. SAMHSA, OAS, *Results from the 2002 National Survey on Drug Use and Health: National Findings,* NHSDA Series H-22, DHHS Publication No. SMA 03-3836; S. A. Dawson, B. F. Grant, F. S. Stinson, P. S. Chou, B. Huang, and W. J. Ruan, "Recovery from DSM-IV Alcohol Dependence: United States, 2001–2002," *Addiction* 100, no. 3 (2005): 281–92.

8. Y. I. Hser, M. Maglione, L. Polinsky, and M. D. Anglin, "Predicting Drug Treatment Entry Among Treatment-Seeking Individuals," *Journal of Substance Abuse Treatment* 15, no. 3 (1998): 213–20.

9. SAMHSA, OAS, *Treatment Episode Data Set (TEDS): 2004 Treatment Discharges,* http://www.oas.samhsa.gov/TEDSdischarges/2k4/TEDSD2k4Chp1.htm.

10. NIDA, *Principles of Drug Addiction Treatment: A Research-Based Guide,* NIH Publication No. 00–4180, http://www.nida.nih.gov/PODAT/PODATIndex.html.

11. J. R. McKay, "Effectiveness of Continuing Care Interventions for Substance Abusers: Implications for the Study of Long-Term Treatment Effects," *Evaluation Review* 25, no. 2 (2001): 211–32.

12. P. Wilbourne and W. Miller, "Treatment of Alcoholism: Older and Wiser?" in *Alcohol Problems in the United States: Twenty Years of Treatment Perspective,* ed. T. McGovern and W. White (New York: Haworth Press, 2003), 41–59.

13. SAMHSA, OAS, *Treatment Episode Data Set (TEDS): 2004 Treatment Discharges.*

14. A. T. McLellan, D. C. Lewis, C. P. O'Brien, and H. D. Kleber, "Drug Dependence, a Chronic Medical Illness: Implications for Treatment, Insurance, and Outcomes Evaluation," *Journal of the American Medical Association* 284, no. 13 (2000): 1689–95; W. White and A. T. McLellan, "Addiction as a Chronic Disease: Key Messages for Clients, Families and Referral Sources," *Counselor* 9, no. 3 (2008): 24–33.

15. "Discharges Who Left Against Professional Advice: 2003," *The DASIS Report* 28 (2006), http://www.oas.samhsa.gov/2k6/leftTX/leftTX.htm.

16. M. Brecht, M. D. Anglin, and M. Dylan, "Coerced Treatment for Methamphetamine Abuse: Differential Characteristics and Outcomes," *The American Journal of Drug and Alcohol Abuse* 31 (2005): 337–56.

17. R. Rawson, A. Huber, P. Brethen, J. Obert, V. Gulati, S. Shoptaw, and W. Ling, "Methamphetamine and Cocaine Users: Differences in Characteristics and Treatment Outcomes," *Journal of Psychoactive Drugs* 32 (2000): 233–38; M. Cretzmeyer, M. V. Sarrazin, D. L. Huber, R. I. Block, and J. A. Hall, "Treatment of Methamphetamine Abuse: Research Findings and Clinical Directions," *Journal of Substance Abuse Treatment* 24 (2003): 267–77.

18. Y. I. Hser, E. Evans, and Y. C. Huan, "Treatment Outcomes Among Women and Men Amphetamine Abusers in California," *Journal of Substance Abuse Treatment* 28 (2005): 77–85.

19. R. Rawson, *Treatment for Stimulant Use Disorders,* TIP Series #33 (Rockville, MD: U.S. Department of Health and Human Services, 1999).

20. J. R. Volpicelli, "Alcohol Abuse and Alcoholism: An Overview," *Journal of Clinical Psychiatry* 62, supplement 20 (2001): 4–10; E. Senay, *Substance Abuse Disorders in Clinical Practice* (New York: W.W. Norton & Co., 1998).

21. M. Schuckit, "The Treatment of Stimulant Dependence," *Addiction* 89 (1994): 1559–63; R. A. Rawson, R. Gonzales, and P. Brethen, "Treatment of Methamphetamine Use Disorder: An Update," *Journal of Substance Abuse Treatment* 23 (2002): 145–50; C. W. Meredith, C. Jaffe, K. Ang-Lee, and A. J. Saxon, "Implications of Chronic Methamphetamine Use: A Literature Review," *Harvard Review of Psychiatry* 13, no. 3 (2005): 141–54.

22. R. Gonzales and R. Rawson, "Methamphetamine Addiction: Does It Work?" *Counselor* 6, no. 5 (2005): 16–23.

23. F. J. Vocci and N. M. Appel, "Approaches to the Development of Medications for the Treatment of Methamphetamine Dependence," *Addiction* 102, supplement 1 (2007): 96–106.

24. Rawson, Gonzales, and Brethen, "Treatment of Methamphetamine Use Disorder"; A. Baker and N. K. Lee, "A Review of Psychosocial Interventions for Amphetamine Use," *Drug and Alcohol Review* 22 (2003): 323–35.

25. J. Shearer, "Psychosocial Approaches to Psychostimulant Dependency: A Systematic Review," *Journal of Substance Abuse Treatment* 32 (2007): 41–52.

26. N. M. Petry, J. M. Peirce, M. L. Stitzer, J. Blaine, J. M. Roll, A. Cohen, J. Obert, T. Killeen, M. E. Saladin, M. Cowell, K. C. Kirby, R. Sterling, C. Royer-Malvestuto, J. Hamilton, R. E. Booth, M. Macdonald, M. Liebert, L. Rader, R. Burns, J. DiMaria, M. Copersino, P. Q. Stabile, K. Kolodner, and R. Li, "Effect of Prize-Based Incentives on Outcomes in Stimulant Abusers in Outpatient Psychosocial Treatment Programs: A National Drug Abuse Treatment Clinical Trials Network Study," *Archives of General Psychiatry* 62, no. 10 (2005): 1148–56.

27. D. M. Donovan and E. A. Wells, "'Tweaking 12-Step': The Potential Role of 12-Step Self-Help Group Involvement in Methamphetamine Recovery," *Addiction* 102, supplement 1 (2007): 121–29.

28. Shearer, "Psychosocial Approaches to Psychostimulant Dependency."

29. J. L. Obert, M. J. McCann, P. Marinelli-Casey, A. Weiner, S. Minsky, P. Brethen, and R. Rawson, "The Matrix Model of Outpatient Substance Abuse Treatment: History and Description," *Journal of Psychoactive Drugs* 32 (2000): 157–64.

30. Rawson, *Treatment for Stimulant Use Disorders;* M. D. Anglin, C. Burke, B. Perrochet, E. Stamper, and S. Dawud-Noursi, "History of the Methamphetamine Problem," *Journal of Psychoactive Drugs* 32, no. 2 (2000): 137–41.

31. R. A. Rawson, P. Marinelli-Casey, and M. D. Anglin, "A Multi-site Comparison of Psychosocial Approaches for the Treatment of Methamphetamine Dependence," *Addiction* 99 (2004): 708–17.

32. P. Frawley and J. Smith, "One-Year Follow-Up After Multimodal Inpatient Treatment for Cocaine and Methamphetamine Dependencies," *Journal of Substance Abuse Treatment* 9 (1992): 271–86.

33. M. L. Brecht, C. von Mayhauser, and M. D. Anglin, "Predictors of Relapse After Treatment for Methamphetamine Use," *Journal of Psychoactive Drugs* 32 (2000): 211–20.

34. R. Rawson, A. Huber, P. Brethen, J. Obert, V. Gulati, S. Shoptaw, and W. Ling, "Status of Methamphetamine Users 2-5 Years After Outpatient Treatment," *Journal of Addictive Diseases* 21 (2002): 107–19.

35. Rawson et al., "A Multi-site Comparison of Psychosocial Approaches for the Treatment of Methamphetamine Dependence."

36. B. Luchansky, A. Krupski, and K. Stark, "Treatment Response by Primary Drug of Abuse: Does Methamphetamine Make a Difference?" *Journal of Substance Abuse Treatment* 32 (2007): 89–96.

37. Cretzmeyer et al., "Treatment of Methamphetamine Abuse," 275.

38. M. L. Brecht, L. Greenwell, and M. D. Anglin, "Methamphetamine Treatment: Trends and Predictors of Retention and Completion in a Large State Treatment System (1992–2000)," *Journal of Substance Abuse Treatment* 29 (2005): 295–306.

39. *Drug Court Activity Update: Composite Summary Information* (June 15, 2006), Bureau of Justice Assistance (BJA) Drug Court Clearinghouse, American University, http://spa.american.edu/justice/documents/1956.pdf.

40. Brecht, Anglin, and Dylan, "Coerced Treatment for Methamphetamine Abuse."

41. J. F. Kelly, J. W. Finney, and R. Moos, "Substance Use Disorder Patients Who Are Mandated to Treatment: Characteristics, Treatment Process, and 1- and 5-Year Outcomes," *Journal of Substance Abuse Treatment* 28, no. 3 (2005): 213–23.

42. Brecht, Greenwall, and Anglin, "Methamphetamine Treatment: Trends and Predictors of Retention and Completion in a Large State Treatment System (1992–2000)."

43. Gonzales and Rawson, "Methamphetamine Addiction: Does It Work?"; P. Marinelli-Casey, R. Gonzales, M. Hillhouse, A. Ang, J. Zweben, J. Cohen, P. F. Hora, and R. Rawson, "Drug Court Treatment for Methamphetamine Dependence," *Journal of Substance Abuse Treatment* (forthcoming).

44. Cretzmeyer et al., "Treatment of Methamphetamine Abuse."

45. McKay, "Effectiveness of Continuing Care Interventions for Substance Abusers"; M. L. Dennis, C. K. Scott, and R. Funk, "An Experimental Evaluation of Recovery Management Checkups (RMC) for People with Chronic Substance Use Disorders," *Evaluation and Program Planning* 26, no. 3 (2003): 339–52.

46. M. D. Godley, S. H. Godley, M. L. Dennis, R. Funk, and L. Passetti, "Preliminary Outcomes from the Assertive Continuing Care Experiment for Adolescents Discharged from Residential Treatment: Preliminary Outcomes," *Journal of Substance Abuse Treatment* 23, no. 1 (2002): 21–32.

47. W. White and E. Kurtz, "The Varieties of Recovery Experience," *International Journal of Self Help and Self Care* 3, no. 1–2 (2006): 21–61; W. White and E. Kurtz, *Linking Addiction Treatment and Communities of Recovery: A Primer for Addiction Counselors and Recovery Coaches* (Pittsburgh, PA: Institute for Research, Education and Training in Addictions, 2006).

48. Donovan and Wells, "'Tweaking 12-Step.'"

49. R. F. Forman, "One AA Meeting Doesn't Fit All: 6 Keys to Prescribing 12-Step Programs," *Psychiatry Online* 1, no. 10 (2002): 1–6; White and Kurtz, *Linking Addiction Treatment and Communities of Recovery.*

50. T. E. Freese, J. Obert, A. Dickow, J. Cohen, and R. H. Lord, "Methamphetamine Abuse: Issues for Special Populations," *Journal of Psychoactive Drugs* 32, no. 2 (2000): 177–82.

51. Brecht, Greenwall, and Anglin, "Methamphetamine Treatment: Trends and Predictors of Retention and Completion in a Large State Treatment System (1992–2000)."

52. Hser, Evans, and Huang, "Treatment Outcomes Among Women and Men Amphetamine Abusers in California."

53. Freese et al., "Methamphetamine Abuse"; R. A. Rawson, M. D. Anglin, and W. Ling, "Will the Methamphetamine Problem Go Away?" *Journal of Addictive Diseases* 21, no. 1 (2002): 5–19.

54. Rawson, Anglin, and Ling, "Will the Methamphetamine Problem Go Away?" 15.

55. Gonzales and Rawson, "Methamphetamine Addiction: Does It Work?"

56. S. Shoptaw, R. Rawson, M. McCann, and J. Obert. "The Matrix Model of Outpatient Stimulant Abuse Treatment: Evidence of Efficacy," *Journal of Addictive Diseases* 13, no. 4 (1994): 129–41; Brecht, von Mayhauser, and Anglin, "Predictors of Relapse After Treatment for Methamphetamine Use."

57.   H. Klee, S. Wright, and J. Morris, "Amphetamine Users in Treatment: Factors Associated with Sustained Abstinence from Street Drugs," *Addiction Research* 7, no. 3 (2001): 239–65.

58.   S. A. Stalcup, D. Christian, J. Stalcup, M. Brown, and G. P. Galloway, "A Treatment Model for Craving Identification and Management," *Journal of Psychoactive Drugs* 38, no. 2 (2006): 189–202.

59.   Klee, Wright, and Morris, "Amphetamine Users in Treatment."

60.   T. D. Gunter, D. W. Black, J. Zwick, and S. Arndt, "Drug and Alcohol Treatment Services for Methamphetamine Abuse," *Annals of Clinical Psychiatry* 16, no. 4 (2004): 195–200.

61.   W. L. White, A. B. Laudet, and J. B. Becker, "Life Meaning and Purpose in Addiction Recovery," *Addiction Professional* 4, no. 4 (2006): 18–23.

62.   W. Miller and J. C. de Baca, *Quantum Change: When Epiphanies and Sudden Insights Transform Ordinary Lives* (New York: Guilford Press, 2001).

63.   W. White, *Pathways from the Culture of Addiction to the Culture of Recovery* (Center City, MN: Hazelden, 1996).

64.   Dennis, Scott, and Funk, "An Experimental Evaluation of Recovery Management Checkups (RMC) for People with Chronic Substance Use Disorders."

INDEX

ABOUT THE AUTHORS

Dr. Ralph A. Weisheit is a Distinguished Professor of Criminal Justice at Illinois State University. He is the author of seven previous books, more than forty journal articles, and numerous book chapters and solicited essays. He appeared in the *Frontline* documentary film series "Busted: America's War on Marijuana" and on the news program *60 Minutes.* His work has also been reported in a variety of magazines and newspapers, including *The Atlantic Monthly, U.S. News & World Report,* and *U.S.A. Today.* His prior research on illicit drugs, combined with his interest in rural issues, led quite naturally to his current research on methamphetamine.

William L. White, M.A., is a Senior Research Consultant at Chestnut Health Systems/Lighthouse Institute and past chair of the board of Recovery Communities United. Mr. White has worked in the addictions field since 1969 and has authored or co-authored more than three hundred articles and fourteen books, including *Slaying the Dragon: The History of Addiction Treatment and Recovery in America* and *Let's Go Make Some History: Chronicles of the New Addiction Recovery Advocacy Movement.* His sustained contributions to the field have been acknowledged by awards from the American Society of Addiction Medicine, the National Association of Addiction Treatment Providers, the National Council on Alcoholism and Drug Dependence, and NAADAC: The Association of Addiction Professionals.

Hazelden, a national nonprofit organization founded in 1949, helps people reclaim their lives from the disease of addiction. Built on decades of knowledge and experience, Hazelden offers a comprehensive approach to addiction that addresses the full range of patient, family, and professional needs, including treatment and continuing care for youth and adults, research, higher learning, public education and advocacy, and publishing.

A life of recovery is lived "one day at a time." Hazelden publications, both educational and inspirational, support and strengthen lifelong recovery. In 1954, Hazelden published *Twenty-Four Hours a Day*, the first daily meditation book for recovering alcoholics, and Hazelden continues to publish works to inspire and guide individuals in treatment and recovery, and their loved ones. Professionals who work to prevent and treat addiction also turn to Hazelden for evidence-based curricula, informational materials, and videos for use in schools, treatment programs, and correctional programs.

Through published works, Hazelden extends the reach of hope, encouragement, help, and support to individuals, families, and communities affected by addiction and related issues.

For questions about Hazelden publications, please call **800-328-9000** or visit us online at **hazelden.org/bookstore.**

ECC Library